D0376759

Eleanor

A SPIRITUAL BIOGRAPHY

Eleanor

A SPIRITUAL BIOGRAPHY

*The Faith of the 20th Century's
Most Influential Woman*

Harold Ivan Smith

31652003214799

WESTMINSTER
JOHN KNOX PRESS
LOUISVILLE • KENTUCKY

© 2017 Harold Ivan Smith

First edition
Published by Westminster John Knox Press
Louisville, Kentucky

17 18 19 20 21 22 23 24 25 26—10 9 8 7 6 5 4 3 2

All rights reserved. No part of this book may be reproduced or transmitted in any form or by any means, electronic or mechanical, including photocopying, recording, or by any information storage or retrieval system, without permission in writing from the publisher. For information, address Westminster John Knox Press, 100 Witherspoon Street, Louisville, Kentucky 40202-1396. Or contact us online at www.wjkbooks.com.

Unless otherwise indicated, Scripture quotations are from the King James Version. Public Domain. Scripture quotations marked NIV are from *The Holy Bible, New International Version.* Copyright © 1973, 1978, 1984, 2011 by Biblica, Inc.® Used by permission. All rights reserved worldwide. Scripture quotations marked NRSV are from the New Revised Standard Version of the Bible, copyright © 1989 by the Division of Christian Education of the National Council of the Churches of Christ in the U.S.A., and used by permission.

Excerpts from a prayer by Chief Yellow Lark and a prayer composed by Australian aborigines are from Eleanor Roosevelt s My Day © Eleanor Roosevelt. Reprinted by permission of UNIVERSAL UCLICK for UFS. All rights reserved. All other excerpts from Eleanor Roosevelt's "My Day" columns are used by permission of the Eleanor Roosevelt Estate. All rights reserved.

Book design by Drew Stevens
Cover design by Marc Whitaker / MTWdesign.net
Cover photo: Eleanor Roosevelt, *Bridgeman Images*

Library of Congress Cataloging-in-Publication Data
Names: Smith, Harold Ivan, 1947- author.
Title: Eleanor : a spiritual biography : the faith of the 20th century's most influential woman / Harold Ivan Smith.
Description: First edition. | Louisville, Kentucky : Westminster John Knox Press, 2017. | Includes bibliographical references.
Identifiers: LCCN 2016041537 (print) | LCCN 2016055185 (ebook) | ISBN 9780664261641 (pbk. : alk. paper) | ISBN 9781611647976 (ebk.)
Subjects: LCSH: Roosevelt, Eleanor, 1884-1962--Religion. | Presidents' spouses--United States--Biography.
Classification: LCC E807.1.R48 S65 2017 (print) | LCC E807.1.R48 (ebook) | DDC 973.917092 [B] --dc23
LC record available at https://lccn.loc.gov/2016041537

♾ The paper used in this publication meets the minimum requirements of the American National Standard for Information Sciences—Permanence of Paper for Printed Library Materials, ANSI Z39.48-1992.

Most Westminster John Knox Press books are available at special quantity discounts when purchased in bulk by corporations, organizations, and special-interest groups. For more information, please e-mail SpecialSales@wjkbooks.com.

With deep appreciation, I dedicate this book to

Robert Clark

Archivist par excellence, then at the FDR Presidential Library, who urged me to set aside another project to explore the spirituality of Eleanor. I took his sage advice.

Sally Higgins

At a moment of indecision, she leaned across the table and said, "Write the book!"

Gregory DeBourgh

Who listened to more Eleanor stories than any nursing scholar should and offered his dining room table, where I spent hundreds of hours writing and editing. His wise counsel helped me clear hurdles throughout the entire process.

Contents

Acknowledgments

It takes a village to publish a book. Over the decade of research and writing, I borrowed a lot of "eyeballs" to read draft after draft.

I owe a great deal to:

Mary Kay Speaks, who proofread the working manuscript and raised poignant "How do you know *this*?" questions and weighed dozens of citations.

Doug Fuehling, an energetic librarian/detective who tracked down books, articles, and ideas—sometimes with only the sketchiest details from my memory.

Rabbi Earl Grollman, who on more than one occasion gave me the Dutch-uncle talk and finally said, "Enough research! Write the *damn* book! I can't wait around for this book." The rabbi is in his tenth decade!

Bill Moyers and Doris Kearns Goodwin, who offered encouragement during their visits to the Bennett Forum sponsored by the Harry S. Truman Library Institute, where I am an honorary fellow. Over the years the Truman Institute led by Alex Burden and the Kansas City Public Library led by Crosby Kemper brought dozens of presidential scholars to lecture at the Truman Forum's incredible presidents and first ladies lecture series.

Virginia Ledwick, archivist at the FDR Presidential Library, who answered many e-mail questions and directed me toward resources for consultation and interpretation.

The host of "Eleanorettes" who read drafts and offered great chunks of encouragement and whose standard question became, "How's Eleanor these days?" including Dennis and Beulah Apple, Brenda Atkinson, Ron Attrell, Ron Benefiel, Dan Boone, John Roosevelt Boettiger, Sharon Bowles, Gray Brechin, Peggy Campolo, Betty Carmack, Tim Cox, Greg DeBourgh, Nina Roosevelt Gibson, Richard Gilbert, Janice Greathouse, Jolane Hickman, Nancy Keller, Jerry Kolb, John and Diane Larsen, Randy McCain-Eddy, Therese McKechnie, Marina McSorley, Rhonda Monke, Nancy Mullins, Jane Norman, Arvil Pennington,

Susan Prion, Rabbi Daniel Roberts, Allison Palandrani Romero, Leslie Stockard, Judy Turner, Mary Grace Williams, and Rosalyn Wilson.

The staffs of the Franklin D. Roosevelt Presidential Library in Hyde Park, the Hyde Park Free Library, the Dwight D. Eisenhower Presidential Library, the John F. Kennedy Presidential Library, the Herbert Hoover Presidential Library, and the Harry S. Truman Library.

The Linda Hall Science Library, a crown jewel for scholars, which provided traditional quiet space for editing and thinking.

The Kansas City Public Library, the Mid-Continent Public Library, and the Johnson County Public Library, which provided space to edit and procured literally hundreds of books, some long removed from circulation.

Author's Note

TWO ABBREVIATIONS

Eleanor's faith was personal, but never private. In her dozens of books and thousands of newspaper and magazine columns, she wrote frequently of Scripture, the example of Jesus, her own prayers, and the divine call to work for a more just and peaceful world. Two regular columns stand out as the venues in which common Americans most often heard from Mrs. Roosevelt, offering a window into not just Eleanor's activities and political views but her very soul.

I have documented most sources cited in this book in the back matter, but to highlight the public nature of Eleanor's spirituality, I have cited quotations from these two publications parenthetically throughout the book and abbreviated them as follows.

MD: "My Day," Eleanor's syndicated newspaper column, ran from December 30, 1935, until September 26, 1962, six days a week until January 1961, then three days a week until a mere six weeks before her death.

IYAM: "If You Ask Me," a monthly column Eleanor wrote from May 1941 until her death in November 1962, was originally published in *Ladies' Home Journal*. A conflict with the publisher led her to take the column to *McCall's* in June 1949.

Introduction

In the mid-1930s, a young child asked to name the President responded, "Franklin Eleanor Roosevelt." The answer wasn't far off the mark.
　　　　　　　　　　　　　　　　　　　—Daniel Patrick Moynihan

Although it was early that November morning in 1938, in Birmingham's Municipal Auditorium people attending the Southern Conference for Human Welfare fanned furiously while craning their necks and twisting in their chairs to watch the entrances. Conferees had walked past parked police cars ringing the building in readiness for a showdown. Commissioner of Public Safety Eugene "Bull" Connor, strutting and growling, boasted that he would "show *her*" who was boss. Birmingham was *his* town. As the program began, some feared she had not come, to avoid a confrontation.

Suddenly a rumble swept the auditorium. There she was! Her smile drew more cheers. Acknowledging the applause, she slowly made her way to the "white" seating section and chose a chair on the aisle. Disappointment whipped the crowd. She had caved in!

In 1938, rigid segregation was the law of the state of Alabama, the law interpreted by Bull Connor, who had announced that he would arrest any white person—even the First Lady—who even attempted to sit on the wrong side of the aisle.

Organizers had worked to prevent confrontation by marking paths on the floor so that speakers walking to and from the platform could avoid accidentally stepping into the wrong racial section.

Slowly, the hubbub died down. The speaker resumed.

A few minutes passed. Then some delegates elbowed individuals sitting next to them and pointed to the aisle. Eleanor's chair had moved.

1

Then moved again. Perhaps she felt crowded or could not see the podium. The chair moved again! The eyes of people in both sections darted from the podium to Mrs. Roosevelt's chair to Bull Connor's officers. Some conferees stood for a better view. Slowly, while nodding in agreement with the speaker, Eleanor continued scooting her chair a few inches at a time. A few more inches. Then a few more.

By the end of the speaker's presentation, the First Lady sat in the middle of the wide aisle between the "white only" and the "Negro only" sections. Connor, a Baptist deacon, itching to cuff her and haul her off to jail, fumed and cursed. Although his deputies were poised to move swiftly, she had not broken Alabama law. Yet.

The First Lady sat there throughout the morning session. Eleanor had demonstrated that she would not be bullied by a racist Southern police chief nor be bound by racism, as had her Georgia-born paternal grandmother Bulloch. By lunchtime, Eleanor's "inching" was the talk of the South. One could imagine the conversations during the break:

"Did you see her?"

"Sure did!"

"Did you see ole Bull Connor's face?"

"Saw that too."

"He was as red as a tomato."

Far beyond the venue, God smiled and said, "*Finally!*"

The incident became legend across the country.

Anna Eleanor Roosevelt Roosevelt (her maiden name was also Roosevelt) remains one of the world's most admired women a half century after her death in 1962. Conrad Black identifies Franklin Roosevelt as "the most important person of the twentieth century" and America's "most accomplished leader since Abraham Lincoln." Other historians add, "If there hadn't been an Eleanor, there wouldn't have been a Franklin."

Eleanor Roosevelt's living and dying, commitments and causes, words and beliefs, still offer inspiration, insight, and vision. In words from the New Testament that Eleanor had memorized as a child, she "being dead yet speaketh" (Heb. 11:4).

Search online booksellers and libraries and you may be surprised at the number of books by and about Eleanor Roosevelt, certainly more than for any other First Lady. Readers, politicians, and scholars still want to know what made her tick. What inspired her activism and made her the most controversial First Lady in American history? How did she live with the ridicule, the criticism, the carping? Where did she find courage to live out her convictions?

Seemingly, scholars, historians, and biographers have explored every nook and cranny of her life. The sheer amount of historical, biographical, and photographic records in her papers in the Franklin D. Roosevelt Presidential Library and Museum in Hyde Park, New York, daunts any researcher. Journal articles, research papers, books, recordings, dissertations, and documentaries, as well as Ken Burns's PBS series *The Roosevelts*, have explored her commitment to civil rights, the needs of minorities, the Democratic Party, Jews, labor issues, women's rights, artists, sharecroppers, and impoverished Americans.

Her investment in the fledgling United Nations and her influence as a power broker in the highest circles of the Democratic Party and Americans for Democratic Action, a group she cofounded after her husband's death, have been studied by numerous writers. Her childhood, her marriage to Franklin, her relationships with Lorena Hickok and the troubled boys of Wiltwyck School, and her political and social activism have been summarized and publicized. Hundreds of thousands of people walk by or stop at her statue at the Franklin Delano Roosevelt Memorial in Washington, DC.

How can any writer believe there is something new to be discovered about Eleanor Roosevelt?

Repeatedly, through researching and writing draft after draft, I have pondered her words, "You must do the thing you think you cannot do." In too many moments during meals, while trying to relax after a long day of editing, and even during sleep, her words have roared through my mind like the midnight coal trains that passed by my childhood home.

What made Eleanor, late that dark night in Tennessee, despite Klan threats to kill her and an abundance of liquored-up good old boys anxious to collect the $25,000 bounty on her head, drive more than eighty miles—without police protection—to speak at the Highlander Folk School near Monteagle?

Why did Eleanor, as an elderly woman, phone Attorney General Robert Kennedy to ask why Martin Luther King Jr. was jailed and what the attorney general was going to do to respond? What made her open her checkbooks—at times, she kept five—to raise bail money for King and his associates?

What drove her to challenge racist property owners so that singer Nat King Cole could buy the house he wanted in Hollywood and entertainer Harry Belafonte could get the apartment he wanted in New York City?

What made Eleanor, on more than one Christmas Eve, slip from the gaiety and comfort of the White House to drive through alleys and slums to distribute trees and gifts to children who lived in dire poverty within the Capitol's shadow?

What made Eleanor trek through the worst hollows in Appalachia to buy meat so that a young boy's pet rabbit would not be his family's dinner?

Why did Eleanor, by the hour, listen and dialogue with angry college students, some dabbling with socialism and communism? Why did she bother to speak with clueless federal bureaucrats?

What prompted Eleanor to speak out vigorously against lynching while her husband chose silence and southern Democrats babbled about "protecting the purity" of white women and "preserving the southern way of life"? What made Eleanor fight until the midnight hour to block one black man's execution?

What made Eleanor visit World War II internment camps holding taxpaying US citizens because they were Japanese Americans?

For Mrs. Roosevelt, the answer, I conclude after a decade of research and reflection, is her spirituality. Eleanor possessed a deep spirituality—not piety or religiosity—initially formed during her decades as a cradle Episcopalian. After leaving the White House in 1945 as a betrayed widow, particularly during her years serving as an American representative at the United Nations, she interacted with people from all faiths and no faith. Her understanding of and appreciation for alternative spiritual paths was stretched long before the word *spirituality* became popular in American culture.

Eleanor was formed by her deep appreciation for the words of Jesus and the New Testament, much of which she had memorized in French. Through spirited conversations during her travels as a United Nations delegate and advocate, she came to appreciate other voices, other myths, and other truths that did not fit into the boxed confines of her Episcopal faith. She became an early voice insisting that Americans must prepare themselves to listen to Muslims, Buddhists, Hindus, and Sikhs. At some point, she acknowledged that the narrow fundamentalist Episcopalian theology of her childhood was an inadequate vessel to hold all of the outrageously extravagant grace of a Creator who could not be bound by theological doctrine, dogma, or liturgy, let alone the shorthand conversation stopper, "*My* Bible says . . ."

Eleanor wrapped her mind and soul around the teaching of Jesus, "Thou shalt love thy neighbor as thyself" (Mark 12:31). Eleanor believed lyrics of the hymns she sang, such as "In Christ there is no east or west, in him no south or north" or "My faith has found a resting place, not in device nor creed" or "This is my Father's world, and to my listening ears all nature sings." Her faith might be particularly summed up in the words of the folk song penned by Peter Scholtes, "They'll Know We Are Christians by Our Love," which was sung during civil rights marches across the South—marches Eleanor would have joined had she been younger and in good health.

Eleanor's spirituality was not an abstract notion but a reality explored, lived, and celebrated. To her, all human beings, all, are the beloved children of God. Therefore, all humans are brothers and sisters. As Eleanor lived out her spirituality, her life and witness gave individuals courage to reassess the moorings of their faiths and to take stands of conscience.

A deep-rooted awareness of the transcendent stirred Eleanor to speak up, speak out, and speak persuasively about a merciful God and about the breadth of the word *all* in the Declaration of Independence, which declares that "all men are created equal." That awareness led her to offer mercy to the most unlikely candidates. She believed that in every audience there was one person—at least *one* person—she could reach with her ideas or hope; people she could invite, perhaps nudge, to think beyond the entrenched biases and shallow prejudices of their environment and their faith constructs.

Not by creeds and dogmas, white papers produced by denominational bureaucrats, committees and commissions, or ecclesiastical edicts, but by a practiced consistent love resting on Jesus' words, "Inasmuch as ye have done it unto one of the least of these my brethren, ye have done it unto me" (Matt. 25:40).

Three millennia ago, Micah, a Hebrew prophet, posed a timeless question: "What doth the LORD require of thee?" Micah's answer was carved deeply on the walls of Eleanor's consciousness: "to do justly, and to love mercy, and to walk humbly with thy God" (Mic. 6:8).

Eleanor acted justly when it was inconvenient.

Eleanor loved mercy and acted mercifully when it was inconvenient.

Eleanor walked humbly with her Creator when it was inconvenient.

This spiritual biography focuses on her zealous commitment to three ancient ideals. Her life is an invitation for spiritual seekers to explore one individual's application of Micah's declaration— which is needed even more today in a shrinking global society where, in the words of a

Christmas carol Eleanor loved to sing, "Hate is strong, and mocks the song / of peace on earth, goodwill to men."

Eleanor opened doors, initiated conversations, and stretched minds to new possibilities of seeing and sensing human need and defining human rights. Eleanor could have followed the traditions of previous First Ladies and been a tea-and-cookie-serving, one-cause, hand-shaking appendage to the president. Instead, she was driven by a longing, captured by the poet Mary Oliver, "I don't want to live a small life."

Because Eleanor Roosevelt chose not to live "a small life," this book explores the legacy of one remarkable child of God whose ripple has never stopped lapping at the shorelines of human souls.

1

What Religion Meant to Her

I think anyone who really thinks about the life of Christ must of necessity be influenced by it. It has always seemed to me that if we ever succeeded in living up to the standards which He set for us we would eliminate much of the conflict in the world. We would certainly get along better in our communities.

—Eleanor Roosevelt

Eleanor was an Episcopalian, from its aristocratic wing. She grew up in a nation she understood to be "a Christian country" (MD, February 16, 1951) and "predominately a Protestant country." Hindus, Buddhists, and Muslims lived in countries overseas, but rarely in Minneapolis, Long Beach, Sioux City, or Birmingham; immigration laws enacted in the 1920s restricted the entry of individuals from countries where those religions were dominant. Eleanor was baptized as a baby in 1884, confirmed as an adolescent in 1903, married as a young woman in 1905, and buried as an elderly woman in 1962, all in rituals that followed the liturgical rubrics of the Book of Common Prayer. The liturgy and prayers read at her funeral were almost identical to rituals for a hundred other Episcopalians memorialized that day and to the rituals for her mother, brother, father, grandmother, and husband in preceding decades. That was *the* way such things were done by Roosevelts—by the book, that is, by the Book of Common Prayer.

In Mrs. Roosevelt's day, attention to the soul, at least in American Protestant circles, was commonly framed by words such as *religion, religiosity, piety, dogma, faith,* or *denomination.* In December 1932, just three months before she moved into the White House, her article "What Religion Means to Me" appeared in the *Forum,* a national periodical. Some had to stop and reread part of the second paragraph: "To me religion has nothing to do with any specific creed or dogma." Eleanor explained:

It means that belief and that faith in the heart of a man which makes him try to live his life according to the highest standard which he is able to visualize. To those of us who were brought up as Christians that standard is the life of Christ.

Spirituality, to Eleanor, was "that feeling of having something outside of one's self and greater than one's self to depend on." She continued, "There never has been a time when that feeling is more needed than it is today. People in trouble need just what little children need—a sense of security, a sense of something greater than their own powers to turn to and depend on."

Her son Elliott Roosevelt dedicated his book *Mother R.* "To F.D.R., a man of conviction, and *A.E.R., a woman of faith.*" Eleanor never hesitated to talk about Christian religion in conversations, in speeches, in articles, or in her column. Her spirituality percolated in a deep, inner, sacred space. She acknowledged having questions about faith and doctrine. Joseph Lash, her friend and biographer, recalled, "Christ's story was a drama that re-enacted itself repeatedly in her thoughts and feelings." Certainly, others saw her as a feminist, a savvy politician, or, in her later years, a stateswoman. To Lash, "she was a woman with a deep sense of spiritual mission. Like Saint Theresa, she not only 'had a powerful intellect of the practical order' but was a woman of extravagant tenderness and piety."

For readers who protest that religious interests are private matters—especially for the nation's First Lady or former First Lady—Eleanor countered, "It does very little good to believe something unless you tell your friends and associates your belief" (MD, May 7, 1945).

Eleanor's beliefs on civil rights, for example, were shaped on the anvil of her faith. It did little good to believe segregation was wrong unless one protested it, particularly in settings where one might encounter objection. One could not look the other way or make nice. She did not consider holding one's tongue a gift of the Spirit. But it was critical to express one's thoughts with sensitivity and clarity. She once confided to Joseph Lash, "It's all very well to have a great many nice ideas but if you can't say them so that any child of five can understand them, you might just as well not have them."

PRACTICES OVER BELIEFS

Serving at the United Nations and the United Nations Association later in her life provided opportunities for interaction and discussion with adherents of all the world's major religions, as well as with individuals who professed to be atheist or agnostic. In those personal encounters, often over a cup of tea, Eleanor learned that religious labels are imprecise and fluid in response to life experiences. I think she would have understood and applauded spiritual migrations that take place across theological polarities today. Joshua Boettiger, her great-grandson, for example, is a Reconstructionist rabbi. That would please her!

Denominational politics and sermonic potshots from ecclesiastical leaders about the numerous divorces and remarriages of her children strained her denominational loyalty. From time to time, church officials sought something from Eleanor: a check, an endorsement for a pet project, a "favorable word," or "intercession with certain government agencies." One bishop irritated Eleanor because his visits focused on gossip rather than issues of faith.

In her essay "What Religion Means to Me," Eleanor demonstrated remarkable religious tolerance, which would eventually prove critical at the United Nations: "To those of us who happen to have been born and brought up under other skies or in other creeds the object to be attained goes by some other name." (The phrase "of us" offers insight into the breadth of her faith.) Eleanor rejected us-versus-them thinking on any topic. Granddaughter Nina Roosevelt Gibson told me that Eleanor always wanted to get beyond "me" or "you" to "you *and* me." Eleanor believed that *all* humans are God's beloved children.

It did not matter to Eleanor what religion one belonged to. It did matter *how* one practiced that religion! And how that religion impacted and nurtured one's worldview, particularly toward people who are marginalized, powerless, or poor. Thus, the institutionalized racism rampant in southern Protestantism befuddled her, particularly when she pondered these words in the book of Galatians: "There is neither Jew nor Greek, there is neither bond nor free, there is neither male nor female: for ye are all one in Christ Jesus. And if ye be Christ's, then are ye Abraham's seed, and heirs according to the promise" (Gal. 3:28–29).

Unlike Franklin Roosevelt, she would not overlook racism. Racism demeaned and wounded the integrity of the racist and the recipient. Consequently, she spent little time in FDR's cottage in Warm Springs, Georgia, because racism was woven tightly into the fabric of daily social interaction there.

Eleanor, much to the chagrin of more fundamentalist Christians, found broad nuances in Jesus' words, "For God so loved the world, that he gave his only begotten Son, that whosoever believeth in him should not perish, but have everlasting life" (John 3:16). *Whosoever* meant inclusion in a generously spacious relationship with God. Eleanor thought John 3:16 could not be read without John 3:17, "For God sent not his Son into the world to condemn the world; but that the world through him might be saved" *and* be more fully human. So, if God did not condemn, why should humans? Joseph Lash noted that later in life, "In general, she seemed to think that all churches as institutions too often seemed to be in conflict with genuine religious feeling, faith, and spirit. Like Tolstoy she felt there was little in common between the organized church and Christ's teachings, except the name."

COUNTERING HER CHRISTIAN CRITICS

I have struggled writing about Eleanor's spirituality because my research and reflection have been filtered through the lens of my own spirituality, as well as my doctoral studies in spiritual formation. Ironically, I grew up in a faith that had little use for Mrs. Roosevelt's "do-gooder" social beliefs. The term "liberal Christian Democrat" would have been considered oxymoronic. While I have, over the years, migrated to a more generous understanding of grace, occasionally I am ambushed by traces of theological residue from my southern Holiness upbringing.

Similarly, many Christian fundamentalists in Eleanor's own day did not believe that she and Franklin were *true* Christians, that is, "Bible-believing, God-fearing" Christians. Some readers of this book, I suspect, will want evidence that proves Eleanor was a "born again" Christian, in the sense of the usage Jimmy Carter injected into the 1976 presidential campaign, or that she would have agreed with former president George W. Bush's identification of Christ as "the greatest philosopher: He changed my life." Eleanor was a *baptized* Christian and a *confirmed* Christian. Some readers may push: "Yes, but was she saved?" Or "had she accepted Jesus as her personal lord and savior?" Or "had she prayed the sinner's prayer?" Few in Eleanor's liturgical tradition would have used that phraseology, as presidential candidate George H. W. Bush, a fellow Episcopalian, discovered in 1988 as he attempted to win the votes of the religious right.

Eleanor was keenly aware of fundamentalist Christians who spent endless time and energy deciding who was and who was not "saved" or arguing about doctrinal cul-de-sacs. Many Christians even today seem unconvinced of the depth and authenticity of Eleanor Roosevelt's faith, not knowing that the strength so many admire in her was born of the alchemy of deep emotional wounds *and* a deep reservoir of enriched spirituality.

Peter Benson and Carolyn Eklin conducted a study of eleven thousand individuals to identify eight core characteristics of a mature Christian spirituality. These markers are used by many in the fields of Christian education and church life to gauge the spiritual health of congregations, and they make an equally useful tool for examining elements in Eleanor's spirituality, lest we think her understanding of religion as "having something outside of one's self and greater than one's self to depend on" and having "nothing to do with any specific creed or dogma" puts her outside the scope of traditional Christianity in any way.

Benson and Eklin suggest that an individual practicing "healthy" Christian spirituality

— trusts in God's saving grace and believes firmly in the humanity and divinity of Jesus;
— experiences a sense of personal well-being, security, and peace;
— integrates faith and life, seeing work, family, social relationships, and political choices as part of one's religious life;
— seeks personal growth through study, reflection, prayer, and discussion with others;
— seeks to be part of a community of believers in which people give witness to their faith and support and nourish one another;
— holds life-affirming values;
— advocates for social and global change;
— serves humanity, consistently and passionately, through acts of love and justice.

These elements were the piers upon which Eleanor's spirituality rested.

Trusts in God's saving grace and believes firmly in the humanity and divinity of Jesus. Admittedly, Eleanor was much more concerned with how one lived one's faith than with the particularities of one's beliefs, but her reverence for Jesus Christ was undeniable. Surfing the Eleanor Roosevelt Papers Project Web site of George Washington University, one finds nine hundred mentions of Jesus Christ. Eleanor mentioned Jesus, by my calculations, in 12 percent of her "My Day" columns. She wrote about and talked about Jesus more than she wrote about some of the major political players of her day. Certainly, she talked about Jesus more and more boldly than did all the other First Ladies combined.

As a faithful Episcopalian, she would have affirmed the historic creeds of the church in hundreds of worship services over her nearly eight decades of life. From the Book of Common Prayer (1892), Eleanor would have recited the Apostles' Creed, with its particular beliefs about Jesus:

> I believe . . . in Jesus Christ, his only Son, our Lord: Who was conceived by the Holy Ghost, Born of the Virgin Mary: Suffered under Pontius Pilate, Was crucified, died, and buried; He descended into hell; The third day he rose again from the dead: He ascended into heaven, And sitteth on the right hand of God the Father Almighty: From thence he shall come judge the quick and the dead.

Eleanor, from years of repetition, could quote both the Apostles' and Nicene Creeds without looking at the prayer book, but she had some reservation on some phrases, for example, "born of the Virgin Mary." Accepting the virgin birth, in Eleanor's view, was not essential to believing and practicing what Jesus taught and lived. She was content to consider the details of Jesus' divinity and salvific work a "mystery."

Reflecting on the similarities and differences of Christianity and Hinduism on a trip to India, she wrote, "Many of us in the West who are Christians believe that, through a mystery we cannot understand, Christ was the Son of God sent to the world to sacrifice His life to save us."

Had someone asked Eleanor if she were saved, she might have flipped the question, "From *what*?" Indeed, I think that she might have tightened the question, "Saved *to what*?" Eleanor understood salvation not as having been "washed in the blood" or "saved from sin," but rather having been freed through God's magnificent grace to be fully human and empowered to live out Jesus' teachings, especially those in the Sermon on the Mount in Matthew 5–7.

Eleanor did not find Jesus' teaching static but ongoing. "The story of the New Testament," she wrote on Christmas Day, 1950, "is the story of His life and teachings. Christ taught from his early youth. He is still teaching each and everyone of us today" (MD, December 25, 1950).

Experiences a sense of personal well-being, security, and peace. "Nobody can make you feel inferior without your cooperation" is among the most widely quoted Eleanorisms. It took decades, however, for Eleanor to become comfortable in her own skin. (Some question if she ever did.) Psychologists agree that attachment to caregivers—particularly parents—shapes one's attachment to God. John Bowlby theorizes that attachment anxiety results from uncertainty, irregularity, and unpredictability in the family of origin; Eleanor experienced all three to a horrifying degree! Because of her mother's persistent verbal abuse and her father's extended absences and irresponsibility (abandonment), it took time for Eleanor to embrace a trustable God who would not abandon her. Lisa Miller argues, "Parenting choices in the first two decades radically affect . . . children's spiritual development in ways that last their entire lives."

It was not ultimately her family or her church that helped her discover this sense of well-being and security, but the influence of Marie Souvestre, the atheist, lesbian headmistress at Allenswood. Eleanor recalled years later, "For three years, I basked in her generous presence, and I think those three years did much to form my character and give me the confidence to go through some of the trials that awaited me when I returned to the United States."

Eleanor found that receiving Holy Communion also offered a sense of peace and well-being. William Turner Levy, a confidante to Eleanor, recalled sitting with her one Sunday morning at St. James' Church: "I could not but sense her complete separation from all earthly ties, caught up in a loving absorption" of the service. Only once, he confessed, had he ever witnessed anyone as "caught up in rapture" of the Eucharist, and that had been T. S. Eliot.

Integrates faith and life, seeing work, family, social relationships, and political choices as part of one's religious life. Eleanor knew individuals whose faith was a Sunday morning experience, who compartmentalized their faith. Her husband fit that category. Episcopal formation and tradition shaped Eleanor and Franklin, but while Eleanor talked about faith, Franklin regarded religion as a private matter. Pressed by a reporter to elaborate on his faith, FDR used nine words: "I am a Christian and a Democrat, that's all." As the mother of five young children, Eleanor fumed over Franklin's nominal faith practices: What kind of example was he setting for their children? Sundays for him—before polio—were for golfing and socializing with friends. She patiently endured the children's protests that they had to attend church and their father did not! Moreover, when her children listened in church, questions arose. On leaving church one Sunday, one Roosevelt child overheard a congregant make a disparaging remark about a neighbor. The child loudly protested to his mother, "That is the thing I can't understand about you grown-ups. You talk one way in church and come out and act another" (MD, June 17, 1939). Years later, a grandchild coming out of St. James' would make the same observation.

Individuals—particularly political leaders—who used faith to rationalize prejudice troubled Eleanor. She was annoyed to learn that when a woman who desperately needed a job applied for a federal position, her congressman informed her that he "would pray over it." What was there to pray about? Give the woman the job! (He nominated someone else.) Eleanor was alarmed by a trio of virulent avowed Christian southern senators—A. Willis Robertson of Virginia, and Theodore Bilbo and James Eastland of Mississippi—who used their faith to write racial prejudices into law and to avoid challenging the entrenched racist bigotry of their white voters or irritating their good-old-boy colleagues in Congress.

When the Wagner-Van Nuys Anti-Lynching Bill—after years—finally came to the Senate floor for consideration in 1938, polling demonstrated that even 65 percent of Southerners thought the time had come to enact a federal statute to eliminate lynching. But senators from the South—all Democrats and Christians—fought the bill tooth and nail. Tom Connally of Texas vowed (in February) to keep the filibuster going until Christmas recess; Senator "Cotton Ed" Smith of South Carolina pleaded for Northerners to understand that Southerners *needed* lynching "to protect the fair womanhood of the South from beasts." Moderate Republicans and Democrats agreed that if FDR "wanted the bill passed, it would go through in two or three days." But the silence from the Oval Office was deafening. Perhaps, at the end of his second term—as a lame duck—he could support such legislation. There were, no doubt, some tense conversations between the Roosevelts on this subject. For Eleanor, it was time for the president to lead! She later wrote: "Too many of us gave lip service to the spirit of Christlike living, but when it actually comes to carrying out His mandates, they are too often forgotten" (MD, December 25, 1950).

Seeks personal growth through study, reflection, prayer, and discussion with others. Biographer Joseph Lash and White House seamstress Lillian Parks report that Mrs. Roosevelt always carried written prayers in her purse, not as a talisman, but as a reminder of her commitments to fit a moment of reflection between appointments. Lash and her grandson John Roosevelt Boettiger describe observing Eleanor close her long, overscheduled days with a prayer containing this phrase, "Forbid us to be satisfied with what we make of life." Eleanor wrote about prayer in "My Day":

> The Lord meant us to pray when we are frightened and when we feel the need of help. None of us in ourselves can feel that we have the wisdom and courage to meet the happenings in our ordinary daily lives, much less to meet those in the troubled world today. But there are many verses in the Bible that would remind us what strength there is in faith. (MD, February 16, 1951)

After a long life, Eleanor observed, "I believe very strongly that faith in God will help us in any situation—physical, mental or spiritual" (IYAM, June 1957). As the apostle Paul compelled his readers, "Be ye transformed by the renewing of your mind" (Rom. 12:2). Eleanor recognized the importance of devotional reading, not only from the Bible and from spiritual classics, but also from fresh voices on the spiritual landscape. The alternative was conformity to shallow, safe thinking. Eleanor knew God could speak through emerging voices whose books she touted in "My Day" columns.

Mrs. Roosevelt often dialogued with clergy members about religious issues and topics. Her responses to letters from ministers frequently required serious reflection. She expressed sadness when the Rev. James Pike, dean of the Cathedral of St. John the Divine in New York City, became bishop of California. She valued Pike's open, expansive spirituality—later branded heresy—that stretched the worldviews of New York Episcopalians; indeed, the New York diocese was the most diverse in the Episcopal Church (MD, February 8, 1958).

Eleanor paid attention to scientific discovery—particularly the development of the atomic and hydrogen bombs—that frightened many Christians and fueled their apocalyptic thinking or obsession. She urged believers to think, pray about, and promote peaceful uses of atomic energy. The atom was not a reality to be feared, but a reality to be appropriated for the improvement of humankind.

Seeks to be part of a community of believers in which people give witness to their faith and support and nourish one another. Throughout her adult life, Eleanor was active in local Episcopal parishes. The seeds of her faith and commitment to social justice were nurtured in the Church of the Incarnation, on Madison Avenue in New York City, the family's parish during Eleanor's early childhood.

Franklin and Eleanor, as young parents, attended St. Thomas

Episcopal Church in Manhattan. During widowhood, while living in Greenwich Village, Eleanor attended the Church of St. Luke in the Fields, the spiritual home for many social activists. Certainly Eleanor's deepest commitment was to St. James' Church, the small parish in Hyde Park, New York. One reason for her loyalty was surely the parish graveyard, less than one hundred feet from the altar, where she had buried the first Franklin D. Roosevelt Jr., her baby, in 1909. While First Lady, she frequently attended St. John's Episcopal Church in Lafayette Square across from the White House.

Mrs. Roosevelt concurred with Martin Luther King Jr.'s assessment that the most segregated hour in American society was Sunday morning when Christians gathered by race for Bible study and worship. Late in life, Eleanor joined the Church for the Fellowship of All Peoples in San Francisco pastored by the Rev. Howard Thurman, an African American theologian and mystic. As a "national" member, she wanted to support this faith community's commitment to ending the racial divide in Protestant churches. Thurman's thinking and writing on spirituality and mysticism fascinated her. She hoped this congregation could become a national model.

Holds life-affirming values. Eleanor had witnessed firsthand the havoc created by World War I when she joined Franklin, then assistant secretary of the navy, to tour French battlefields. After World War II, when the United Nations Commission on Human Rights was in recess, Eleanor walked the rescarred landscape of Europe to see the devastation, one of the first American women to do so. Perhaps she remembered Jesus chiding, "Having eyes, see ye not?" (Mark 8:18). The carnage that Eleanor smelled and breathed, touched and tasted, the pleas of individuals to whom she listened, the sad, hungry children, accelerated her commitment to peacemaking. The next war would be one no one could win.

As the Cold War intensified, Eleanor reflected, "It probably would be extremely helpful if each of us prayed for the ability 'to love those who hate us'" (MD, July 26, 1949). People, Eleanor asserted, must invest in peacemaking by praying *and by working* for peace.

Nightly she prayed, "Show us a vision of a world made new." Traditional understandings of international political order were no longer sufficient to maintain peace in a dramatically redrawn world. Rights, Eleanor argued, must be clearly established through a Universal Declaration of Human Rights monitored by the United Nations—a tall order, given the postwar reshuffling of the political, religious, and ethnic landscape. Repeatedly, she reminded herself of Jesus' beatitude, "Blessed are the peacemakers," aware that their being called "the children of God" might not occur in her lifetime (Matt. 5:9).

Advocates for social and global change. Eleanor understood the need for global responsibility. To her last breath, she advocated personal involvement in four venues: local, state, national, and global. She lobbied for social change so that humanity could assume responsibility for one another as brothers or sisters. In *The Moral Basis of Democracy*, written in 1940, she contended that "Christ-like living" was essential for democracy's survival. How did she define this phrase? At a speech at Foundry Methodist Church in Washington in 1942, she declared that faith gives us "a sense of obligation to live with a deeper interest in the welfare of one's neighbor."

Eleanor had the spiritual gift of showing up, advocating for social justice through her very presence. Moreover, by showing up she attracted the media and shed light on intolerable injustices.

In February 1938 when the Wagner-Van Nuys Anti-Lynching Bill finally came to the Senate floor for consideration, the First Lady pointedly sat with African Americans in the Senate gallery throughout the seven days of debate. She called her action "paying witness." In 1939, when Missouri sharecroppers went on strike, Eleanor showed up to support them camped alongside two highways, and she wrote about their courage in "My Day"—much to the consternation of Missouri's Democratic governor, Lloyd Stark, who wanted her to lighten up on him, given his campaign against the incumbent US senator, Harry Truman.

During that same Southern Conference for Human Welfare where Eleanor inched her chair to the center of the aisle of the segregated meeting space, Eleanor boldly argued with Alabama Gov. Bibb Graves that *all* Alabama residents had the right to vote and then took on Congressman Luther Patrick. Patrick took the position that passing an anti-lynching law would scapegoat Southerners and would give northern racial prejudice "a pass." Eleanor finally had enough and stood to ask the politician "why the solution doesn't lie in the hands of the people of the South." Could not Alabama lead the way? Eleanor zeroed in on the sweating congressman to ask, "Had there ever been a real effort by Southern lawmakers to pass an anti-lynching law" which could be a model that other legislatures could follow to end the injustice?

Serves humanity, consistently and passionately, through acts of love and justice. In addition to her national and international advocacy for justice at the systemic level, Eleanor was committed to personal acts of charity to help the less fortunate. Where Washington bureaucrats saw statistics, Eleanor saw individuals loved by God. Joseph Lash reports that Mrs. Roosevelt "felt a responsibility to help everyone in distress who appealed to her." I doubt if anyone—including her children and secretaries, Malvina Thompson, Edith Helm, and Maureen Corr—knew the identities of many recipients of Mrs. Roosevelt's checks and kindnesses; they certainly did not know the names of individuals who stopped her on the street, and to whom she gave cash!

Lash observes that evading an issue or an appeal for help was never an option, and "in every situation she asked not only what was to be done but what she herself must do."

One recipient of such help was Nicholas Stephanos Vasilakos, who had operated a peanut stand on the sidewalk by the northeast corner of the White House grounds since Uncle Theodore was president. Now the District Chamber of Commerce wanted to evict him because his stand was "an obstruction to traffic flow."

The vendor had developed friendships with customers from all walks of life. Eleanor Roosevelt, while walking her dogs, frequently stopped, chatted, and bought peanuts. After reading about the eviction in the *Washington Evening Star*, the First Lady clipped the article, attached a four-word memo, "Must this man go?" and sent it to FDR.

Vasilakos stayed at that spot selling peanuts. Eleanor's victory must be shared with Irvin Henry McDuffy, the president's valet, also a long-time customer, who had urged the president to intervene. Imagine a First Lady who had time to respond to a sidewalk vendor's predicament!

Sometimes, "acts of love" occur in distant places; at other times, close to home.

A LIVED SPIRITUALITY

Eleanor had friends who, alarmed by the darkening war clouds across Europe, concluded that the answer to the world's problems was "a great religious revival," much like the Great Awakenings that took place in the eighteenth and nineteenth centuries. Eleanor conceded that while these friends *might* be right, the need was for "great religious revivals which are not simply short emotional upheavals lifting people to the heights then dropping them down again below the place from which they rose." Revivals require, she argued, "a fundamental change in human nature."

While such change "will come *to some people* through religion," she acknowledged, "it will not come to all that way, for I have known many people, very fine people, who had no formal religion." Eleanor reflected, "The change must come to some, perhaps, through a new code of ethics, or an awakening sense of responsibility for their brothers." Eleanor pointed to Cain's snarl in the Genesis narrative, "Am I my brother's keeper?" She answered resoundingly, "Indeed, you *are!*" And to the brothers and sisters you know *and* those you do not know.

Eleanor understood Jesus to call his followers to live differently despite traditions and cultural norms, disappointments, and tragedies. Eleanor, a survivor of a pathetic childhood and twenty-one significant deaths, well knew faith-enshrouded dysfunction. The dysfunctional Halls, in whose home she was raised, attended church every Sunday, but their religion was lived "on a Sunday" and had little to do with everyday life. To Eleanor it was about living faith the other six days as well. And the goal in her mind was clear: to "follow the life of the Man who was always unselfish, who really cared how the downtrodden suffered." The world would change when individuals would live as if "they really wished to follow in Christ's footsteps."

Spirituality measured in beliefs, congregational involvement, and a personal sense of security is incomplete—in Benson and Eklin's terms, "immature" or "unhealthy"—without spirituality lived out in service and justice. Eleanor knew from repeated readings of and reflection on the book of James in the New Testament: "Religion that God our Father accepts as pure and faultless" is *not* about dogma and doctrines or adherence to denominational interpretations and policies. No! James declared the goal of "pure" religion was "to look after orphans and widows in their distress and to keep oneself from being polluted by the world" (Jas. 1:27 NIV).

To Eleanor there was never a better time than the present moment to live out one's faith and fulfill Charles Wesley's lyrics in "A Charge to Keep I Have": "To serve the present age, my calling to fulfill, O may it all my powers engage, to do my Master's will." Eleanor noted in "What Religion Means to Me":

When religion becomes again a part of our daily lives, when we are not content only with so living that our neighbors consider us just men, and when we really strive to put into practice that which in moments of communion with ourselves we know to be the highest standard of which we are capable, then religion will mean in each life what I think it should mean. We will follow the outward observances because they give us help and strength, but we will live day by day with the consciousness of a great power and of greater understanding than our own to guide us and protect us and spur us on.

2

A Childhood from Hell

Eleanor's Early Years

Mine was a very miserable childhood. I wanted to be loved so badly,
and most of all I wanted to be loved by my father.
—Eleanor Roosevelt

I do not feel she has much chance, poor little soul.
—Edith (Mrs. Theodore) Roosevelt, predicting Eleanor's future

One day in 1886, James and Sara Roosevelt welcomed distant cousin
Elliott Roosevelt and his wife, Anna, and two-year-old daughter, Eleanor, to Hyde Park, New York. Elliott wanted to see four-year-old
Franklin, his godson. At one point during that visit, Anna, scolding
her daughter, called her "Granny," explaining that Eleanor was "such
a funny child, so old-fashioned." When Franklin invited Eleanor to
climb onto his back for a "horsey" ride, the parents laughed. Who
would have predicted these children would someday marry, step onto
the world stage, and impact history?

No one should experience a childhood like Eleanor's. That children
still experience such childhoods, a century and a quarter after Eleanor's birth, shows how powerful families can be in hiding their darkest
secrets. But for the grace of God, Eleanor would have reacted to her
upbringing in a more rebellious and violent way and, perhaps, earned
a different type of fame.

Eleanor told Joseph Lash—her friend and biographer—that she had
survived "a very miserable childhood." Corinne Robinson Alsop commented that her cousin did not "realize how ghastly it was" because
she had little interaction with other children. Eleanor, at age fifty-five,
reflected, "It is useless to resent anything in this world; one must learn
to look on whatever happens as part of one's education in life and make
it serve a good purpose in the formation of character."

HER CHILDHOOD SHOULD HAVE BEEN IDYLLIC

Anna Eleanor Roosevelt was born on October 11, 1884, to Elliott Bulloch Roosevelt and Anna Rebecca Hall Roosevelt, members of New York City's social elite. Guests at their December 1883 wedding ceremony had included the Cornelius Vanderbilts, the John Astors, the William Astors, and the James Roosevelts. Elliott, the younger brother of future president Theodore Roosevelt, lived a dashing sporting life thanks to trust funds from his father, Theodore Roosevelt Sr., who had died in February 1878. Eleanor's younger brother Elliott Jr. was born on September 23, 1889, and another brother, Gracie Hall, on July 18, 1891.

The deaths of Martha Bulloch Roosevelt, the family matriarch, and Alice, Theodore's first wife, of unrelated causes just hours apart on Valentine's Day 1884, two days after Alice had given birth to baby Alice Lee, staggered the privileged Roosevelt tribe, particularly Elliott. Some feared that Theodore, age twenty-five, a member of the New York Assembly, would not survive this double heartbreak. Eleanor's birth and baptism six months later brought some light into the family darkness.

New York society expected great things from Theodore Sr.'s sons Elliott and Theodore. Theodore Sr.'s literal interpretation of Jesus' words, "For unto whomsoever much is given, of him shall be much required" (Luke 12:48), had driven his vigorous commitment to doing good works and philanthropic generosity—not just by writing checks but by "hands-dirty" involvement.

The Roosevelts hoped Anna Hall could settle Elliott down, especially after Eleanor's birth. Instead, Elliott spent much of his time away from wife and baby pursuing a good time hunting, yachting, clubbing, and imbibing with pals. Today his drinking habits would be considered an addiction; only the family's social status prevented Elliott from being called a drunk. Repeatedly Theodore chastised his brother to "act like a man" and live up to his responsibilities as husband and father.

For the wealthy, extended trips in Europe could be a subterfuge for finding the right spa or treatment to dry out or, at least, to hide an alcoholic from the public eye. On May 18, 1887, Elliott, Anna, and Eleanor sailed for Liverpool, England, on the SS *Britannic*. The second day at sea, in intense fog, the SS *Celtic*, another steamer, rammed their ship three times, killing twelve and injuring twenty.

In the chaotic evacuation of the *Britannic*, Elliott, standing in a lifeboat, repeatedly yelled to a sailor on an upper deck dangling Eleanor over the rail to drop her. Eleanor clung to the sailor. She never forgot the trauma "of plummeting from the deck high above the pitching lifeboat below" and, thankfully, into her father's arms.

The Roosevelts returned to New York City and booked passage on another vessel. Geoffrey C. Ward describes Eleanor's hysteria upon overhearing her parents' plans: "The traumatized little girl now wept and shook at even the thought of going to sea again." Given the child's distress, Elliott and Anna left her with family. During their absence Great-aunt Gracie took Eleanor on an outing to Oyster Bay. As their carriage neared the water, Eleanor wailed: "Baby does not want to go into the water. Not in a boat!"

Anna and Elliott, seeking a cure for Elliott's numerous physical complaints—which he medicated generously with alcohol—extended their stay in Europe. That nine-month absence was the first of several abandonments that shaped Eleanor's childhood. Blanche Wiesen Cook assesses a little girl's fear:

> Without the immediate opportunity to face her terror again, the accident left Eleanor with a fear of heights and water that connected to a lifelong sense of abandonment. If she had not cried, if she had not struggled, if she had not been afraid, if she had only done more and been better, she would be with her parents.

Elliott's alcoholism and irresponsibility, mixed with the pressures of being Theodore Roosevelt's brother, wrecked the marriage. While rehearsing a stunt for an amateur circus, Elliott broke his leg. Because physicians failed to set the leg properly, his leg had to be rebroken. During a prolonged recuperation, Elliott relied on morphine, laudanum, and alcohol to relieve pain. Seeking another fresh start, the couple sailed to Europe—again without Eleanor. That cure was short-lived.

In 1890, when the Roosevelts traveled to Europe a third time, six-year-old Eleanor accompanied her parents. Although Elliott had sworn off alcohol, Eleanor watched her father sipping a large stein of beer in a German café. Pointing to German children tasting beer, she asked for a taste. Elliott replied, "Very well, but remember if you have it, you have to drink the whole glass." Eleanor wrote, "Never since then have I cared for beer."

Eleanor idolized her debonair father, who called her "my Little Nell" after a character in Dickens's *Old Curiosity Shop*. Eleanor recalled, "I never doubted that I stood first in his heart." That Elliott lavished love generously on his daughter but frugally on his wife may explain Anna's resentment of husband *and* daughter. Nina Roosevelt Gibson, Eleanor's granddaughter and a psychologist, reflected, "Her father made her feel special . . . made her feel loved. He didn't make her feel unattractive or shy. She felt very secure in his presence." Eleanor said her father, "who looked upon [her] short-comings with a much more forgiving eye," gave some "badly needed reassurance." Their time together created cherished memories, particularly of Venice. "I remember my father," Eleanor recalled, "acting as a gondolier, taking me out on the Venice canals, singing with the other boatmen, to my intense joy."

Because the Roosevelts prized horsemanship, children learned to ride at an early age. One day in Italy, Elliott, riding a horse, and Eleanor, on a donkey, plodded along a mountain trail. At some point, frightened by the steep descent, Eleanor balked. Her father, in a tone she described as "incredulous," snapped, "You're not afraid, are you?" Before the frightened child could answer, "A steely look came into the man's eyes, and in a cold voice he said, 'You may go back if you wish, but I did not know you were a coward.'" Elliott rode off, leaving Eleanor, her "donkey boy," and nurse to return to the lodge. Eleanor commented on that experience, "As I pondered the look in my father's eyes, I think my realization that fear was shameful and a thing to be overcome, began."

Decades later, Joseph Lash, discussing the incident with Eleanor, caught a twist in Eleanor's story that she had not included in her autobiography. In this version, her father asked, "How could a child of mine be a coward?" "Child of mine" had implications, given rumors of unfaithfulness by both parents. Lash, over a long friendship, concluded that Eleanor never overcame the shame of disappointing her father on that trail. Cook, Eleanor's definitive biographer, adds, "It seemed never to occur to her, even years later, that her father's expectation" of a child's riding skills, particularly in that treacherous setting, "had been unreasonable, and his impatience cruel."

TENSIONS BETWEEN PARENTS ESCALATE

After learning that Anna was again pregnant, Elliott either fell off or jumped from the proverbial wagon. To limit Eleanor's exposure to their arguments, Anna placed her in a French Catholic convent school. Eleanor felt abandoned; "the convent experience was a very unhappy one." After observing the nuns' reaction to a student who had swallowed a coin, Eleanor declared that she, too, had swallowed a coin. The nuns summoned Anna and expelled Eleanor, who later noted, "I realize how terrible it must have seemed to her to have a child who would lie!" One can imagine Anna's anger, "As if I don't have enough problems with your father, *now you do this*!" Anna had repeatedly scolded Eleanor, "You have no looks, so see to it that you have manners." Now the child had failed at manners!

The more the couple argued, the more Elliott drank. In desperation, Anna committed him to a sanitarium in Vienna, from which he escaped. He fled to Paris and took up with a married American woman who, over time, became his mistress.

Theodore and wife Edith—an adult child of an alcoholic—lost patience with both Elliott and Anna. In July 1889, Theodore confessed to his sister (also named Anna, but always called Bam, Bamie, or Bye) that he was at "wits end to know what else to do" about their brother's lifestyle, which he branded "a perfect nightmare." Theodore railed that his sister-in-law Anna was "an impossible person to deal with. Her utterly frivolous life has, as was inevitable, eaten into her character like an acid."

Anna's latest pregnancy was the last straw for Theodore. The couple, he insisted, as only he could insist, *must* separate. Anna and Elliott, he thundered, "have no right to have children now. It is a dreadful thing to bring into the world children under circumstances such as these. It must not be done. It is criminal."

Theodore's distress escalated when Catherine "Katie" Mann, a family maid, disclosed that she was pregnant. When she named Elliott as the father, Theodore was outraged that she would make such a preposterous allegation! After weighing Elliott's denials, Theodore dispatched a messenger to see the child. That messenger reported that the child was probably Elliott's; therefore, the Roosevelts "would be wise to pay whatever it took to settle the case." Quickly. At this point, Betty Boyd Caroli reports, "most of Elliott's family gave up on the idea of ever being able to help him."

The Roosevelts wrote a large check to make Catherine and the baby "go away." Eleanor never met her half brother, Elliott Roosevelt Mann, or his daughter, who wrote to her soon after she became First Lady in 1933. Any response more than a form letter would have contradicted Eleanor's fiercely protected image of her father.

Anna and the children sailed home. The Roosevelts' troubles stirred society chatter. The *New York Sun* reported Anna's decision to sue for divorce with this headline: "Elliott Roosevelt Insane"; other newspapers provided lurid details. Theodore's decision to seek a "writ of lunacy"—something like power of attorney—stimulated more headlines and fresh gossip. Given the way Elliott was squandering his inheritance, Theodore acted to protect what was left for Anna and the children. (That action insured Eleanor's inheritance, which would provide some financial independence from her mother-in-law.)

Elliott, from Europe, drafted a defense for the *New York Herald* stating that he was neither insane or an alcoholic. Riding injuries, he insisted, had sparked "a nervous condition." Theodore dismissed this assertion and denounced his brother as "a maniac and a flagrant man-swine" who had lost the family's respect.

If petitioning for divorce had been an attempt by Anna to force her husband to change, she failed. Rumors, spun by socialites, appeared as fact in the *New York Herald* on August 18, 1892: "Elliott Roosevelt demented by excess. . . . Wrecked by liquor and folly . . . is now con-fined in an Asylum for the insane."

Anna and the three children moved in with her mother, Mary Lud-low Hall. The Hall family divided their time between a New York City home and an estate in Tivoli, halfway between New York City and Albany. Now Eleanor's spiritual development would be overseen by her grandmother, a fundamentalist Episcopalian.

HELL AT THE HALLS'

Although Eleanor never knew her grandfather Valentine Hall, from the grave he controlled Mrs. Hall and molded the severe religiosity Eleanor would experience in their home. In the family library—filled with Val-entine Hall's theology books—Eleanor discovered a Bible containing graphic drawings of hell and massacres of the unrighteous. She recalled, "The Bible illustrated by Doré occupied many hours—and I think, probably gave me many nightmares."

Mrs. Hall conducted family prayers in the morning and evening, expecting every servant in the house and even the coachman to come at least once a day. As soon as she could read, Eleanor followed and recited the prayers in family worship. Joining Episcopalians around the country to pray from the Book of Common Prayer every morn-ing and evening shaped young Eleanor. Although Eleanor, over time, "abandoned the severe religiosity" of her grandmother, she retained

Mrs. Hall's appreciation for regular prayer and the Book of Common Prayer. Years later, Eleanor reflected that she had "really enjoyed learning the Bible verses and the hymns, which always had to be memorized for Sunday morning." Eleanor's youngest son, Elliott, expressed his amazement: "It was something of a marvel to me that religion had not been driven out of her when it was drilled in so hard at Tivoli."

Strict Sabbath observance was demanded, "a day set apart from other days." Especially in rural communities like Tivoli, one's behavior on Sunday attracted the notice or criticism of neighbors, and Grandmother Hall's Sundays were the gold standard of religious days in Eleanor's memory. After morning prayers at home with the Book of Common Prayer, the family went to St. Paul's Church. Eleanor recalled, "I had to sit on the uncomfortable small seat in my grandmother's large Victoria [carriage] … five miles to and from church." Eleanor remembered "hating every minute of that five mile drive. It seemed so long and I had to sit so still!" (MD, July 13, 1950). Mrs. Hall's approved Sabbath activities included taking children for walks and reading books aloud in wintertime, around the fireplace, but activities that resulted in noise or fun were not permitted! Grandmother Hall decided which books were appropriate for Sunday reading. Any book Eleanor was reading at bedtime on Saturday night had to be closed until Monday morning—a rule she did not always obey.

Eleanor's childhood curiosity sometimes made the family nervous. She never forgot her family's discomfort at dinner when she asked what *whore* meant.

Mrs. Hall sputtered, "It is not a word that little girls should use."

"Well," Eleanor retorted, "*it's* in the Bible." (Years passed before classmates at Allenswood explained the word's meaning to Eleanor.)

Rejecting Grandmother Hall's belief that every word of Scripture be taken literally, Eleanor gradually found her own way to weigh the words of the Bible. One must, she thought, be open to serious reflection, conversation, and challenge.

AN IMPOSSIBLE STANDARD

Beyond the rigidity that might be expected in a home of such social status and religiosity, Eleanor's mother presented, both overtly and implicitly, a standard to which the child could never hope to measure up. She repeatedly sought what Anna was unwilling, or unable, to give.

"No matter what she [Eleanor] did," Blanche Wiesen Cook reports, "it was never enough really to please Anna." Affirmation was never freely given, but could perhaps be earned.

Eleanor disclosed:

> I slept in my mother's room, and remember well the thrill of watching her dress to go out in the evenings. She looked so beautiful, I was grateful to be allowed to touch her dress or her jewels or anything that was part of the vision which I admired inordinately.
>
> My mother suffered from very bad headaches, and I know now that life must have been hard and bitter and a very great strain on her. I would often sit at the head of the bed and stroke her head. People have since told me that I have good hands for rubbing, and perhaps even as a child there was something soothing in my touch, for she was willing to let me sit there for hours on end.

Those "hours on end," historian Geoffrey Ward contends, reinforced Anna's assertion "that the way to be loved was to be useful"—a lesson that "stayed with [Eleanor] all her life" and affected every relationship she had.

The Halls relied on physical beauty as insurance for a female's future. Eleanor opened her first autobiography, "My mother was one of the most beautiful women I have ever seen." In cousin Alice Roosevelt's opinion, Anna was "one of the most beautiful women of her time," exquisite but "empty headed." "From my earliest days," Eleanor reminisced, "I knew that I could never hope to achieve my mother's beauty" or the beauty of her aunts. Anna Roosevelt was always "a little troubled" by her daughter's plain looks. Consequently, "she tried very hard to bring me up well so my manners would in some way compensate for my looks." Unfortunately, "I fell short in so many ways of what was expected of me."

Eleanor acted out. In Anna's indictment the child was "stubborn and spiteful." During a tutor's demonstration for mothers, Frederic Roser called on Eleanor to spell several words—spellings she knew. Eleanor "stood there in agony, the room heavy with anxiety and shame." Finally, Roser told her to be seated. Anna took her aside and "whispered severely" that she "feared to think 'what would happen if I did not mend my ways!'"

The misbehavior intensified. Eleanor "put sugar on her cereal, lied about her behavior, stole candy meant for dinner guests by the entire bagful out of the pantry. When her mother tried to get her to go to parties with other children, she resisted and burst into wild sobbing. On several occasions, she had utterly unbecoming and embarrassing tantrums in public."

Anna repeatedly humiliated Eleanor in front of guests. After one incident, Eleanor said that she "wanted to sink through the floor in shame, and I felt I was apart from, different than" her brothers.

"I felt," Eleanor confessed, "a curious barrier between myself and these three [my brothers and my mother]." Over time, the family branded the "introverted, painfully shy, and gawkily tall" child their "ugly duckling," although Aunt Edith observed, "The ugly duckling may turn out to be a swan." Four decades later Eleanor recalled the emotional bruising:

> By nature I was always a timid child, afraid of the dark, afraid of dogs, afraid of horses, and of snakes, afraid of being scolded, afraid that people would not like me! It was a long time before I came to the realization that this fear really paralyzed growth. If you are always thinking of what might go wrong, or what people will think, you are not giving yourself a fair chance to think freely and develop an independent personality.

However, in a draft of an article eventually published in *Look* magazine, Eleanor sanitized reality:

> I suppose it is natural for any child to feel that the most vivid personalities in early youth were those of his parents. This was certainly so in my case. My mother always remained somewhat awe-inspiring. She was the most dignified and beautiful person. But she had such high standards of morals that it encouraged me to wrongdoing. I felt it was utterly impossible for me to ever live up to her!

Scoldings from her mother only intensified the child's longings for her father's loving affirmation. It seems that Elliott too felt the futility of satisfying the Hall women. He pleaded with his mother-in-law to allow him access to his children:

> Please Mother dearest I am doing all I can. . . . I know it seems very little but if you only knew the agony of shame, repentance, and the love hunger you would pity me. Bear with me for it is a hard fight to make alone, even with God's promise of help to cheer one. . . . I know I was wrong and all of you right. . . . I pray for forgiveness. I am so sorry.

Elliott expressed annoyance with family members who discouraged any reunion with the children:

> There seems also to be still a strong feeling of suspicion as to my desire to lead a correct life. . . . They have all told me that they would like to see the proof given for another year of my capability to live rightly and of the earnestness of my desire to do so.

Elliott vowed to convince the family "of my sorrow for sin and to prove beyond doubt my worthiness to possess my Babies."

LONGING FOR FATHER

Neither Anna nor Mrs. Hall acknowledged that Elliott's absences were harming Eleanor. The young mother had little energy to deal with a stubborn girl whose preference for an absentee father never wavered. "Perhaps, in rejecting Eleanor's fervent love for her father," Doris Kearns Goodwin speculates, "Anna was rejecting that part of herself that had fallen" for such an "untrustworthy" but vivacious man.

In early 1892, Theodore sailed to Paris to confront his brother. If Elliott signed over a significant portion of his wealth, Theodore promised, the divorce suit and the lunacy petition would be quashed. Second, Elliott must submit to Dr. Leslie Kelley's "Bi-Chloride of Gold Cure" treatment—a program in Illinois designed for wealthy alcoholics. Third, following treatment, Elliott must go into exile for two years to work on the family's mining properties in southwestern Virginia.

Elliott, realizing that declining Theodore's terms might keep him from seeing the children, vowed to prove himself worthy in the eyes of Theodore and his mother-in-law; Anna, however, would be difficult to win back. A broken, repentant Elliott arrived in New York City to discover that no family reunion awaited the prodigal. Anna had taken the children to summer in Bar Harbor, Maine.

Elliott wrote to his daughter on her eighth birthday:

> My darling little Daughter
>
> Many happy returns on this birthday little Nell. I am thinking of you always and I wish for my Baby Girl the greatest joy and the most perfect happiness in her young life. . . . Take good care of yourself and little Brothers, Ellie and Brudie [Hall] and kiss them

for me. Love dear Mother for me and be very gentle and good to her 'specially now while she is not well.

He apologized for not being present to celebrate Eleanor's birthday:

Because Father is not with you is not because he doesn't love you. For I love you tenderly and dearly. And maybe soon I'll come back all well and strong and we will have such good times together, like we used to have.

Eleanor treasured the signature, "Your devoted Father."

A few weeks later, in November 1892, Anna underwent surgery. Despite Elliott's pleas to see his wife and children, Mrs. Hall turned him down: Anna needed rest more than she needed Elliott's presence. As Anna's physical and mental condition deteriorated, she disclosed to Mrs. Hall and her sisters shocking details of the marriage. Nine years after her wedding had been celebrated on the front page of the *New York Times*, Mrs. Hall groused that the marriage "had been pure torture." Anna died on December 7, 1892, of diphtheria and typhoid fever.

Grandmother Hall did not permit the children to attend their mother's funeral or burial in the family crypt at Tivoli, New York; she kept Eleanor from seeing headlines in New York newspapers: "Mrs. Roosevelt's Death. Her Last Years Saddened by Her Husband's Insanity. One of the Favorites of New York Society."

Eleanor never forgot how she learned that her mother had died. "Cousin Susie [Mrs. Henry Parish Jr., her second cousin] told me. . . . She was very sweet to me, and I must have known that something terrible had happened." Death, Eleanor recalled, "meant nothing to me, and one fact wiped out everything else—my father was back [for the funeral] and I would see him very soon." Anna had expressed her wish—with Theodore's concurrence—that Mrs. Hall be named guardian for the children. According to Joseph Lash, Theodore promised to keep "hands off"—unless Elliott tried to take the children. In that event, Theodore and Aunt Bam would join Mrs. Hall to stop him.

While some in the family hoped that Anna's death would have a sobering effect on Elliott, grief stimulated more drinking. Occasionally, under strict supervision, Elliott visited his children in Mrs. Hall's residence. During one visit, Elliott told Eleanor that the two of them—not the four—must keep close because "some day" they would "be together."

He asked Eleanor to write often and "not to give [Mrs. Hall] any trouble, to study hard, to grow up into a woman he could be proud of."

In 1893, when her brothers contracted scarlet fever, Eleanor was sent to Susie Parish's home. Elliott Jr.'s death on October 17, 1893, devastated Eleanor. She was not permitted to attend her brother's funeral. Many years later, she framed the loss, "My little brother, Ellie, was simply too good for this world, and he never seemed to thrive after my mother's death."

Elliott tried to alleviate his daughter's grief: "We bury little Ellie tomorrow up at Tivoli by Mother's side. He is happy in Heaven, with her so now you must not grieve or sorrow," paraphrasing the biblical injunction in 1 Thessalonians 4:13. Elliott pressed, "You will have to be a double good Daughter to your father and good sister to [Hall] who is left to us." Those words motivated Eleanor to become Hall's surrogate mother until he died of alcoholism in late September 1941.

Elliott returned to New York City and lived under an alias with a "Mrs. Evans," outrageous behavior for a Roosevelt. In letters exchanged between the Roosevelts, they expressed fear that Elliott was about to "sink to the lowest depths." Although Elliott swore he had reformed, on one rare visit, when father and daughter walked his three large dogs, Elliott asked Eleanor to watch the dogs while he went inside the Knickerbocker Club, a private men's establishment, for a few minutes. She waited on the steps for six hours before seeing her drunken father carried out. Seeking a quick libation, he drank until he passed out. The doorman sent Miss Eleanor home in a cab. Although Eleanor never complained, Mrs. Hall raged furiously.

In the remaining months of his life, Elliott continued to consume large amounts of wine and liquor. When delusional, he became paranoid, thinking that armies were chasing him. Once he struck his mistress with a stick. And one day Elliott showed up at Mrs. Hall's townhouse asking to take Eleanor—but not his son—for a drive. The governess let Eleanor go with him. After that episode, even Elliott's sister Corinne—his staunchest defender—insisted that Mrs. Hall *never* allow Eleanor and her father to be alone.

Kathleen Dalton, a biographer of Theodore Roosevelt, hints that some family members may have suspected or been aware of "hints of abuse worse than [Elliott's] violent rages." Edith Roosevelt applauded efforts to keep the children from Elliott, a man she and Theodore did not want around *their* children. She confessed, "I live in constant dread of some scandal of his [Elliott's] attaching itself to Theodore." Despite

Edith's concern for Eleanor's safety, she made no effort to remedy the threat.

ELLIOTT'S DEATH

On August 13, 1894, Elliott, suffering delirium tremens, tried to jump out a window. Then he ran up and down the stairs in the house where he was living. A family legend persisted that, in his last hours, Elliott, assuming his daughter to be somewhere in the building, knocked on one resident's door to ask if his daughter was there. He responded, "If she is out, will you tell her father is so sorry not to see her." Finally, he suffered a seizure and lost consciousness. Twenty-four hours later, Eleanor and Hall were orphaned. Blanche Wiesen Cook, in a lecture at the New York Historical Society, grimaced, "One has to pause to wonder how much alcohol you have to drink to die at age thirty-four." Douglas Brinkley says the death was, in essence, a suicide.

William Turner Levy, Eleanor's close confidante, insisted that "for the rest of her life she mourned his loss and venerated his memory." Eleanor, according to Betty Boyd Caroli, rehearsed good memories and ignored the bad, a process psychologist J. William Worden labels "selective forgetting." Four decades after her father's death, Eleanor dedicated her autobiography to her father. "I have a curious feeling," she wrote, "that as long as he remains to me the vivid, loving person that he is, he will . . . be alive and continue to exert his influence which was always a gentle, kindly one."

Details of Elliott's last days outraged the Roosevelts. It would not do for the politically ambitious Theodore to have his brother die in the arms of a woman the family considered a prostitute. So, with some persuasion, the *New York Times* reported: "Elliott Roosevelt Dies of Heart Disease." When Theodore viewed the corpse, his sister Corinne reported, he was "more overcome than I have ever seen him"—more than at the viewings of his wife and mothers' corpses. The future president "cried like a little child for a long time."

The Roosevelts moved to get the prodigal in the ground as quickly as possible. Pointedly, they did not bury Elliott next to "the pure, longsuffering" Anna in the family vault in Tivoli. Informed that her father had died, a subdued Eleanor whispered, "I did want to see father once more." Years later Eleanor recalled that day. "[I] simply refused to believe it, and while I wept long and went to bed still weeping, I finally went to sleep and began the next day living in my dream world as usual."

Because Grandmother Hall once again did not allow Eleanor and Hall to attend the funeral, Eleanor later wrote, "I had no tangible thing to make death real to me. From that time on I knew in my mind that my father was dead, and yet I lived with him more closely, probably, than I had when he was alive." One grandson summarized the death, "There was no closure provided, and none allowed." Eventually Eleanor named a son after her father—a troubled son who became her favorite.

Eleanor grieved for her deflated fantasy that someday she and her father would live together—a longing that had made life in Mrs. Hall's home bearable. Franklin D. Roosevelt III, a grandson, commented that at times Elliott had "reappeared briefly and swept Eleanor up in his arms, told her again how wonderful she was, and that everything was going to be all right. . . . And that really gave her the hook on which she could hang her life." Her father *would* show up again.

All humans maintain assumptions about how the world works. Ronnie Janoff-Bultman studied the impact of the collapse of an individual's assumptive "world." Eleanor had to grieve for *what had been* and for *what now would never be*. As I argue in an earlier book, "Three traumatic deaths, in less than twenty-four months, permanently challenged Eleanor's capacity to trust and to love." Consequently, future traumas, tragedies, and disappointments rekindled the emotional residue of Elliott Bulloch Roosevelt's death.

A GRANDMOTHER'S DAMAGE

Few biographers have pondered the emotional damage Mary Livingston Ludlow Hall inflicted on her grandchildren. Admittedly, given Elliott's irresponsibility, someone *had* to protect the children. Since they were already living with Mrs. Hall, making other arrangements after Elliott's death would have resulted in fresh instability. Aunt Bam might have been Eleanor's preference, but she lived in London, and besides, Grandmother Hall didn't like Eleanor spending even short amounts of time with her father's family. Before her father's death, Eleanor had enjoyed spending Saturdays with her paternal Aunt Grace. Mrs. Hall stopped those visits because she wanted her ward to "be at home as much as possible." Eleanor later hinted at a deeper motivation:

"Perhaps she feared we might slip away from her control if we spent too much time with our dynamic Roosevelt relatives."

In fact, because Mrs. Hall disapproved of those rambunctious Roosevelts of Oyster Bay, and to some degree blamed them for her son-in-law's egregious behavior, she determined to protect her grandchildren by limiting their contact with their father's family. For their part, Theodore and Edith had six children and could not, or would not, take Eleanor and her brothers.

Mrs. Hall, obsessed with the conclusion that she had failed to raise her five children properly, vowed that she would not fail with her grandchildren. However, the four adult children who still lived under their mother's roof, generally, were emotionally out of control, obsessed with the frills and fluff in New York's social orbit. In a lecture at the New York Historical Society, Blanche Wiesen Cook blasted the "obnoxious aunts and uncles who were drug addicts" and who did "insane things" with some degree of regularity. Given memories of her father's drinking, Eleanor became afraid of them. Her uncles, amateur tennis champions, got away with outrageous behavior because Mrs. Hall indulged them, always believing their latest promises to stop drinking. Uncle Vallie "liked to crouch in an upstairs window and fire his shotgun at anyone who happened to be on the lawn." Eleanor and her brother Hall "learned to stay close to the trunks of the big sheltered shade trees whenever they ventured outside."

It is hard to understand how Mrs. Hall could loathe Elliott's drinking and yet ignore her own alcoholic sons. *Dysfunction* would be too mild a label to describe the environment in which Eleanor and her brothers lived. Because Valentine Hall, the patriarch, died without a will—and had treated his wife as a child while he was alive—Mrs. Hall lived in financial chaos despite having two large homes. Whether in the New York City house or at Tivoli, Mrs. Hall spent most of her day sequestered in her darkened bedroom. She emerged only to give instructions to servants and to conduct the family's mandatory morning and evening prayer services.

Despite her severe religiosity, Mrs. Hall could not nurture the young, grieving children. The rule *"Don't talk, don't feel, ignore the obvious!"* was continuously reinforced.

Corinne Roosevelt Robinson, Eleanor's cousin, labeled Eleanor's childhood "the grimmest childhood I had ever known." Robinson, who visited Eleanor a few times, admitted that she resisted going because of "the grim atmosphere of that house. There was no place to play games, unbroken gloom everywhere. We ate our suppers in silence. The general attitude was 'don't do this.'" Eleanor, despite having a trust fund, "learned to ask for nothing" as a psychological defense against Mrs. Hall's habitual nos. Mrs. Hall dressed her in the aunts' hand-me-downs—long out of style.

Eleanor's autobiographical writings make almost no mention of childhood friendships or even playmates other than her younger brothers. A young girl Carola de Peyster, who lived five miles away, was allowed to visit Eleanor *one* day each summer; Eleanor was allowed to visit that child for one day. Eleanor admitted, "When I was a child, I had few playmates of my own during the long summer months in Tivoli." Because Eleanor's formal childhood education was sporadic, she lost opportunities for developing socialization skills with other girls, a problem neither Mrs. Hall nor other relatives sought to remedy. Edith discouraged contact between Alice, her stepdaughter, and Eleanor, cousins only eight months apart in age—both of whom had experienced a mother's death. After Elliott died, Edith wrote her mother, "As you know I never wished Alice to associate with Eleanor so [I] shall not try to keep up any friendship between them." Edith's insensitivity came at a critical psychospiritual point when Eleanor needed a cousin and an affirming "normal" aunt. Edith's actions led to lifelong tension between the cousins and fueled Alice's bitterness toward Eleanor's achievements. Aunt Edith did suggest one intervention with potential: "If anything . . . can be done for Eleanor it will be by a good school." Unfortunately, years passed before anyone acted on that suggestion.

I contend Mrs. Hall's tight grip on her grandchildren was motivated by her fear that a grandchild might slip up and disclose the ongoing pathological toxicity in the Hall residence, such as being shot at by two alcoholic uncles. Eleanor, for some reason, rationalized her grandmother's decision, suggesting that modes of transportation made "getting [her] about" difficult.

Eleanor was often on her own until evening. The rolling hills around Mrs. Hall's home in Tivoli offered safe places to read, dream, and wander. Eleanor preferred a particular cherry tree not simply for its shade and delicious cherries. The tree provided "a comfortable perch where she could not be seen" reading and from which she could spot "the approach of any grown up who might disapprove of the type of literature [she] had chosen" from the large family library, which could be thought "unsuitable" for a young lady. It seems, perhaps, she had good reason to hide.

Eleanor's bedroom door had three locks. Why would an adolescent, in 1898, in a pious, socially elite family need *any* lock, let alone three? Who installed the locks? When? And why? Laura Chanler White described a night spent as Eleanor's guest in Mrs. Hall's home. When White asked Eleanor to explain the locks, Eleanor answered: "To keep my uncles out."

Blanche Wiesen Cook comments, "Whether or not ER's 'lurching' uncles ever succeeded in molesting her or were sexually abusive cannot now be known. But that she recognized the need to create physical barriers to their presence indicates a far more embattled adolescence than we have heretofore understood."

A NANNY TO BE FEARED

A succession of nannies and teachers likewise rained havoc on the child's fragile emotional security. Eleanor's French teacher, Mlle. LeClerq, made Eleanor spend a significant portion of her day memorizing New Testament passages in French. Eleanor recalled, "I thought this a great waste of time, but later found very useful the well-trained memory which all this learning things by heart gave me." Paradoxically, that knowledge of Scripture would shape Eleanor's faith and commitment to social justice. Traces of Scripture can be found throughout her writing. One can hope some verses brought her a bit of comfort in an otherwise dismal childhood.

Eleanor's life became more complicated when Eleanor's formidable great-grandmother, Maggie Ludlow, came for a visit and bellowed her disapproval of Eleanor's academic progress. Nor, to Mrs. Ludlow's consternation, did Eleanor's cooking and sewing abilities meet her standards. Ludlow immediately dispatched Madeleine Bell, her French maid, whom Blanche Wiesen Cook describes as "stern, unsmiling, and impatient"—hardly the treatment Eleanor needed—to be responsible for the children. Madeleine was sweet with Hall, but tyrannized Eleanor and soon became a menacing presence in her life. "I was not supposed to read in bed before breakfast," Eleanor later wrote, "but as I woke at five a.m. practically every morning in summer and was, I am afraid, a self-willed child, I used to take a book with me and hide it under the mattress. Woe was me when Madeleine caught me reading!"

Madeleine evaluated Eleanor's sewing skills on dish towels and socks. Whenever Eleanor made a mistake, the nanny angrily cut a larger hole for the child to mend. Eleanor remembered, "Many a tear I shed over this darning." If Eleanor was late getting ready for bed, Madeleine scolded her "unmercifully and pulled her hair." Corinne recalled that Madeleine berated her cousin "so violently that when Eleanor did something wrong, she preferred punishment at the hands of her grandmother," who "would scold me less severly." Eleanor was "desperately afraid" of Madeleine, although she later wrote that she could not remember "precisely why."

Biographer Geoffrey Ward, in light of today's understanding of child abuse, concludes that Madeline was a bigger nemesis than Eleanor acknowledged in her autobiography. Ward focuses on Eleanor's statement that she had "no recollection":

> If she remembered Madeleine's petty cruelties, what else was it that had been so terrible that her conscious mind could not later summon it up? Had there been more physical abuse than hair-pulling? Might there have been an element of molestation . . . something that might help account for her later deep ambivalence about sex?

Maxia Dong and Robert Anda have researched adverse childhood experiences (ACE)—the accumulation of stress agents such as parental death, divorce, illness, or abuse that thwart a child's development. Survivors of ACE "may have difficulty recalling certain [painful] events as a protective mechanism" to avoid bringing memories of distressing events into focus or possibly to prevent scandal. Thus, ACE survivors "are likely to underestimate actual occurrence" or subconsciously create narratives blaming themselves for adverse experiences. Using the inventory designed to assess ACE, Eleanor soars off the charts.

Adults block painful childhood or adolescent memories, particularly if the wound is linked to a sense of helplessness or the failure of adults to protect them. With Mrs. Hall isolated in her bedroom for much of the day, the children's nannies had little supervision.

So, was Eleanor molested? If so, was Madeleine a perpetrator? The *only* perpetrator? Few biographers or historians are dually trained in psychiatry or clinical psychology. K. Elan Jung, a psychiatrist, after studying Eleanor's childhood, stated that her biographers have found "little reason" to assume the nanny sexually abused Eleanor. That may not be true for the next generation of biographers. On the other hand, surviving the "terrors of her childhood" gave her a keen capacity "to feel the pain of others."

Almost a third of a century has passed since Blanche Wiesen Cook explored Eleanor's childhood and adolescence in the first volume of her definitive biography. Unless a future researcher stumbles on something in Eleanor's papers at the FDR Presidential Library and discloses the discovery, there may be no documented proof of sexual abuse. However, sexual abuse cannot be dismissed as unthinkable.

Robert Anda insists that individuals who report "any single category of adverse childhood experience"—such as a parent's alcoholism or the death of a parent—"were likely to have suffered multiple other categories." Anda's observation warrants further exploration. "When a child is wounded" and is taken from one insecure home environment and thrust into another insecure home environment, "the pain and negative long-term effects reverberate as an echo of the lives of people they grew up with." Eleanor, whose father was an absentee alcoholic, now had to interact daily with two resident alcoholics, maybe three, counting one aunt.

A particular element deserves a closer look. Geoffrey Ward spotted a nuance in Eleanor's descriptions of Madeleine's severity. In the 1939 edition, Eleanor wrote that she told her grandmother of the terror, "between sobs." In the 1958 edition, Eleanor reported that she "confessed it" to Mrs. Hall. *Confessed* is a far more indicting term than the sterile *told*. Eleanor's daring, desperate attempt to seek her grandmother's assistance—perhaps fearing her grandmother would not believe her—coupled with intense sobbing, hints at more.

Admittedly, one must be cautious when applying today's sensitivities to that historic period. Yet, given the Halls' social status, any disclosure would have further blemished the family's reputation. Some things were best left unspoken.

THE EFFECTS OF A DARK-SHADOWED CHILDHOOD

Troubling experiences during Eleanor's childhood shaped her understanding of sexuality, femininity, and intimacy. Given that a child's understanding of gender and personal worth are shaped in early childhood, what must it have been like for young Eleanor to be repeatedly verbally dismissed as ugly by her own mother?

No wonder Eleanor sucked her thumb and bit her fingernails.

Can one accurately assess the lasting damage of particular experiences in childhood? For Eleanor, serial losses at a young age—mother, brother, father—and her grandmother's *hyper*negativity and *hyper*religiosity ruled out opportunities for her to have a happy childhood like other girls in her social class. William Chafe, a feminist historian who has studied presidential couples, observes, "Public figures are shaped by private experiences. . . . Personal experiences infuse and inspire the choices that political figures make. *What goes on in the family where a child grows up helps define in fundamental ways how that child responds as an adult to moments of political or moral crisis*" (emphasis added).

As Eleanor herself later wrote, "It is the way we meet adversity, not adversity itself, which counts." Although countless girls experienced—and continue to experience—childhoods as miserable as hers, few grow to have such an influence on the world as Eleanor Roosevelt.

These early losses, it could be argued, are what sensitized Eleanor to the needs of orphans and refugee children before, during, and following World War II. Years later, as a vigorous advocate for the rights of children, Eleanor observed to Joseph Lash, "In a world as troubled as that of today, anything one can do to make the lives of children happier must be done with a feeling of great satisfaction, because if there is one time in life when you should have a sense of security it is when you are a child."

Eleanor never felt such a sense of security. Two questions must have darted frequently through Eleanor's mind: "Who will die next?" and "Then what will happen to me?" Memory of these fears may have driven her commitment as chair of the United Nations committee drafting the Universal Declaration of Human Rights to include generous provisions for children:

> Motherhood and childhood are entitled to special care and assistance. All children, whether born in or out of wedlock, shall enjoy the same social protection. (art. 25.2)
>   Everyone has the right to education. (art. 26.1)
>   Education shall be directed to the full development of the human personality and to the strengthening of respect for human rights and fundamental freedoms. (art. 26.2)

Claudia Black wrote a book titled *It's Never Too Late to Have a Happy Childhood.* Perhaps it is never too late to let one's inner child loose. After the Universal Declaration of Human Rights was passed in Committee Three at 2:00 a.m. on December 10, 1948, Eleanor was one of the last delegates to leave the Palais des Nations in Geneva. She paused to admire the shiny marble floors in the long grand lobby. Eleanor

Roosevelt II describes what happened next. Aunt Eleanor, sixty-four years old, handed her purse and briefcase to an aide. "My aunt's feet were long and narrow, and her low-heeled shoes had leather soles. She ran, gathering momentum, and then slid down the hall, her arms outstretched in triumph. It was so much fun that she did it again."

Perhaps some slivers of her wounded childhood were shaken free that triumphant night in Geneva.

3

Nourishing a Parched Soul

Eleanor in Adolescence

Just as I am, though toss'd about
With many a conflict, many a doubt,
Fightings and fears within, without,
O Lamb of God, I come!

—Charlotte Elliott, "Just As I Am"

It was the first time since her infancy that an adult had been truly interested in Eleanor Roosevelt for herself, and she responded by living up to Souvestre's expectations.

—Russell Freedman

President Theodore Roosevelt stared at the tall, young woman. Who was this? Surely not the fearful niece he had ordered to jump into Oyster Bay near his Sagamore Hill home after learning that she could not swim—an experience that exacerbated her long fear of water. How proud Elliott would be of his daughter, this confident Miss Eleanor. "Delightful!" Theodore exclaimed after receiving a light kiss on his cheek from his favorite niece, now home from London.

The words of Charlotte Elliott's hymn "Just As I Am," sung at Elliott Roosevelt's funeral in 1894, capture the fragility of the adolescent who sailed in the fall of 1899 *for* England and, more critically, *away* from the chaos in her grandmother's home. The Atlantic Ocean, which she had feared as a young child, offered a path to the opportunity on her horizon.

As she stood on deck for hours, each large breaking wave brought her closer to Allenswood, Mlle. Marie Souvestre's progressive boarding school near Wimbledon, in London. The years 1899 to 1902 would offer a fertile, safe environment for happiness and a spiritual rebirth.

Although women in the Hall and Roosevelt social circles knew Marie Souvestre by reputation, Anna and Elliott Roosevelt had met the educator in France in 1891. That Anna, on her deathbed, had expressed the wish that Eleanor have this educational opportunity—a wish others overheard—trumped Mrs. Hall's reluctance to send Eleanor so far from *her* control.

43

The *under*told narrative is that Eleanor's enrollment may have been decided by more than a dying mother's last wishes. Perhaps Anna Hall had realized that if she had gone to finishing school, like her friends, she might not have married Elliott Roosevelt. If her mother's home had not been so chaotic, she might not have seized Elliott's love and charisma as an escape. Grandmother Hall, in a letter seeking Eleanor's admission, disclosed troublesome details of the family narrative and expressed fears for Eleanor's "uncertain future." Those letters would become a filter through which Souvestre listened to Eleanor talk about her family and to her silence when classmates talked about their families.

Mrs. Stanley Mortimer (Aunt Tissie, her father's sister) accompanied Eleanor to London and saw her settled. What was going through Eleanor's mind as she watched her aunt's carriage drive away? Did thoughts of those troubled days in the French convent school intrude on that moment?

Not every grieving child or adolescent has a positive adjustment to boarding school. But Eleanor immediately discovered Allenswood would suit her "better than any home she had known since early childhood." James Roosevelt observes that although his mother "lived in many places" during childhood, "none of which was home to her." The word *home* would take on new psychospiritual meaning at Allenswood.

"This," she later reminisced, "was the first time in all my life that all my fears left me. If I lived up to the rules and told the truth, there was nothing to fear."

More troubling wording is found in Eleanor's disclosure that, once free from her grandmother's negativity, "I felt that I was starting a new life, *free from all my former sins and traditions*" (emphasis mine). Admittedly, her grandmother's piety shaped Eleanor's understanding of sin, but one wonders what "former sins" so sheltered an adolescent could have experienced, or what sins committed against her she may have internalized.

Five years had passed since Aunt Edith Roosevelt had urged Mrs. Hall to send Eleanor to a boarding school—*any* boarding school! Unfortunately, during this delay, incredible emotional damage had been inflicted on young Eleanor. Why did Mrs. Hall hesitate? Clearly, not for financial reasons, since Mrs. Hall received $7,500 annually from trusts Elliott had established for his children, the equivalent of $211,000 in 2016 dollars. Perhaps something happened—or *almost happened*—that forced Mrs. Hall to send Eleanor to a boarding school far away in Europe; finishing schools in New England would have been more convenient. Mrs. Hall's inability to control Valentine (Vallie) and Eddie, her alcoholic sons, may have triggered anxiety for Eleanor's safety.

Early adolescence—and the antics of her uncles—heightened Eleanor's self-consciousness as her body was developing, despite Mrs. Hall's attempts to camouflage that by dressing Eleanor in children's clothing. Moreover, Eleanor's posture brought new attention to her breasts. Because the family feared curvature of the spine, Eleanor had worn a corrective steel back brace for almost a year. She had been "made to walk up and down the River Road [in Tivoli] for hours at a time, with a stick behind her shoulders hooked at her elbows." Grandmother's tastes, coupled with young Eleanor's height, made the girl more self-conscious. Eleanor's grandson, David, reports that on the few occasions his grandmother visited Uncle Teddy's family, "she felt socially awkward, shy, and unsophisticated in dress compared with her more lively cousins." This lack of peer relationships is essential in understanding the sheltered, nervous adolescent who arrived at Marie Souvestre's school in 1899.

HOME AT ALLENSWOOD

Thomas Moore, a noted writer on spirituality, describes personal spiritual development as "the discovery of a new room in the soul, some area of life that has great potential but has just been found." Allenswood offered fifteen-year-old Eleanor not only a new room but a new home. Souvestre emancipated this bruised adolescent through the classroom, conversation, travel, and affirmation. Souvestre taught her how to think and, more important, valued what Eleanor thought. Allenswood offered Eleanor her first positive socialization with girls her age, and she became, as her cousin Corinne Robinson discovered, the most popular girl in the school, "beloved by everybody." In time, Souvestre considered Eleanor her "supreme favorite."

Eleanor's years in England, 1899–1902, were magical because Souvestre gave the girl freedom to be a fifteen-year-old. Quickly, "You *may*" replaced Mrs. Hall's "No!" David Roosevelt adds, "At Allenswood, under the loving care and gentle guidance of Mlle. Souvestre" the girl branded "an ugly duckling" began "her transformation into a swan," paradoxically as Aunt Edith had predicted.

If one were to search for a woman who was the precise opposite of

Mary Ludlow Hall, Marie Souvestre more than fit the bill. Four words capture that difference: *educated, progressive, irreligious,* and *lesbian.* Souvestre dismissed the conventional thinking of wealthy families that education threatened girls' mental health and, indirectly, their physical health.

Rubbish! fumed Souvestre. By exposure to "a truly unique liberal arts education" not readily available in other girls' schools, Souvestre shaped a generation of alumni whose children, grandchildren, and great-grandchildren would challenge and rewrite social expectations. On the eve of a new century that would radically reframe opportunities for women, Souvestre and her faculty challenged students to reexamine worldviews shaped by privilege. Students had to think vigorously, write clearly, and defend ideas. In class, she never hesitated to tear into pieces any student assignment she judged inferior. To encourage thinking, Souvestre required students to lie on their backs on the floor for ninety minutes, during which her charges focused their minds "on a single thought," which would then be discussed at the afternoon teatime.

Mrs. Hall did not know, let alone suspect, that the headmistress was a lesbian who lived with a partner, Paolina Samaia, at the school. Otherwise, Eleanor would never have attended Allenswood. Certainly, in this era, some women lived as lifelong partners in what was termed "a Boston marriage." One wonders at what point Eleanor sensed Souvestre's relationship with Samaia was different. D. A. Steel suggests that Eleanor, given her sensitivity and intuition, may have noticed Souvestre's "lesbian proclivities," given the amount of time she spent with her. Although historian Russell Freedman insists, "There is no evidence that Eleanor, as a student," knew the couple's sexual orientation, the student may have intuited more than she acknowledged.

Souvestre had had at least two partners, both involved in her schools: Caroline Dussaut in France, and Paolina Samaia at Allenswood. In fact, tensions between Souvestre and Dussaut led Souvestre to abandon her French school and launch Allenswood. After Souvestre's death in 1905, Allenswood continued under Samaia's leadership until 1948, which suggests she was considerably younger.

Allenswood exposed Eleanor to women who thought radically differently than the Hall women or any women Eleanor knew. Allenswood women were interested in ideas and causes. She confessed that from her father's death, "I never again had that sense of adequacy and of being cherished until I met Mlle. Souvestre." This extraordinary teacher began "to give me back some of the confidence which since my father's death I had not felt." At Allenswood, both in the classroom and in social interaction, Eleanor thrived. And she learned from Souvestre a lesson that forever shaped her life: "that the underdog was always the one to be championed!" Eleanor handwrote an exclamation mark on the typed manuscript.

AN ATHEIST'S INFLUENCE

It is unclear what role religion played in daily lives at Allenswood; certainly students were given time to attend church on Sundays. While Souvestre declared herself an atheist, which shocked many students, Eleanor questioned the accuracy of that self-definition. After attending Christmas Mass with her at St. Peter's Basilica in Rome, Eleanor concluded "with considerable relief" that Souvestre "was not an atheist at heart for she was as much moved as we were by the music and the lights." In today's lexicon, Marie Souvestre might have described herself as "spiritual but not religious."

Souvestre thought that Christians, in general,

> were rather to be looked down upon because they did right for gain. It might not be gain in this world but it was for gain in the next, and therefore the only people of real virtue were those who believed that there was no future life, but who wished to help those around them to do what was right purely through an interest in their fellow human beings and a desire to see right triumph just because it was right.

Far from dousing young Eleanor's faith, Souvestre's influence challenged her to lifelong examination of her beliefs. Three decades after Allenswood, Eleanor reflected on her teacher's position and gave her reply. "I was too young to come back then with the obvious retort that making those around you happy makes you happy yourself," she wrote. Thus,

> You are seeking a reward just as much as if you were asking for your reward in a future life. . . .
>
> Perhaps what we know as good in life and what we here think of as praise-worthy will not be counted at all as a spiritual achievement by some more understanding judge. That is why we all of us, whether we are willing to acknowledge it or not, do crave the belief in some power greater than ourselves and beyond our

understanding—because we know in our hearts that deeds and outward things mean little and that only someone who can gauge what striving there has been can really judge of what a human soul has achieved.

That Souvestre held and expressed political views shocked some pupils. She ignored prevailing British interests to voice support for the Boers in South Africa who were warring against British colonizers. On the other hand, Souvestre did not douse British girls' assumptions of the correctness of their nation's policies. Instead, Souvestre created teaching moments to explain "her theories on the rights of the Boers or of small nations" to thrive. Souvestre realized that if her pro-Boer stance got back to parents, the school's financial stability would be threatened. Decades later, Eleanor reported that echoes of Souvestre's views—and her tenacity in expressing those views—"still live in my mind."

Souvestre sparked Eleanor's lasting distaste for postwar colonialism, particularly of the Winston Churchill stripe, and empowered her work to protect the interests of small nations in the United Nations. The hospitality to ideas that Eleanor participated in while dining at Souvestre's table led her to host delegates from small nations in her home for tea or meals. She learned from her guests just as she had learned from the views of other students over meals at Allenswood.

Marie Souvestre was a forerunner for another perspective of femininity. She modeled a woman who, although connected to many of the elite in British and European families, deplored the pomp and shallowness of the sheltered privileged. Souvestre not only planted intellectual seeds but vigorously enriched the soil of her students' thinking and creativity about their social world.

Instruction and conversation were conducted in French, which Eleanor spoke fluently; she also studied German and Italian. At the end of the day, students had to confess if they had used more than two words of English. This grounding in thinking and speaking in French would prove valuable during Eleanor's service at the United Nations, since French was then *the* diplomatic language.

Nina Roosevelt Gibson, Eleanor's granddaughter, assessed the impact of her grandmother's experience at Allenswood: "My grandmother was absolutely taken by Mlle. Souvestre, because she saw this elegant, brilliant woman who was interested in her and what she had to say. And she blossomed at Allenswood. She became the beginnings of the woman that she would become later in life."

Souvestre, like a jeweler examining a raw diamond, saw potential in Eleanor, a recognition that would come to bless the whole world.

TRAVELING TOGETHER ON HOLIDAYS

During holiday vacations, Souvestre and Eleanor traveled across Europe, visiting palaces, cathedrals, museums, and galleries, and sampling local life—a perspective Eleanor would *never* have experienced with members of her family. Souvestre wanted Eleanor to *see, sense,* and *taste* Europe—the Europe missed by the eyes and ears of many young women in privileged families. They lodged in accommodations that would have displeased Mrs. Hall. Frequenting cafés, galleries, and museums, walking through gardens, and strolling along streets became the classroom du jour. This travel acquainted Eleanor with terrain on which two world wars would be fought, terrain Eleanor would later see war-scarred.

Souvestre let Eleanor plan trips, make arrangements, and prioritize the day's schedule. In an era when girls from wealthy families were constantly chaperoned, Souvestre urged her protégé to wander, particularly in Rome and Florence, to see what interested her and not just what Souvestre thought she *should* see. Repeatedly she instructed Eleanor, "The only way to know a city really is to walk its streets." When Eleanor returned to their lodging, the two discussed what she had observed.

From Souvestre, Eleanor learned spontaneity. On one excursion in Italy when their train stopped at Alassio, Souvestre nudged Eleanor, "Let's get off." Souvestre had remembered that her friend, religious modernist and social activist Mrs. Pumphrey Ward, lived there; perhaps, she was home. Eleanor reported, "We simply fell off onto the platform, bag and baggage . . . just before the train started on its way." Although Mrs. Ward was not home, teacher and pupil spent a "wonderful hour down on the beach" breathing the Mediterranean air and gazing into the star-dazzled night. Souvestre developed a cold from the exposure to the night air, but neither regretted taking a chance on enchantment. Traveling with her teacher, Eleanor learned that some of life's richest moments cannot be planned.

One day in Paris, the Thomas Newbolds, friends of Mrs. Hall, spotted Eleanor strolling unchaperoned. Horrified, they thought it their duty to report this to Mrs. Hall. Infuriated, she bristled that Souvestre allowed too much freedom and sent a letter demanding Eleanor return to New York at the end of the term. Too bad if that meant missing the coronation of King Edward VII.

RETURN TO DYSFUNCTION

As the term ended, Mrs. Hall sent her daughter Edith, known to the family as Aunt Pussie, to escort her niece home. On top of the sadness of leaving Allenswood, Eleanor witnessed yet another romantic melt-down for Pussie; actually, Eleanor chaperoned her aunt home. Pussie was the family's raging drama queen. Her poor choices in romance had more potential for scandal than did Eleanor walking alone! "One talent she had above all others," Eleanor recalled, "was always falling in love with the wrong people, very often with gentlemen who were already married." Sitting in a hotel lobby, Eleanor witnessed the latest married gentleman Pussie "loved" end the relationship "on the spot." Pussie did not take rejection well; her heart was "shattered again."

As Eleanor and her aunt approached the dock to board their ship, Pussie announced, "I am going to commit suicide on the way home.'" So, a frightened seventeen-year-old spent the cruise "watching every time [Pussie] started for the door, and making sure she was not going" to attempt to jump overboard.

Mrs. Hall decided to remain in Tivoli to keep Vallie away from New York City bars and taverns. So, Eleanor stayed with her aunt in the city and gained "a liberal education in how a person who is really probably emotionally unstable can make life miserable for the people around them." Periodically Pussie would abruptly retire to her bedroom—imi tating Mrs. Hall—and refuse to speak to or see anyone. Eleanor and the household staff walked on eggshells. Then, days later, Pussie "would emerge perfectly delightful and bright and happy as a May morning," offering no explanation for her latest hibernation. Of course, Eleanor suspected it was from breaking up with her latest "gentleman of the moment."

Eleanor must have longed to be back at Allenswood having stimu-lating conversations or traveling with Souvestre. Eleanor found it dif-ficult to interact with New York girls whose interests were so radically different. Their conversations bored Eleanor. Surely none of her class-mates were spending the summer as a "lifeguard" for a distraught fam-ily member. Because Eleanor had experienced a saner, safer world at Allenswood, the Hall family dysfunction stood in clear relief.

At some point that summer, Aunt Pussie, under the influence of a great deal of alcohol and thoroughly depressed by the collapse of another romance, viciously turned on her niece, hurling family secrets and dirty linen at Eleanor. Pussie's interpretation of the details of Elliott Roosevelt's last years, which the family had hidden from Eleanor, were aired like intimate garments on a clothesline on a windy day. Pussie shredded the memories that Eleanor cherished of her father. It was time, Pussie insisted, that Eleanor knew "the truth" about that despicable scoundrel Elliott Bulloch Roosevelt who had disgraced the Hall family! Oh, she grandly emoted, *what* he put her poor sister through!

Eleanor would grieve that night, the next night, and thousands of nights for the father Pussie had drawn and quartered—the *only* family member who had loved Eleanor.

Humuhumu in the Hawaiian language means "fitting the pieces together." The word captures how Eleanor spent that summer—sorting through shards of the family's collective narrative and her own fantasies and reconstructing a story that was uniquely hers. It was as if she had eaten, as had Eve, from the tree of knowledge of good and evil and had her eyes opened. Knowing that biblical account well, Eleanor knew she could not return to the innocence of her personal garden of Eden. Over that summer, what Blanche Wiesen Cook calls "the mysteries of her childhood" popped like soap bubbles. At last Eleanor understood her father's prolonged absences, the hushed conversations between family members, and Grandmother Hall's animosity toward Elliott Bulloch Roosevelt. It all began to make horrible sense.

As a result of Pussie's despicable verbal assault, Eleanor gained a new appreciation for the nursery-rhyme character Humpty Dumpty. She could not put Elliott Bulloch Roosevelt "back together again." As a result, Eleanor emotionally unraveled. Cousin Susie Parish, with whom Eleanor spent alternating weeks that summer, "had her hands full trying to console me," but there was no consolation to be had.

Eleanor *pleaded* to return to Allenswood; challenging Mrs. Hall's initial rejection of the idea demonstrated the emotional growth Eleanor had experienced. Finally, Mrs. Hall, weary from policing two alcoholic sons, two drama-queen daughters, and a brokenhearted granddaughter, booked passage for Eleanor's return to England.

Unfortunately, the weather made for a difficult crossing. So how did this adolescent—who had had such a fear of water—deal with the rough crossing? Eleanor sat in a deck chair lashed to the railing "for hours watching the horizon rise and fall." She ate most of her meals on deck to avoid overpowering odors along the ship's corridors. But the unpleasantness could be endured because she was returning to Allenswood!

OVER TOO SOON

That school year flew by too quickly. Eleanor dreamed of teaching at Allenswood and putting an ocean between herself and certain family members, but Grandmother Hall would not bend: Eleanor *must* come home to prepare for her coming out as a debutante, an eligible woman for a suitable suitor. Mrs. Hall's rigidity broke Marie Souvestre's heart and Eleanor's.

Souvestre cautioned Eleanor that the New York social scene could "take you and drag you" like an undertow "into its turmoil." Souvestre warned, "And even when success comes . . . bear in mind that there are more quiet and enviable joys than to be among the most sought-after women at the ball." Souvestre could have pointed to the Halls for proof of that point. That guidance paid rich dividends when Eleanor rejected the opportunity to have her wedding in the White House and later opportunities to be *the* sought-after hostess during two stints in Washington. She was able to avoid falling into the traditional roles that had been imposed on previous First Ladies.

The debutante experience proved as dreadful as Eleanor had feared. She knew that the Hall women had experienced the glittering gauntlet of dinners and balls, teas and parties as head-turning belles of the ball. Over the years, New York's eligible wealthy males had stumbled over each other to dance with a Hall, but not this year. Eleanor described the experience as "utter agony" with no Cinderella ending. "For long intervals" at events, Eleanor "sat awkwardly at the side of the room, while other girls, pretty and smiling, waltzed by with attentive partners." She and her maid left parties early.

Eleanor described her chagrin: "I was the first girl in my mother's family who was not a belle, and though I never acknowledged it to any of them at that time, I was deeply ashamed."

While preparing to marry Franklin on Saint Patrick's Day 1905, Eleanor learned that her beloved teacher had liver cancer and was dying. Eleanor had looked forward to seeing her during an extended European honeymoon that summer. On March 30, 1905, two weeks after the wedding, Marie Souvestre died. Three months later, in London, while visiting Marjorie Bennett, an Allenswood roommate, Eleanor realized that, caught up in the details of marrying Franklin, she had not had time to mourn her mentor's passing. In Eleanor's words, "It had been a great sorrow . . . when life was so full I had little time for repining."

As the newlyweds visited sites and places Eleanor had first seen with Souvestre, "This trip brought home the loss, and made me long for her more than once."

Souvestre helped emancipate Eleanor spiritually. The nurture her mother, grandmother, and aunts could not give, Souvestre had generously lavished. "Whatever I have become since," Eleanor confidently reminisced, "had its seeds in those three years of contact with a liberal mind and strong personality." Eleanor honored Mlle. Souvestre's memory by keeping her picture on her desk and carried Souvestre's letters—along with her father's—for the rest of her life. Souvestre's influence, according to one obituary, "counted for much in the lives of many women coming from the best of the governing class of England," as well as those from America, France, and Germany. Souvestre's spirited teaching shaped Eleanor's teaching at Todhunter School (1928–1932). Blanche Wiesen Cook assesses a beloved teacher's lasting influence: "Eleanor Roosevelt never turned away from the memory of Marie Souvestre. Her influence and spirit burned deeply within ER, and her teachings continually pointed in the direction of what was possible by way of independence, self-fulfillment, public activity, and human understanding."

WHAT ALLENSWOOD GAVE YOUNG MISS ROOSEVELT

Daniel Gilbert, in *Stumbling on Happiness*, contends that one of the amazing capacities of human beings is an ability to imagine a future that may not exist now. Allenswood instilled in this orphan the confidence to imagine a next period of her life far better than her troubled childhood and early adolescence predicted. Allenswood, especially that last year, endowed Eleanor with alternative maps with which she could navigate the world. That metamorphosis would not be fully evident, however, until the mid-1920s. William Youngs describes the stretching of Eleanor's world on the eve of a new century: Eleanor "had always taken the public world for granted. Now it turned out that political life could be talked about, even criticized. People were not simply caught in the stream of history, hopeless observers of the great events about them. They could evaluate, criticize, even influence public affairs."

"They" included women. Souvestre had modeled that reality. And what was true of public affairs was true in religion. Spirituality was not a staid form into which one was poured but a living willingness to respond authentically to the challenges of the day. The Episcopal faith, as practiced by the Halls, would go under the microscope as Eleanor navigated her future. Just as Eleanor's views on Scripture evolved, so did her perspectives on doctrine, ritual, dogma, the practical ways one lived out faith, and the commitments one embraced.

In Souvestre, Eleanor admired a woman who knew her own mind. And Eleanor would know *her* own mind about applications of what one believed. Three years studying with a woman who said an enthusiastic yes to life led Eleanor to say as fervent a yes to life.

Eleanor never publicly disparaged her tradition as an Episcopalian. She reflected, no doubt referring to the years at Allenswood, "As I grew older I questioned a great many of the things that I knew very well my grandmother . . . had taken for granted." Eleanor once told Father William Turner Levy that her grandmother's unshakable belief that *every* word in the Bible was literally true "discouraged me from asking questions, and that was a very unhealthy situation."

In January 1949, Eleanor's "My Day" column underscored a teacher's opportunity to influence the next generation. She chose to quote, at length, from *Some Memories of Marie Souvestre*, written by Allenswood alumni. This teacher put "such a salt and savour into life, that it seemed as if we could never think anything dull again" (MD, January 27, 1949).

Paradoxically, this summation of Souvestre's life, in time, could equally have been written of Eleanor:

> She went into the world; she travelled; she was on intimate terms with many of the ablest minds of the day in many countries, and wherever she went she brought the keenness of her mind, her refreshing and sometimes alarming sincerity, her irrepressible spirits. And through all the direst quarrels of the day, though she "took sides" vehemently, she never lost a friend, and if she made enemies, it was never of those who were worthy or able to understand her. (MD, January 27, 1949)

Allenswood was a providential way to redeem Eleanor's traumatic childhood and early adolescence. These three years gave young Miss

Roosevelt, in the ancient words of the prophet Jeremiah, "a future with hope" (Jer. 29:11 NRSV).

Souvestre, by teaching Eleanor *how* to think—rather than *what* to think—taught her how to read the same Bible as her grandmother. While Eleanor had arrived constrained by her grandmother's dogmatism, three years honoring questions changed her. She learned that questions may be more important than answers. John D. Morgan, a philosopher, describes the process of spiritual metamorphosis:

> Each one of us has been raised in a tradition of some sort, whether that tradition is Buddhism, Christianity, consumerism, or hedonism. Each of us decides how much of that tradition s/he is going to adopt. Spirituality is our ability to decide for ourselves how much I'm going to take from A, from B, from C . . . and try to put together some sort of consistent whole.

Souvestre was the midwife for a reborn Eleanor—testing, embracing, and discarding what she had believed and what she could believe. Eleanor navigated a middle path between her grandmother's dogmatic Christianity and Souvestre's dogmatic atheism.

The time with Marie Souvestre prepared Eleanor for a life beyond imagination. Eleanor called her brief formal education a "second period of my life." One could reasonably argue that this unlikely mentor—a French atheist, lesbian, thinker—gave Eleanor a spiritual footing.

In those eucharistic meals she attended during childhood and adolescence, Eleanor repeatedly had heard the promise for "newness of life." She found that gift at Allenswood. "Never again," Eleanor insisted, "would I be the rigid little person I had been theretofore."

4

A Woman of Faith

Eleanor's Theology

What did she believe? I know she believed in God . . . with wide margins.
—Allida Black

Challenged by Marie Souvestre to question and discover her own spirituality, Eleanor cultivated an adult faith grounded in Jesus' call to care for "the least of these," nurtured by regular prayer and Bible reading. She was confirmed in the Episcopal Church on May 3, 1903, after returning from Allenswood. She would become what her son Elliott would one day call "a woman of faith." But the progressive theology of this cradle Episcopalian and political liberal could never satisfy some. Eleanor would receive criticism throughout her adult life for not being the kind of Christian many people thought she should be.

Although she regularly attended and financially supported St. James' Church to the end of her life, in the judgment of some Christians that was insufficient to make her a "true Christian" or a "Bible-believing Christian." Even today, some conservative Protestants are suspicious of the liturgical focus and liberal tendencies of Episcopalians. During the civil rights era, critics dismissed the Episcopalians as "Catholic lite," more committed to social justice than "getting people saved." Episcopal priests were frequently photographed in the front rows of marches or rallies—a role Eleanor applauded. Had she been younger and her feet in better condition, she would have considered joining them.

But while she agreed with her denomination's social actions and found meaning in its prayer and ritual, Eleanor knew that the moniker on one's church—or whether one attended a church at all—was not determinant of a faith's worth or sincerity. She abhorred denominational pride and ecclesiastical arrogance. Eleanor summed up her personal credo: "The way your personal religion makes you live your life is the only thing that matters" (IYAM, August 1947).

This was certainly not the message imparted by Grandmother Hall, for whom Bible reading and daily prayers seemed to be pious ends unto themselves, unrelated to one's human relationships. The faith apparent in Eleanor's work as First Lady would inextricably link these core practices of religion with active care for people in need, both at home and abroad.

PASSING ON THE FAITH

Eleanor's and Franklin's perspectives on faith formation for their children differed because of their own childhood experiences of church. The religious environment at the Halls' was not harmful in itself, but it left Eleanor with spiritual baggage to overcome in addition to her family trauma. At one point, Eleanor, concerned about the spiritual development of their children, engaged Franklin in serious conversation on the topic. She outlined the potential harm of what the Roosevelt children were being taught in church school, particularly about how one reads the Bible.

Franklin listened, then asked, "What you were taught never hurt you, did it?"

"No," Eleanor acknowledged, but "it never gave me any chance to think these things out for myself."

"Well," Franklin followed up, "since it didn't hurt you, why not let the children have the same kind of teaching and then think things out for themselves when they have grown up, just as you did."

That conversation somewhat relieved Eleanor's anxiety. Religious practices may have been drilled into her uncomfortably at Tivoli, but some practices had value that should be passed on to future generations.

"I think it is important for all our children to learn something about their religions," she wrote in a 1959 "My Day" column. "The Bible is shared by Roman Catholic, Protestant and Jewish groups, and certainly we have all learned that this is a book that is important as history, as literature, and for spiritual understanding and guidance" (MD, February 21, 1959). And not only one's own faith, but that of others. "It is vital," she admonished, "in a democracy for each of us to know what the other believes, for tolerance can only exist through understanding" (citing *Reader's Observer*, a pamphlet published by Consumer's Book Cooperative, in MD, October 10, 1941).

To achieve these ends, Eleanor lent her support to several causes designed to advance the accessibility and understanding of Scripture. In December 1944, Eleanor donated to and endorsed an appeal by the American Bible Society to raise $3.25 million above its budget to provide Bibles around the world, particularly in devastated war zones. The society felt, and Eleanor agreed, "that above all other books, this book must be furnished now to men and women in the services, to prisoners of war, and to civilians at home in every country which can be reached. Later, of course, there will be great demands for the Bible by churches and ministers as they try to rebuild their congregations in war-torn countries" (MD, December 8, 1944).

Eleanor, although deeply appreciative of the King James Version of the Bible she had memorized as a child and had read in her father's New Testament, recognized the emerging need for more readable translations to increase biblical literacy. Christian fundamentalists, on the other hand, resisted those moves. Eleanor conceded, after attending the rollout celebration for the Revised Standard Version of the Holy Bible (RSV) in 1952, that for "many of us the King James Version had seemed fully satisfying" (MD, October 3, 1952). However, the RSV translation team had worked diligently to offer the exact meaning of the Old and New Testaments based on rigorous study of ancient manuscripts, bringing it greater accuracy as well as readability for modern audiences.

Eleanor applauded the priorities of David J. Fant, general secretary of the New York Bible Society, who had overseen the translation process. If, as Fant suggested, this new version could reach more readers and make "more people familiar with the Scriptures," Eleanor wrote that this new translation "might well make this a more important event in the world's history than battles lost or won, financial crises met, or even the result of Presidential elections."

Eleanor closely studied the changes made in her favorite passages. In 1 Corinthians 13, for example, *charity* had been changed to *love*. She approved because for years she had known that *love* was a more accurate translation from the Greek. She commented, "It does not really affect the meaning a great deal, since charity has always been a practical demonstration of love," but "I think it is a very pleasant change" (MD, October 3, 1952).

The publishers of the RSV had reason to hope that Eleanor's insights would impact early acceptance and sales; Christian fundamentalists, however, dismissed this "false Bible" because it did not plainly support the virgin birth of Jesus.

ELEANOR'S READING OF SCRIPTURE

Eleanor took the Bible too seriously to take it literally. Rather than fearing new scholarship and biblical interpretation, Eleanor applauded the developments, particularly by young scholars. Higher criticism of scriptural texts, a strong curricular emphasis in Episcopal seminaries, attracted scorn from fundamentalists. A reader, Eleanor believed, had to apply recent scientific discoveries to a particular text and give attention to the change in word meaning over the centuries. Fundamentalist Protestants, then and now, believe that *every* word in the Bible is true and, moreover, has been included under the direct inspiration of the Holy Spirit. Protestant fundamentalists repeatedly pointed Eleanor to this verse: "All scripture is given by inspiration of God, and is profitable for doctrine, for reproof, for correction, for instruction in righteousness" (2 Tim. 3:16).

Readers of Eleanor's regular magazine columns felt comfortable sending her questions about the Bible, even when she was First Lady. Eleanor's answer in *Ladies' Home Journal* to a reader's inquiry, however, ignited a flurry of protest. Specifically, this questioner wondered if Eleanor believed that Adam and Eve had been "real people."

In June 1942, a reader challenged Eleanor, "How can you reject parts of the Bible and accept others? Does your belief in the story of Adam and Eve as an allegory," the writer mused, "interfere with your faith in Jesus as the world's Redeemer?" (IYAM, June 1942).

Eleanor conceded that while she appreciated the beauty of the garden narrative of the first couple, she believed the Genesis account was allegorical because it would be difficult intellectually to accept the story "in any other way." The factuality of the "story of Adam and Eve," she insisted, "does not in any way affect my belief in the beauty and divine inspiration of Christ's life."

"Upon what basis do you say 'We know the Adam and Eve story is not true?'" another reader demanded.

"On the basis of science," Eleanor answered, going on to explain that an allegory is "true" in its own way but that "when taught without interpretation, as many children learn it, it is not true" (IYAM, March 1947).

If, as fundamentalists claimed, the Bible is "unchanging," how, Eleanor wondered, did one explain the change in thinking on slavery? The default retort, "that was *then*," annoyed Eleanor. Any serious reader had to consider the times in which particular passages were written and the cultural circumstances the text addressed. Eleanor knew that her paternal ancestors, the Bullochs of Georgia, owned slaves and that many Southerners quoted the apostle Paul's straightforward admonition to servants, "Be subject to your masters" (1 Pet. 2:18), as definitive! Southern Christians pointed to Paul's example when he sent Philemon, a Christian runaway slave, back to his owner. Nothing, Southerners argued, in this inspired biblical narrative condemned owning slaves!

"The Bible is a remarkable book, you can always find something that suits the subject you are discussing," she noted (MD, July 16, 1955). However, "attempts to justify discrimination by quotations from the Bible . . . hardly coincides with much of the teaching in the New Testament" (MD, September 2, 1955).

That teaching, particularly verses urging compassion toward those Jesus called "the least of these," stimulated Eleanor's faith and imagination to find ways to care for the marginalized "least" in American society. This, she understood, was what a Christian *must* do. In 1937, she argued, "There is very little actual fundamental law. Really only 'Love one another.' The rest is all interpretation—even the ten commandments" (MD, February 13, 1937).

When Eleanor called her own knowledge of Scripture "superficial" because her reading was "confined often to sections which I like particularly and not to sections which are particularly concerned with the reasons for my beliefs" (MD, October 10, 1941), a "very indignant reader" chastised Eleanor for demeaning Bible study. Eleanor responded:

> I wonder how many people would dare to say otherwise. Few people can claim a real study and knowledge of that book, which is probably the most widely read book in the world and, frequently, the least understood. . . . It is because I have such a deep appreciation of what real knowledge of the Bible implies, that I would never presume for a minute to consider it possible for me to claim anything beyond a very superficial study. (MD, October 22, 1941)

ELEANOR ON PRAYER

Readers of Eleanor's columns often questioned her about prayer as well: whether she believed in the power of prayer, whether prayers were really answered, and whether God provided direct guidance for those who seek it.

To the latter question, Eleanor answered, "I am sorry to say that I have never been able to feel that I was important enough to receive any kind of special guidance" (IYAM, June 1958). Eleanor acknowledged having acquaintances, however, who felt that, through prayer, "they can ask for specific favors. I have always thought," she noted, "this required either a very childlike faith or an amount of arrogance hardly excusable in a mature person" (IYAM, September 1958).

The questions of whether one's prayers had any efficacy in the real world were hardly hypothetical during wartime, when many Americans' prayers for a loved one's safety had proved futile while others' prayers seemed to have been answered—at least for the time being.

Eleanor knew the assertion, "The effectual fervent prayer of a righteous man availeth much" (Jas. 5:16), and carefully answered her anxious reader:

> It depends entirely on how you pray, whether prayer is answered or not. If people pray for special things, I doubt if anyone could be quite sure whether his prayer had been answered or not. If we pray, however, for the things that I think one can legitimately pray for—for instance, courage to meet whatever the day may bring—then I think we can find in our hearts the knowledge whether our prayers were really answered or not. (IYAM, November 1944)

During World War II, thousands of mothers wrote to the First Lady, knowing that as a mother of soldiers herself, she would understand their trepidation. Many shared prayers they had found meaningful, and Eleanor reprinted many of them, including one urging blood donation, and another imagining a fallen son walking hand in hand with God's Son in heaven. One such wartime prayer she carried in her wallet for the rest of her life:

> Dear Lord,
> Lest I continue
> My complacent way,
> Help me to remember,
> Somehow out there
> A man died for me today.
> As long as there be war,
> I then must

Ask and answer
Am I worth dying for?

Eleanor once told her friend Joseph Lash (who considered himself "an agnostic Jew") that "a prayer was not something to be recited only in church," temple, or religious setting. Rather, prayer "should be a continuous influence, something carried in the heart and mind all the time," an application of the apostle Paul's teaching to "pray without ceasing" (1 Thess. 5:17).

STRENGTH FOR THE JOURNEY

Eleanor's own prayers were often "for guidance, for strength, and for the inspiration to do right" (IYAM, September 1958). She believed that in a complex world, when access to data sometimes is limited and there are competing agendas, it can be difficult to know what is the right action; so, one prayed for insight.

After reading for the first time Francis of Assisi's famous prayer that begins "Lord, make me an instrument of thy peace," Eleanor asked her secretary to make two copies: one she carried in her purse and the other she placed on the nightstand beside her bed. Joseph Lash thought that Francis's prayer summarized Eleanor's faith and philosophy of life. He commented after Eleanor's death that her life's desire—which might be phrased in today's vernacular, *her purpose*—"to make life better for more of our people" was more spiritually driven than politically motivated. Eleanor, "driven to the Lord for strength, had transformed despair and loneliness into that selfless gift described in the Prayer of St. Francis, of love and charity without measure."

The confidence and self-discovery Eleanor gained during her years at Allenswood could not insulate her from more pain and more loss, but the faith she discovered and confirmed as a young woman would sustain her through marriage, motherhood, and the political spotlight and empower her to become an instrument of peace, hope, and justice throughout the world.

5

Challenged and Betrayed

Eleanor and Franklin before the White House

I had very high standards as to what a wife and mother should be and not the faintest notion of what it meant to be either a wife or a mother, and none of my elders enlightened me.

—Eleanor Roosevelt

The radiant young couple expected their wedding guests to line up to offer hearty congratulations. However, as soon as the Rev. Endicott Peabody declared, "I now pronounce you man and wife," Uncle Theodore headed for the refreshments. Like children after a pied piper, guests followed his booming voice. Alice Roosevelt, a bridesmaid, lamented—for once agreeing with her siblings—that her father always "wanted to be the bride at every wedding and the corpse at every funeral." Today was no exception; in fact, "he stole the show."

Eleanor and Franklin married on March 17, 1905, because President Theodore Roosevelt would be in New York City for Saint Patrick's Day festivities. He had wanted to host his niece's wedding at the White House, but the couple had chosen the residence of Mrs. Henry Parish, Eleanor's second cousin and godmother Susie. Unfortunately, because of crowds along the parade route and the security for President Roosevelt, many guests did not arrive before the vows were exchanged.

Eleanor and Franklin looked at each other, shrugged, and joined the group as Uncle Teddy regaled the guests with stories and opinions on issues of the day. He congratulated Franklin for "keeping the name in the family."

Guests expected the young Columbia law student and his bride to go places in New York society. No one would have predicted that within three decades the couple would be branded "traitors to their class." No one would have predicted that in a century the couple would be included in *Time* magazine's millennium poll of the twenty most influential leaders and revolutionaries in the world!

THE MRS. ROOSEVELT

How would Eleanor and Franklin's marriage and, perhaps, the history of the nation, have been different had James Roosevelt not died in 1900 while his son was at Harvard? Or had Franklin had siblings to diffuse his mother Sara's obsessive affection? While Eleanor, Franklin, and Sara were surely familiar with the Scripture read in the wedding ceremony, "Therefore shall a man leave his father and his mother, and shall cleave unto his wife: and they shall be one flesh" (Gen. 2:24), Eleanor could never penetrate the bond between mother and son.

Eleanor was hardly Sara Roosevelt's choice for a daughter-in-law, nor was the time right, in her eyes, for Franklin to marry. According to Eleanor's grandson Curtis Roosevelt, Sara expected Franklin to finish law school, pass the New York bar exam, and establish himself in one of the city's elite law firms. Then he could think about marriage.

Franklin, while conceding that he had caused Sara pain, stood up to her. Geoffrey Ward and Ken Burns noted that Sara had promised to love and adopt Eleanor fully "when the right time comes." In Sara's eyes, however, that "right time" never came.

Eleanor expected Sara to be the mother she had never had—a longing quickly extinguished. There would be only one Mrs. Roosevelt, Sara informed the servants: herself! Calling Sara a strong personality would be an understatement. The one who controlled the purse strings, as Sara did, held the power. Certainly, Sara had effective ways of bending her son and her grandchildren to please her.

In 1906, Sara built the couple a townhouse attached to her townhouse with connecting doors on three floors. Eleanor quipped, "You were never quite sure when she would appear, day or night." Franklin Jr. told Lash, "Those were the years when Granny referred to us as 'my children'" and told her grandchildren, "Your mother only bore . . . you." Sara undercut Eleanor and Franklin's authority by giving the grandchildren money and expensive gifts, especially "things their parents had withheld as a form of discipline." And there were promises of gifts to come after her passing. "From behind a façade of total generosity, submission, and love," Sara ruled!

Two chairs faced the fireplace at Springwood, Sara's home at Hyde Park—one for Franklin, the other for Sara. At meals, Franklin sat at the head of the table, Sara at the opposite end. Eleanor Roosevelt II recalled arriving for dinner and hearing Sara direct her aunt Eleanor, "You may choose wherever you want to sit along either side, my dear," the same instruction she gave grandchildren and guests.

When tensions flared between the two women, quite often, Franklin fled to his stamp collection. More than once, Eleanor left a meal in tears. Ironically, Franklin and his mother could not be in the same room for very long before an argument erupted. Little wonder that Franklin's stamp collection kept growing.

THE BABIES

Eleanor soon began giving Sara grandchildren: Anna Eleanor in 1906, James in 1907, Franklin Jr. in 1909, Elliott in 1910, Franklin Jr. II in 1914, and John in 1916. Eleanor described the early years of the marriage as "either getting over having a baby or getting ready to have one."

On March 18, 1909, Eleanor gave birth to Franklin Jr., an eleven-pound son she described as "the biggest and the most beautiful of all the babies." Unfortunately, the baby had heart problems. On November 1, Franklin Jr. died from complications of influenza and pneumonia. Sara observed, "Poor Eleanor's mother's heart is well-nigh broken. She so hoped and cannot believe her baby is gone from her." In her grief, Eleanor crafted an indictment that haunted her for the rest of her life: baby Franklin "might have lived" if only she had nursed him longer than a month.

Losing both parents, a brother, a mentor, a nephew, *and* a baby by age thirty constituted "grief overload." William Turner Levy, a friend, commented on Eleanor's lasting "devotion to the memory of her third baby." She never forgot burying him three weeks before Thanksgiving and the start of the holiday season. In 1939, Eleanor wrote, "To this day, so many years later, I can stand by his tiny stone in the churchyard and see the little group of people gathered around his tiny coffin, and remember how cruel it seemed to leave him out there alone in the cold."

Eleanor described her anguish to Isabella Ferguson, a close friend: "Sometimes I think I cannot bear the heartache which one little life has left behind but then I realize that we have much to be grateful for still, and that it was meant for us to understand and sympathize more deeply with all of life's sorrows."

In *This Is My Story*, her autobiography, Eleanor reflected on those dark days:

> I was young and morbid and reproached myself very bitterly for hav-
> ing done so little about the care for this baby. . . . in some way I must
> be to blame. I even felt that I had not cared enough about him, and
> I made myself and all those round me most unhappy during that
> winter. I was even a little bitter against my poor young husband who
> occasionally tried to make me see how idiotically I was behaving.

Although losing a baby—or multiple babies—was common in that era, Franklin's assessment that Eleanor was behaving "idiotically" was insensitive. Eleanor got pregnant immediately with a baby she named Elliott, after her father. The birth, however, failed to diffuse her grief. A grandson later commented, "The deep sorrow she felt at the death of her baby boy had reawakened the melancholy of her relationship with her own father."

FRANKLIN THE AMBITIOUS

Franklin disappointed Eleanor when he decided not to complete law school. He passed the bar exam and, through family connections, joined the prestigious Wall Street firm Carter, Ledyard, and Milburn. He soon informed colleagues that someday he would be president, confidently explaining that he would follow Theodore's path: New York State Assembly, assistant secretary of the navy, governor of New York, then president.

In 1910, Franklin, after informing party leaders that he would have to consult his mother first, accepted a long-shot opportunity to run for a New York Senate seat as a Democrat in a district that had long elected Republicans. He did not consult Eleanor.

FDR threw himself into campaigning—innovatively crisscrossing the district by automobile. Voters who assumed he was Theodore Roosevelt's son contributed to his victory; 1910 would not be the last time that confusion benefited Franklin.

That victory gave Eleanor a welcomed distance from Sara, who had no desire to move to Albany to be around a bunch of politicians. So, in a large house near the state capitol, Eleanor offered hospitality to politicians eating, smoking, drinking, arguing, and crafting political strategy until the wee hours. Eleanor sat for hours in the Senate gallery observing speeches, debates, and parliamentary procedures to better understand Franklin's world. They also became a foundational learning experience for her own political career.

In 1912, Senator Roosevelt won reelection clinging to the presidential coattails of Woodrow Wilson, rather than Uncle Theodore, and then lobbied successfully for a position in the Wilson administration, specifically, Theodore Roosevelt's old office, assistant secretary of the navy. Because the navy had only one assistant secretary, Franklin had enormous responsibilities and powers. Eleanor exhausted herself trying to supervise children and fulfill the outdated social demands on cabinet wives. On Sunday nights, the Roosevelts' dining room drew Washington power brokers for Eleanor's scrambled eggs—which she cooked herself at the table, salad, and dessert but, more importantly, networking.

Franklin, brilliantly assessing the trajectory of the European war that had erupted in August 1914, concluded that the navy and the nation were unprepared for war. At times clandestinely, FDR brokered deals behind Secretary of the Navy Josephus Daniels's back for increased appropriations for new ships and ports, increased manpower, and more authority for himself.

The United States entered the war on April 6, 1917, after the Germans sank unarmed US vessels without warning. Franklin, knowing that Theodore had resigned as assistant secretary to fight with the Rough Riders in the Spanish-American War, sought an officer's commission. Secretary Daniels and President Wilson, however, thought young Roosevelt "more valuable" where he was—behind a desk.

War changed everything in American homes. Eleanor pared down her household staff to just ten servants. She spent long hours volunteering at the Red Cross canteen near Union Station, distributing cigarettes, coffee, and sandwiches, and conversing with soldiers passing through the city. No volunteer put in as many hours—often from early morning until late at night. Eleanor also coordinated knitting groups in Washington for the navy and the Red Cross. The Roosevelts met one another going and coming. Fatigue, complicated by the birth of two more sons by 1916, doused the romantic flame in the marriage.

I WAS SICK, AND YOU VISITED ME

As a cabinet wife, Eleanor had opportunities for persuasion. Soldiers had been gassed in the trenches in France. The pathetic treatment of soldiers suffering shell shock—a forerunner of post-traumatic stress disorder (PTSD)—was scandalous. Scores of soldiers were locked in unimaginable squalor in St. Elizabeth's Hospital, a federal mental facility in Washington. At the request of a navy chaplain, Eleanor agreed to visit some patients. Geoffrey Ward and Ken Burns report, "She never forgot the sound of the door locking behind her or the sight of the dark ward filled with shattered men, some chained to their beds, muttering, staring." Other cabinet wives would never have returned. Yet, week after week, Eleanor squelched her fear and visited the patients. The deplorable conditions, inadequate sanitation, stench, and lack of medical treatment angered her.

At a dinner one night, she was seated next to Franklin K. Lane, secretary of the interior, whose department had oversight for St. Elizabeth's. During the meal, Eleanor graphically described the conditions and pushed Lane to investigate. Soon St. Elizabeth's, after a significant boost in appropriations, offered better care. The soldiers on those wards and their families never forgot Eleanor's compassion and advocacy. Others saw, smelled, and shuddered; Eleanor lived Jesus' words.

This experience demonstrated Eleanor's ability to concretize her faith when confronted by a particular individual's need. Eleanor knew the biblical warning: "If anyone has material possessions and sees a brother or sister in need but has no pity on them, how can the love of God be in that person?" (1 John 3:17 NIV). On numerous occasions she insisted it was not enough to see someone in need. One *must* respond!

FDR AND LUCY MERCER

Soon after the Roosevelts arrived in Washington in 1913, Eleanor had hired twenty-three-year-old Lucy Mercer to serve as her social secretary and a part-time nanny for the children. Lucy was keenly acquainted with the city elite's traditions as well as social minefields and came highly recommended by Aunt Bam. The Roosevelts welcomed the vivacious woman as family. Lucy dined with them frequently when an extra female was required, charming many young naval officers and one assistant secretary—FDR. Her youth and beauty offered a stark contrast to Eleanor's stiffness.

After the outbreak of war, Woodrow Wilson expected cabinet families to model frugality. So, Eleanor terminated Lucy, who immediately secured an assignment as a yeoman in Franklin's office! Secretary Daniels, either suspicious or having heard rumors about FDR and Lucy, after four weeks abruptly terminated her position.

In the era before air-conditioning, Washington summers were unbearable; politicians, civil servants, federal employees, and their dependents fled to cooler climes. The Roosevelts had, for years, summered on Campobello Island, in Canada. After the United States entered the war in 1917, Franklin, claiming the demands of his office, stayed in Washington despite repeatedly promising Eleanor he would try to get away.

When Eleanor was out of town, according to son James, FDR "openly met [Lucy] after working hours." One day Alice Roosevelt Longworth, Eleanor's blabbermouth cousin, spotted the couple alone in a car, miles from Washington. Alice teased Franklin about his "friendship" and invited the pair to her home for dinners. Alice snarled, "Franklin deserved a good time. He was married to Eleanor." Even when Eleanor was in Washington, Franklin socialized late into the nights, while she preferred to work at the canteen.

Foreseeing being asked in the future as a candidate, "What, Mr. Roosevelt, did *you* do during the war?" Franklin knew that the response "I commanded a desk in Washington" would not attract voters. In late 1917, Franklin sailed to France to evaluate the utilization of American war supplies. On several occasions, he witnessed intense combat. Upon completing this assignment, he expected to receive an officer's commission.

Franklin returned from France on a stretcher, suffering from pneumonia. Eleanor received a cable to meet his ocean liner, the SS *Leviathan*, with a physician and ambulance. As the epidemic swept the world, 25 percent of Americans contracted influenza; over five hundred thousand Americans died. Worldwide morbidity estimates ranged between fifty and one hundred million deaths in addition to the war dead.

The Roosevelt social class distrusted hospitals, so Franklin was transported to Sara's townhouse; Franklin and Eleanor's townhouse had been leased out. Unpacking her husband's bags, Eleanor found a packet of letters and recognized Lucy's handwriting. No one knows how many letters Eleanor read, but it was enough to conclude that her husband had been unfaithful.

Marc Peyser and Timothy Dwyer quip that in the nation's capital, "the only thing harder than keeping your job is keeping a secret." Eleanor soon learned that Franklin and Lucy had flaunted the relationship by attending social gatherings as a couple, particularly when she and "the chicks," that is, the children, were at Campobello or Hyde Park. That discovery fanned the embers of Eleanor's entrenched insecurities. Eleanor Roosevelt II, her niece, reflected: "The way that my Aunt Eleanor felt about Franklin was the way she had felt about her Father."

It was the fantastic love that she felt would be total. . . . She was so stunned and didn't know where to put this hurt." In the PBS documentary *Eleanor Roosevelt*, Trude Lash comments, "The greatest hurt was that Franklin had broken his word. It was like her father, who had made promises and not kept them." She had to have remembered sobbing to cousin Ethel Roosevelt before marrying FDR, "I shall never be able to hold him. He is too attractive." That fear became reality.

THE UNPLEASANT MATTER

The confrontations about the future could not have been pleasant for the five principals: Eleanor, Franklin, Sara, Lucy, and Louis Howe, FDR's political strategist. Eleanor naturally did not mention the experience in her autobiography published in 1937. Later, in a conversation with Joseph Lash, she alluded to the affair: "The bottom dropped out of my own particular world and I faced myself, my surroundings, my world, honestly for the first time. I really grew up that year."

Now Eleanor experienced a hint of what her mother must have felt upon discovering her father's infidelity. When FDR admitted that he loved Lucy, Eleanor offered a divorce. She knew, of course, that Mercer, a Roman Catholic, could hardly marry a divorced man with five children without scandal. Not to mention that Secretary Daniels, the hyperfundamentalist who had banned alcohol on US naval vessels, would fire Franklin without hesitation!

Louis Howe, obsessed with guiding Franklin's political ascent, stepped forward to negotiate, pointedly reminding Franklin that a divorce—or even a public acknowledgment of the affair—would sink his potential to be elected to any public office.

The crisis intensified when Sara Roosevelt—as guardian of the family wealth and reputation—declared that she would disinherit him if he divorced Eleanor. Franklin, who relied on his mother's generosity to underwrite his lifestyle, weighed the threat cautiously. During long, restless nights, Eleanor wondered who in their social circle knew. If Alice knew, who had she *not* told? Were people laughing at her naiveté?

Within the Episcopal polity of that day, FDR's unfaithfulness met criteria for a permissible divorce for the "wronged" spouse. With the ball in her court, Eleanor upped her demands. Franklin must promise never to see Lucy again. If she ever learned that he had seen Lucy, she *would* divorce him! Elliott says that his parents moved into separate bedrooms and were never sexually intimate again; others have suggested that they already had separate bedrooms—for birth control—since sometime after John Roosevelt's birth in 1916. Whatever the details, Eleanor confided in her friend Esther Lape that she had not loved Franklin "since discovering the Lucy Mercer affair."

The stubborn Dutchman took his time weighing his options: love and sexual zest or celibacy and an appearance of propriety. He could imagine himself in the governor's chair in Albany. "Franklin must have agonized over the prospect of losing" either the lovely Miss Mercer or a political future. James de Kay comments on the high stakes: "Rarely, if ever, has a domestic decision between two private people held such profound consequences for the future of so many billions of people the world over."

Eleanor understood Franklin's motivations for remaining married: Sara's money and his ambition. Although Eleanor had her own trust fund, raising five children would have been challenging. Moreover, the children, who adored their father—and Lucy!—would be emotionally scarred, if not stigmatized, by a divorce. In her travail—surely an accurate descriptor for her experience—the insanity of her parents' dysfunction haunted her. She had vowed in an Episcopal marriage ritual to "take" Franklin "for better or for worse." Now she fumed at the tail of the vows, "to love and to cherish till death us do part."

From time to time, Eleanor joked that she possessed the memory of an elephant (ironically, the Republican Party symbol). Almost a century after the affair, Geoffrey Ward and Ken Burns suggest, "It became almost a measure of one's intimacy with [Eleanor] to have been quietly told what he had done and how she had dealt with it." At some point, Eleanor told Anna enough detail to soften estrangement between mother and daughter.

Eleanor was cognizant of apostle Paul's stern admonition against taking Holy Communion "unworthily"—a warning priests read aloud before serving Eucharist. Aware of her unforgiving attitude toward her husband, she took the words to heart and did not partake for some time, a significant self-imposed restriction. Surely other congregants, given the small St. James' nave, noticed that she had not walked forward to the altar to receive bread and wine.

IN THE ASHES

A question haunted Eleanor: *Now what?* Slowly, but resolutely, she apprenticed independence and redefined her relationship with Franklin, and with Sara. Doris Kearns Goodwin reports, "No longer would she define herself solely in terms of his wants and needs. A new relationship was forged, on terms wholly different from the old," provoking public curiosity and commentary. No longer would Eleanor's identity be Mrs. James Roosevelt's daughter-in-law.

Eleanor's resolve was reinforced by the death of Mary Livingston Ludlow Hall on August 14, 1919. Remembering the misery of her stern maternal grandmother stirred regret for the life she had not lived. Mrs. Hall's life had revolved around her four surviving children and three grandchildren. "Her life was a sad one in many ways," Eleanor eulogized. Eleanor later candidly reflected:

> I wondered then and I wonder now, if her life had been a little less centered in her family group, if that family group might not have been a great deal better off. If she had had some kind of life of her own, what would have been the result? . . .
>
> My grandmother's life had a considerable effect on me, for even when I was young I determined that I would never be dependent on any of my children by allowing all my interest to center in them. The conviction has grown through the years.

Her grandmother's pathetic life energized Eleanor's determination to be independent. Mrs. Hall's rigidity had anchored deep emotional deficits in Eleanor's soul; Mrs. Hall's inability to give love, in Curtis Roosevelt's assessment, harmed Eleanor's ability to love her own children. Simply, "If you've never experienced free and easy love, how are you going to give it to a child?"

In the 1920s, Eleanor would be mentored by a network of female social activists. By 1926, she lived, at times, in her cottage in Hyde Park—two precious miles from Sara's Springwood—and in an apartment in New York City.

Slowly, the Roosevelt marriage evolved into what Peter Collier and David Horowitz call "a joint venture" and, in time, in the assessment of Geoffrey Ward and Ken Burns, into "one of the most powerful political partnerships in American history" if not world history.

Despite Franklin's promise, the relationship with Lucy went underground. She became a governess for Winthrop Rutherfurd, a wealthy widower with six children, whom she married in 1920. Winthrop, an invalid for several years, died in 1944. Mrs. Rutherfurd attended four inaugurations as FDR's special guest. From time to time, a "Mrs. Paul Johnson"—Lucy's Secret Service code name—visited the president at the White House, and White House telephone operators immediately put through "Mrs. Johnson's" calls to the president.

During the last year of World War II, Lucy and Franklin, in Eleanor's absence, visited and laughed over meals and long conversations in the White House on more than one dozen occasions. Taking advantage of the wartime ban on reporting the president's movements, Franklin visited Lucy at her estates in New Jersey and South Carolina.

FDR, daughter Anna, staff members, and the Secret Service colluded to hide the visits from Eleanor. James Roosevelt qualified the deception, "I doubt father felt he was doing anything wrong in seeing Lucy but he believed mother would take it badly and would be hurt." Curtis Roosevelt reported that Anna, his mother, while serving as gatekeeper to the Oval Office toward the end of FDR's life, given the stress of the war, was under "great pressure to do whatever it would take to make his life easier."

In the Roosevelt era, no organized profession of marriage counseling existed. Some individuals might have confided in a minister, rabbi, or priest, but neither Roosevelt would have ever contemplated such vulnerability. They were Roosevelts! Consequently, a ghost named Lucy permeated the last twenty-seven years of their marriage as well as Eleanor's early widowhood. According to Peter Hay, Eleanor "never got over the hurt." Some would contend that she *never permitted* herself to get over the hurt. Doris Kearns Goodwin disagrees. After FDR's death, "Eleanor was able to reach deep within herself and forgive Franklin for resuming his friendship with Lucy Mercer in the last year of his life." Son James contends that his parents had "an armed truce that endured to the day he died."

Late in his life, Franklin hoped they might have a fresh start after the presidency, perhaps living in the Middle East, where he thought he could broker peace and launch reforestation projects. Eleanor declined to embrace his wish.

Given Eleanor's smoldering resentment, the next crisis came too soon: the 1920 Democratic National Convention selected Franklin to be the vice presidential running mate of Governor James Cox of Ohio. That nomination demonstrated how few knew about Franklin and Lucy. FDR campaigned vigorously across the country—at times with Eleanor standing silently at his side as a prop. The campaign train became a tutorial on the rails for Eleanor as she experienced the underbelly of political strategy and horse trading.

American voters craved change. Warren G. Harding and running mate Calvin Coolidge, promising "a return to normalcy," trounced Cox-Roosevelt, 404 to 127, in the Electoral College in 1920. On the positive side, Democratic Party leaders, bosses, and voters far and wide now knew the name, energies, and ambitions of Franklin Delano Roosevelt.

A VACATION TURNS INTO A NIGHTMARE

In summer 1921, Campobello offered the Roosevelts opportunities to test physical endurance and competitive spirit from sunrise to sunset. For a rare period, the young Roosevelts commanded full parental attention. Vigorous swimming, hiking, games, and sailing filled the laughter-packed days. One afternoon, as FDR and the children sailed back from an outing, they spotted a fire on a small island. They landed on the beach and put out the fire with wet cloths and tree limbs. On reaching their own dock, covered in soot, FDR plunged into the ice-cold water and then ran almost a mile to the cottage. Complaining of fatigue, he turned in early.

The next morning FDR awoke to find his legs would not move. Three days later, his muscles from his chest down to his toes were paralyzed; he had a fever and significant pain. "He was in agony, too, and terrified."

Scattered in the sprawl of the thirty-four-room "cottage," the young Roosevelts sensed something was seriously wrong. Given the remoteness of the island, Eleanor became resident nurse. Louis Howe scoured the nearby resorts until locating Dr. Robert Lovett, a prominent Boston physician. After examining Franklin, Lovett delivered his diagnosis: a disease that generally killed or crippled thousands of children every summer—infantile paralysis, or polio.

For three weeks, around the clock, Eleanor and Louis cared for Franklin, knowing it was imperative to embargo knowledge of his paralysis lest residents panic. The physician prescribed massage, so Eleanor and Louis Howe took turns massaging his legs. Although their efforts were torture, FDR never complained. Eleanor carefully inserted catheters to drain his bladder and administered enemas; she shaved him and brushed his teeth. Her husband's fragile vulnerability trumped her resentment and may have been the raw material for her widely quoted observation, "You must do the thing you think you cannot do." Some betrayed wives might have interpreted the paralysis as the Lord smiting a wayward husband.

Eleanor worked to suppress her anxieties and defuse the children's fears and Sara's after she arrived from Europe. Exhaustion fueled Eleanor's fears and drained her soul. No one knew how extensive or lasting FDR's paralysis would be; Sara assumed the worst. Although Peter Carlson reported that FDR "emerged from this ordeal a warmer, more compassionate man," Eleanor did not know this as she emptied his bedpans!

On those long August nights, as Eleanor slept fitfully on a cot near Franklin, she could not imagine him, the two of them, or the family overcoming polio. He would be branded a cripple. Any sense of security, underwritten by wealth and social status, any political potential, shattered like fine crystal dropped on a marble floor. Franklin struggled to hide his feeling that God had abandoned him.

By stealth, Louis Howe arranged to move FDR by boat and private railroad car to New York City. Howe disguised the severity of FDR's illness. A single newspaper story could torpedo Howe's hopes for Franklin's future and leave Howe with nothing for years of work. From that point on, some thread of deception would be woven into FDR's narrative.

Because Louis Howe managed a friendly relationship between the Boss and the press, particularly after 1928, full disclosure by reporters was hardly a threat. Anyone who dared photograph Roosevelt being lifted out of or into a car found his shot physically blocked by other reporters. On occasion, a Secret Service agent confiscated the film. Few photos of FDR sitting in a wheelchair have survived; four are owned by the FDR Presidential Library. William Binning, Larry Esterly, and Paul Sracic note, "Large numbers of Americans, even through his presidential years, were not aware of the extent of his disability."

THE "MRS. ROOSEVELTS" BATTLE

Mrs. Franklin Roosevelt and Mrs. James Roosevelt squared off in a fierce tug-of-war for custody of Franklin. Sara, who never doubted that she knew what was best for her son and her grandchildren, convinced herself that since "Franklin was going to be an invalid for the rest of his life," he should go home to Springwood, just as his father had after suffering a heart attack. Hyde Park offered privacy where Franklin could be a gentleman farmer, write, and tend his collections.

Eleanor, however, rejected that notion as the worst-possible existence for Franklin. And for her! Conversations about FDR's care became "somewhat acrimonious on occasion" because Eleanor thought it unlikely that Franklin would—or even could—"stand up" to his mother. Doris Weatherford describes the two women tussling "over Franklin's soul" and control of "their futures" as individuals and as family. Fortunately for the nation, Howe sided with Eleanor and tipped the scale: two against one. *The* Mrs. Roosevelt lost! She would be a poor loser.

Louis Howe periodically released disingenuous news of Franklin's progress, which reporters assumed to be fact. Understandably, Franklin, he spun, must step away from politics to focus fully on regaining his health. Still, Howe kept Franklin engaged in vigorous correspondence with party leaders he had met during the 1920 campaign.

In search of health—and maybe to be away from Sara's all-knowingness—Franklin spent long periods of the winters on his boat, the *Larooco,* in the Florida Keys. Missy LeHand, his secretary, and a valet accompanied him. FDR swam, sunbathed, fished, played poker, and entertained guests. Through such activities he masked his depression. In fact, FDR often slept or stayed in his dark cabin until noon, LeHand later told Francis Perkins, "before he managed to pull together the buoyant manner to which his guests had become accustomed."

Eleanor found the *Larooco* one step above a floating stag party—with huge mosquitoes. She stayed away. Setting anchor in the Florida Keys, as waves lapped against the boat, Franklin must have wondered at times if, perhaps, his mother did know best. Missy had her hands full being full-time therapist, cheerleader, and companion.

Pointedly Eleanor refused to abandon the independent life that nourished her soul to be Franklin's permanent nurse or companion or, in the traditional sense, wife. If Missy wanted to fill those roles, fine. Once Eleanor had tasted independence she was not going back.

WARM SPRINGS

In 1924, Franklin visited a run-down resort in Warm Springs, Georgia, where Native Americans had once convalesced in the warm spring-fed waters. After spending a few hours swimming in water he thought magical, FDR fell for the place, rented a ramshackle cottage, and installed Missy LeHand as hostess and, some contend, surrogate wife.

Doris Kearns Goodwin reports that whether on the boat or in New York, "Missy did all the chores a housewife might do, writing Franklin's personal checks, paying the monthly bills, giving the children their allowances, supervising the menus, sending the rugs and draperies for cleaning." Missy had one priority: providing companionship for F. D., as she called him. Goodwin acknowledges the accuracy of Eliot Janeway's conclusion, "In terms of companionship, Missy was the real wife. She understood his nature perfectly." She was always where she wanted to be—with Franklin—until she suffered a stroke in 1941. Eleanor "accommodated" Missy, Hamby argues, because Eleanor did not think they had a sexual relationship. Because Missy came from a different social class, she was not the threat to Eleanor that Lucy Mercer had been.

Soon FDR was spinning ideas about developing the Warm Springs property commercially for two markets: polio sufferers and vacationing guests.

Eleanor would not ignore the entrenched racism of Georgia, despite her family connection to the area. (Martha Bulloch Roosevelt, Eleanor's paternal grandmother, had grown up in a slave-owning family on a plantation near Atlanta. Warm Springs had originally been called Bullochville in honor of the family.) Franklin, on the other hand, accommodated the white good old boys' prejudices and sipped locally produced libations—to be neighborly—despite the Eighteenth Amendment. Neighbors and, in time, Georgia's Democratic politicians grew to like Franklin. FDR spun stories for hours, stirring raucous conviviality while savoring the relaxed way of life and weather. He quickly became "Frank" rather than "that damn rich feller" from New York. However, Eleanor's constant questions about living conditions for Negroes in the community offended "local white sensibilities." As one local person said, "We didn't like her one bit."

When Eleanor called him on his tolerance of racism, FDR countered that these people were now "our" neighbors. Racism, he thought, could be eliminated only by a new southern economy. And that would take time. He intended to be a change agent by offering his ideas about agriculture. Eleanor dismissed such thinking.

In 1927, over Eleanor and Sara's vigorous protests, FDR sank a major portion, perhaps two-thirds, of his personal wealth—some $200,000 ($2.5 million in 2016 dollars) into purchasing the property and some farmland. When Eleanor protested, "You have four sons to educate!" Franklin responded angrily. He heard her objections to buying Warm Springs as objections to his quest to walk again, to regain his old life. It took some reflection while walking in the Georgia pines for Eleanor to realize how much Franklin needed to know that he had tried everything to regain his mobility. Moreover, he needed to invest his time and energy in pursuing a big, successful project that could mean so much not just to him but also to others with polio. Eleanor caved; surely Mrs. Roosevelt would pay for the boys' educations.

With Basil O'Conner, his friend and lawyer, Franklin created the Warm Springs Foundation to run the resort as a polio treatment center. As word spread of Roosevelt's "recovery," patients began showing up at the small train depot seeking treatment. Soon FDR basked in his new moniker, *Doctor* Roosevelt.

ELEANOR AS POLITICAL PLACEHOLDER

Aboard the Roosevelt campaign train in 1920, Louis Howe had realized that there was more to Eleanor than met the eye. While politics was a "man's game," the recent passage of the Twentieth Amendment providing women's suffrage would alter the playing field. Howe made time to chat up Eleanor and test ideas with her. Howe urged her to join the League of Women Voters and try her hand at writing political tracts, articles, and pamphlets for women. In time, Eleanor became editor of the *Women's Democratic News* and emerged as a strong leader, particularly in the Dutchess County delegation to the New York State Democratic Convention.

Howe literally pushed Eleanor onto speaking platforms. The tough tutor-critic sat in the back of the room, monitoring audience response. He ruthlessly critiqued her, especially for an annoying nervous habit of laughing during her speech. Howe helped her hone ideas, structure arguments, discipline her nerves, and lower (somewhat) her high-pitched voice. His advice was straightforward: "Have something you want to say, say it and sit down."

Louis Howe encouraged Eleanor's independence, musing that he might get *two* candidates for the price of one. Sara Roosevelt, however—and the Roosevelt children, particularly Anna—despised Howe (that "dirty little man") as well as political operatives like Huey Long ("that awful man") who began showing up at her table.

Howe helped Eleanor imagine the potential of women working on issues important to them and their families and, then, confidently stepping into polling places and voting Democratic.

Eleanor rejoined the Consumer League, an organization devoted to the needs of impoverished women. Meanwhile, Eleanor made friendships—deep friendships—with women, some of whom were lesbian and partnered and some who were not of the Roosevelt social class. Labor lawyers and radicals like Mary Elisabeth Dreier of the Women's Trade Union League and Mary "Molly" Dewson of the Democratic women's clubs affirmed Eleanor. She learned from activists like Esther Lape and Elizabeth Read of the League of Women Voters, and Rose Schneiderman and Maud Swartz of the Women's Trade Union League. Eleanor stretched her arms toward a new political horizon and a new identity.

Gradually Eleanor Roosevelt came to know and be known by every Democratic leader in New York State. She edited and subsidized Democratic periodicals for women and advocated policy positions. Eleanor engaged with female friends in long, vigorous conversations about the future of women and of individuals over countless cups of tea.

Initially, the party patriarchs were dismissive of women. Eleanor challenged that prejudice, borrowing Abigail Adams's words to her husband, John, "Remember the ladies!" Energy that Eleanor might have invested in restoring her relationship with Franklin or her children, she lavished on women's organizations and causes and on political fund-raising.

1924: "HE'S BACK!"

In 1924 Franklin returned briefly to the political arena. In Madison Square Garden's stifling summer heat, he electrified the Democratic National Convention by "walking"—while leaning on a cane and grasping tightly the arm of a son. Twenty thousand people in the vast hall held their breath, fearing he would fall. When he reached the podium, spectators erupted into frenzy. Although carefully staged, that "excruciating charade"—complete with props: the wide grin, the cigarette holder, the upthrust chin—won the hearts of thousands of Democrats: "He's *back*!" "I tell you, I saw the man walk!" delegates informed skeptics on returning home. Roosevelt stirred the souls of Democrats with his ringing call to nominate New York's Catholic governor, Al Smith, for president.

Eleanor, meanwhile, chaired the Democratic women's platform

committee, which developed progressive planks calling for the elimination of child labor, adoption of the minimum wage, maximum hours for women to work, and care for mothers and infants. Although an all-male platform committee rejected Eleanor's proposals, she learned negotiating skills she would wield later. Women would be heard in 1928!

Sitting in a gallery watching the clamor, Eleanor could never have imagined that someday she would chair a national platform committee, keynote a Democratic convention, or emerge as a major power broker in the Democratic Party.

After Smith lost the nomination, FDR returned to Warm Springs to resume rehab. Gail Collins concludes that FDR's obsession with walking freed Eleanor "to become the woman we know in history" because from then on her primary duty, as she would famously explain, was to serve as his legs, to go where he could not go. "She was no longer expected to live at home with her unfaithful spouse and his difficult mother and a houseful of children whom she loved but never seemed to feel entirely comfortable with."

Thus, during the 1920s, Eleanor laid track in New York on which Franklin's political locomotive would run: to Albany, 1929–1933, and then to the White House. Her activism provided one fringe benefit. Had Eleanor remained a traditional "Yes, dear" wife, she would have been expected to participate enthusiastically in women's groups in the Episcopal church, especially in their local parish. While Franklin served as head of the vestry for St. James' throughout his life, raised funds for Cathedral of St. John the Divine in New York City, and served on a national church commission on social welfare, Eleanor declined opportunities Episcopalians traditionally considered women's work, such as the Altar Guild and chairing this or that bazaar or hosting teas in the church hall.

BACK ON THE BALLOT

In 1928, Al Smith, again running for president, needed Franklin on the ballot to rally voters to vote the straight Democratic ticket in New York, given the number of its electoral votes. If Smith lost the presidency and Roosevelt won the governorship, he reasoned, FDR would need him and "his people" to run the state.

In Louis Howe's grand strategy, 1932 was the year for FDR to run for governor and 1936 for president. FDR dutifully turned down Smith's entreaties, insisting that his first priority was regaining his health. Roosevelt believed he would again walk!

In September 1928, during the New York State Democratic Convention, FDR, in Warm Springs, refused to accept Smith's telephone calls. Finally, a desperate Smith recruited Eleanor to get her husband on the phone.

"Franklin?" She spoke quickly—she always thought long-distance telephone rates exorbitant—"The governor wants to talk to you. Bye." She handed the receiver to Smith and dashed to catch her train. Under the governor's barrage, FDR finally gave in and agreed to accept the nomination to be the Democratic candidate for governor of New York, for an election only seven weeks away!

Working on Smith's national campaign staff, Eleanor encountered ugly raw anti-Catholic bigotry. What difference, she fumed, should a candidate's religion make? Rather, the question should be: Does he practice his religion? Is Al Smith a good Catholic?

In 1928 Eleanor did not campaign for her husband, although there were a few pictures of her standing beside him at events. Rather she campaigned for Herbert Lehman for lieutenant governor. Smith lost New York by one hundred thousand votes, but FDR won the governorship by twenty-five thousand votes. Herbert Hoover's landslide victory in the presidential race delighted Louis Howe because it pushed Governor Smith off the national stage, leaving only one New Yorker with national potential: Franklin D. Roosevelt.

Reporters seeking comment from the governor-elect's wife were puzzled and stunned by her response: "I am not excited about my husband's election. I don't care. What difference can it make to me?" Eleanor was not about to surrender her independence to meet the political establishment's expectations for a tea-pouring, hand-shaking First Lady in Albany! Eleanor vowed to redefine or escape those traditions.

The Roosevelts reached a pragmatic compromise. From 1929 to 1933, during the school year Eleanor spent Wednesday night through Sunday afternoon at the governor's mansion. On Sunday nights, she caught the late train to New York City to teach American history and English literature at the Todhunter School on Monday, Tuesday, and Wednesday; Eleanor shared ownership of the school and her home with her friends Marion Dickerman and Nancy Cook. She told one reporter she liked teaching "better than anything else I do."

AND THEN CAME 1932

Given the stock market crash in 1929 and resulting economic chaos, 1932 shaped up to be an ABH election—*anybody* but Hoover! Al Smith threw his hat in the ring, as did John Nance Garner, a cigar-chomping, bourbon-swigging conservative Texan and Speaker of the House of Representatives. Democratic bosses, however, wanted a fresh face. Momentum—fanned by Louis Howe—built for the "do something" New York governor.

As the economy worsened and Hoover was vilified as incapable of leading, Roosevelt's attraction soared. In June 1932, when the Democrats gathered in Chicago, Franklin had a majority of delegates' votes on the first three roll calls, especially from southern delegates, but no support from the large New York delegation. Convention rules required the nominee to win two-thirds of the delegates. Finally, William Randolph Hearst and Joseph P. Kennedy Sr. persuaded Garner to withdraw from the race. If he endorsed Roosevelt, he would have the vice presidential nomination. He agreed.

During the campaign, Hoover stayed close to the White House—some said *hid in*—while FDR stumped the country promising "Happy Days Are Here Again." If the Roosevelt touch worked in New York, voters increasingly believed, it would work in Washington!

FDR's robust promise of a New Deal sent Hoover packing, by 57.4 to 39.7 percent in the popular vote and 472–59 in the Electoral College. Eleanor later wrote, "I was happy for my husband, of course, because I knew that in many ways it would make up for the blow that fate had dealt him," that is, polio. However, Eleanor moaned,

> I cannot say that I was pleased at the prospect. By earning my own money, I had recently enjoyed a certain amount of financial independence, and had been able to do things in which I was personally interested. The turmoil in my heart and mind was rather great that night, and the next few months were not to make any clearer what the road ahead would be. Life began to change immediately.

WAITING FOR INAUGURATION

The economy grew even worse between FDR's victory in November 1932 and the inauguration in March 1933. More banks closed, more workers lost jobs, more farms and houses were foreclosed. Americans begged for jobs; millions stood in soup lines. Fathers sold apples. "Mister, can you spare a dime?" became an oppressive mantra.

The interim strained the Roosevelt marriage. It was one thing to be a governor's wife balancing her own schedule with ceremonial duties, but quite another to be First Lady of the nation. Eleanor stewed. In her mind she heard her mother's warning that she had to be useful to be loved. Well then, now she must be useful to Franklin.

She asked for "a real job" in the administration, perhaps handling her husband's mail. Impossible, FDR snapped briskly. That would intrude on Missy LeHand's turf. "I knew he was right that it would not work," Eleanor noted, "but it was a last effort to keep in close touch and to feel that I had a real job to do." James Roosevelt reports that his mother's distress deepened after Franklin insisted she give up serving on the Democratic National Committee, the League of Women Voters, and the Women's Trade Union League. FDR's hardest demand was that she give up teaching at Todhunter. Give it up she did, although she remained an owner until 1938, when disagreement between the three owners forced her buyout. And she had to give up flying lessons. Eleanor agonized as Franklin pared down her independence.

Eleanor heard the chains of tradition rattling as she pondered following Republican First Ladies Florence Harding, Grace Coolidge, and Lou Hoover. Slowly, Eleanor sank into a depression, which she labeled her "Griselda" mood. While Eleanor and Franklin had no financial worries—compared to most Americans—could faith sustain her in the days ahead as she navigated uncharted waters? She remembered the spiritual that Mary Bethune's students sang:

> This little light of mine,
> I'm going to let it shine,
> Let it shine, let it shine, let it shine.

But how? Where? By early 1933, critics blasted her professional career as "ER's commercialism." She despaired, "I'll just have to go on being myself, as much as I can." Repeatedly, Eleanor told friends that she would not be "the first lady" but "just plain Mrs. Roosevelt."

THE PSYCHOLOGICAL PRESSURE ESCALATES

Two undercurrents inflated Eleanor's distress. First, through her observations of Aunt Edith Roosevelt, First Lady from 1901 to 1909, she had some awareness of what it took to run the White House well; consequently, she feared being compared to Edith. Further, Alice, Eleanor's acid-tongued cousin, had crowned herself *the* resident Roosevelt in the nation's capital; these two Hyde Park Roosevelts were trespassers! Alice also nursed a grudge: her brother, Theodore Jr., might have been headed to Washington if Eleanor had not campaigned so deceitfully against him for New York governor in 1924.

The bigger hurdle for Eleanor was returning to the city where Franklin had betrayed her. Fifteen years away had not been long enough to heal her wounds. Besides, the "cave-dwellers," the permanent residents of Washington who wielded social influence regardless of who resided in the White House, had long memories of Franklin and Lucy as dinner guests in some of their homes. Thus, for Eleanor—and some Republican Washington residents—FDR's presidency would be a cross to be borne.

That might have proven true had Eleanor not met Lorena Hickok, a top female reporter, who, in a series of conversations, sensed Eleanor's angst. Hickok became Eleanor's confidante during the transition; some say she became more.

Eleanor's disclosure on the eve of the inauguration, "I did not want my husband to be president," offers insight into her mental state in early 1933. Her daily schedule had been stripped of meaningful activities. As she told Hickok, "I cannot say that I was pleased at the prospect." She knew the rumors that she had been the force pushing FDR's political ambitions. No, Eleanor protested. "I never wanted to be a President's wife, and I don't want it now."

Blanche Wiesen Cook concludes, "ER prepared for her new life in Washington with a determination that masked her sense of dread." When reporters questioned why she kept her commitment at Cornell University the day after an assassination attempt against FDR in February 1933, she informed them, "I have the habit of doing things I have said I will do." In the coming years, Eleanor would restate that sentence many times, despite death threats against herself.

There had never been a White House family like these Roosevelts. There had never been a First Lady like Anna Eleanor Roosevelt. Within hours of getting settled in the White House, staff members were shaking their heads and rolling their eyes. After the formal, stilted Hoovers, this might be interesting.

At 7:15 in the morning before her husband's inauguration, Eleanor snuck out the back entrance of the Mayflower Hotel and slipped into a cab, where Lorena Hickok waited. Eleanor instructed the driver, "Rock Creek Park." Looking over her shoulder out the back window, Eleanor expressed relief that no reporters were in pursuit.

The cabbie thought the park an odd destination for two women before daylight. Inside the park, Eleanor directed him to a grove of trees and then asked him to wait. Eleanor and Lorena walked across wet grass toward a tall sculpture, commonly called "Grief." Henry Adams had commissioned the work to commemorate his wife, Marian "Clover" Adams, who committed suicide after she learned he was having an affair. Hickok knew of Augustus Saint-Gaudens's masterpiece, but she did not know the story behind it. Nor did she know Eleanor's affection for this place. They sat in silence. Finally, Eleanor spoke:

> In the old days, when we lived here, I was much younger and not so very wise. Sometimes I'd be very unhappy and sorry for myself. When I was feeling that way and if I could manage it, I'd come out here, alone and sit and look at that woman, and I'd always come away somehow feeling better, stronger.

Eleanor blurted out that she could not go through the inauguration, she could *not* be First Lady! She should have followed through on her threat before the Democratic convention to divorce Franklin. She should not have listened to Louis Howe, who had talked her out of it.

In the cold darkness, Eleanor concluded she had no choice. Maybe, like Herbert Hoover, Franklin would serve only one term. She and Hickok walked back to the taxi and rode back to the hotel in silence. In a little more than twenty-four hours, Eleanor Roosevelt became the First Lady.

Eleanor's depression did not dissipate like a morning fog; but slowly, in God's good time, it lifted. The God who had not abandoned Eleanor as a child, adolescent, young wife, grieving mother would not abandon her once she walked through the door of the White House on March 4, 1933.

6

Helping the Little People

Eleanor in the White House

Dear God, please make Eleanor a little tired.

—Joke in Washington

It has been said that Eleanor Roosevelt viewed the world as one vast slum project. She was always flitting around here and there, coming to some community whose condition she didn't like, and tut-tutting about it and insisting that something must be done. She seemed to have a large political equivalent of the housewife's desire to redecorate.

—William Rusher

Out of the bags of mail addressed to Eleanor Roosevelt at the White House, one letter seized the First Lady's attention. Frank Brodsky, from Brooklyn, appealed for help for Bertha, his fourteen-year-old sister who was battling scoliosis, a crippling degeneration of the back. The word *scoliosis* leaped off the page. Eleanor's beloved Aunt Bye had struggled with the disease and Eleanor, as a young adolescent, had worn a back brace.

After meeting the family, Eleanor discovered they survived on meager earnings from the disabled father's newspaper route; any treatment was beyond their means. Eleanor forwarded Frank's letter to the head of New York's Orthopedic Hospital—the hospital her grandfather, Theodore "Big Heart" Roosevelt Sr., had founded. Surely, a bed could be made available for Bertha at no charge!

"Of course, Mrs. Roosevelt," the head physician responded. When Eleanor visited the hospital postsurgery, although she found Bertha ensconced in a full-body cast, the patient's eyes danced. The girl and the family became beneficiaries of Eleanor's heart: flowers, fruit, candy, books, and holiday gifts. Over the ten months Bertha was hospitalized, Eleanor dropped in for updates. Eleanor personally signed the girl's junior high diploma and sent her to camp. Eleanor, through friends, found jobs for Bertha and Frank.

The First Lady stayed in touch, marveling at the girl's improved gait. Bertha eventually fell in love, and a beaming Eleanor attended the wedding; in time, the First Lady became godmother for the couple's first child. Many "Berthas"—one at a time—were recipients of Eleanor's skills as a door opener.

No First Lady brought more awareness of poverty to her official duties than Eleanor—ironically, the Eleanor with a trust fund. As a child, she had accompanied her father to events at charities he sponsored. She helped serve meals to the poor. More importantly, she observed her father make time to listen to the individuals he assisted. Upon returning from Allenswood, she plunged into serving New York City's poorest, particularly immigrants. While many young women from socially prominent families dabbled in social work at the shallow end of the pool, Eleanor dove into the deep end. In time, Eleanor developed an understanding of rural poverty through operating, with her friends Marion Dickerman and Nancy Cook, a furniture factory at Val-Kill, between 1927 and 1936, to provide work during the winters for struggling farmers in Hyde Park; she wanted the craftsmen she employed to have wages with dignity. (She had hoped to expand the experiment to other locations, but unfortunately the Depression decreased demand for high-end furniture.) Eleanor spent time with poor Americans, and never forgot what she saw, smelled, tasted, sensed, or heard.

FINDING A WAY TO BE USEFUL

In late autumn 1932, as it became apparent that FDR would send Herbert Hoover packing, Eleanor had plunged into her deep "dark night of the soul." Aware of Martha Washington's lament, "I am more like a state prisoner than anything else," Eleanor feared that she, too, would be imprisoned at 1600 Pennsylvania Avenue. Eleanor expected that Washington insiders would criticize her for not being more like Aunt Edith Roosevelt, considered one of the most successful First Ladies for her efforts from 1901 to 1909. (Ironically, in time, future presidential spouses would be "evaluated" in light of Eleanor's accomplishments.) Aunt Bye, long a source of political guidance behind the scenes in Washington as Teddy Roosevelt's sister and confidante, offered Eleanor sage advice for surviving Washington: "My dear, you will never please everyone in this world, if you think this is the right thing to do, go ahead and do it." Eleanor later told Genevieve Forbes Herrick that although initially "terrified," she had turned a corner after deciding, "I would be lost if I pretended to be anything I was not."

Early in the transition, Eleanor had warned Associated Press reporter

Lorena Hickok, "I'm afraid that you won't have much to write about. I'll not be doing anything very interesting" or worth criticizing, she might have hoped—a significant understatement. Doris Kearns Goodwin credits Hickok, the first friend, with helping Eleanor "transform the role of first lady from ceremonial to activist." Traveling the nation as the president's ears, eyes, and legs, Eleanor not only gathered information about how the Great Depression was affecting common people but also translated statistics and charts in government reports into stories about individuals.

Eleanor did not see the mass of "the unemployed," whatever the number in newspaper stories and government reports, as a faceless mass to be pitied—or worse, condemned as lazy or in any way deserving of their condition. Rather she saw *this* particular unemployed man named Joseph or *this* particular unemployed woman named Lillian—particular Americans stigmatized as "the less fortunate" or "underprivileged." She fumed, "I often wonder how we can make the more fortunate in this country fully aware of the fact that the problem of the unemployed is not a mechanical one." Rather, she argued, "It is a problem alive and throbbing with human pain" (MD, April 29, 1936).

Harry Hopkins had worked for FDR in New York and became a close confidante of both Roosevelts. Eleanor and Hopkins believed that the answer to "the suffering of the unemployed" was not the dole but rather dignity-conferring jobs. Both conceded that some make-work jobs had to be created, even if that invited criticism. They joined minds to promote and defend FDR's New Deal. Hopkins headed three agencies for Roosevelt: the Federal Relief Administration, the Civil Works Administration, and the Works Progress Administration. Hopkins was the go-to individual who could make things happen for those Eleanor met in her travel who needed a door opened. Hopkins shared Eleanor's special interest in the poor, the young, and women. They had—at least in the years before the war—a deep confidence in one another's vision. As a result of their efforts, the women's division in the Works Progress Administration and the National Youth Administration were created.

ELEANOR'S WHITE HOUSE

The White House was far less attractive in Eleanor's era. J. B. West, then chief usher, described it as "dingy, almost seedy." (The glory would come through extensive restoration in the early 1960s supervised by Jackie Kennedy—an effort Eleanor applauded.) Although presidential families were appropriated funds to refurbish the family quarters, Eleanor knew that Mary Lincoln had received scathing criticism for her lavish redecorating early in the Civil War. The mansion at 1600 Pennsylvania Avenue, West lamented, resembled a tired "Grand Hotel," with hundreds of guests coming and going; others, however, thought it more of a boardinghouse, given the number of friends and staff of the Roosevelts who lived there from time to time. Immediately after Franklin's "so help me God" on March 4, 1933, Eleanor went to work making the family quarters and the third-floor bedrooms more Roosevelt-friendly. Eleanor did not just direct staff on the placement of furniture; she astounded staffers as she shoved and pulled furniture into place.

In a decision that would rankle her mother-in-law and Washingtonians who dined at the White House from time to time, Eleanor hired Henrietta Nesbitt, a baker from Hyde Park, to be housekeeper and head the kitchen. Mrs. Nesbitt thought "a proper diet" consisted of "plain foods, plainly prepared" or, as some remembered, thoroughly overcooked. Mrs. Nesbitt recalled, "Mrs. Roosevelt and I had our economy program all mapped out and we were going to stick to it. With so many Americans hungry, it was up to the head house of the nation to serve economy meals and act as an example."

Eleanor's decision led to what Laura Shapiro labeled "the most notorious era in the culinary history of the Presidency." Guests described the White House food as "awful," "boring," or "predictable." J. B. West recalled, "Mrs. Roosevelt didn't pay much attention to the food, but the President did. He couldn't stand it." After many meals FDR groaned, "I wish we could do something about Mrs. Nesbitt." Often potential guests declined invitations on Monday nights, when the entrée was tongue with caper sauce, or Thursday nights, when sweetbread (animal thymus or pancreas) was served. The wine and champagne Ernest Hemingway sipped there were inexpensive and the servings limited. He described one meal: "rainwater soup followed by rubber squab, a nice wilted salad, and a cake some admirer had sent in." He dismissed the White House cuisine as "the worst I've ever eaten."

Given that so many Americans—too many—were hungry, formerly well-fed merchants stood in long soup lines, and children were malnourished, it was important to Eleanor that the White House table offered the "humble, wholesome meals" developed by Cornell University home economics faculty. In contrast, Herbert and Lou

Hoover—and their guests—had dined in formal dress every night in the White House, although meals were brief to accommodate the First Workaholic.

This, Eleanor insisted, was a time to demonstrate sensitivity to economic realities and solidarity with the poor. Mrs. Nesbitt periodically served a seven-cent meal consisting of stuffed eggs and a prune dessert. Lunch at the White House might be broiled kidneys on toast or curried eggs on toast.

Food meant little to Eleanor; rather the primary focus of meals was conversation and networking. By seating an individual with an issue next to the president, the issue often could be resolved by the time they finished soup. Eleanor would not develop an appetite for fine cuisine until her United Nations service in Paris. Franklin, however, had been spoiled by Mama Roosevelt's cooks who had prepared gourmet meals, much of the food grown or raised on the estate. Laura Shapiro notes that the president certainly "knew the taste of excellent food and missed it badly." Nevertheless, FDR ate what Mrs. Nesbitt served until Sara's death in 1941; then he installed Mary Campbell, his mother's cook, in a new small kitchen on the third floor. Nevertheless, he claimed he was running for reelection in 1944 to have a chance to fire Mrs. Nesbitt.

Once World War II began, Eleanor put the White House on food rationing, particularly for meat, sugar, butter, cheese, and coffee. The Roosevelts provided Nesbitt $2,000 a month ($34,000 in 2016 dollars) to feed and house their guests—and there were always guests at *every* meal, including soldiers Eleanor met on the streets on her walks.

Early in the administration, Eleanor demonstrated that the White House was her turf; periodically she reminded Franklin of their agreement on that division of labor. Therefore, she would welcome all—and not just the politically powerful and the socially elite.

There were impoverished guests like the hitchhiker Eleanor rescued along the Virginia highway and women laborers attending a convention in Washington. Even when she would not be in town, Eleanor would invite people, "Why not stay at the White House?" That sometimes led to reassigning bedrooms like musical chairs and Nesbitt's lament, "every nook and cranny" was filled with houseguests.

The Roosevelts' oldest child, Anna, and her children moved into the White House as her marriage to Curtis Dahl was ending; Dahl would be banned from the White House. (The dissolution of the marriage came as no surprise to Eleanor; Anna had married too young. The five Roosevelt offspring would ultimately rack up nineteen marriages, a moral blemish—in that day's perspective—that reporters *and* clergy would deride. The presence of two young grandchildren captured public interest and offered moments of welcomed delight for Franklin and Eleanor.

The widowed Harry Hopkins and his six-year-old daughter Diana moved into the White House in 1940. Given Hopkins's poor health, Eleanor became guardian of the child until Hopkins remarried in 1942. Despite his health, he evolved into something of a minister without portfolio. Like Louis Howe, FDR's alter ego and strategist, Hopkins was a friend to both Roosevelts and served as the link—sometimes negotiator—between two strong-willed political partners. When Eleanor realized that Hopkins had shifted full allegiance to the president, becoming an adversary to and critic of her, she was devastated and took to bed for days and in Tommy Thompson's words, "turned her face to the wall." Another betrayal by a man she had trusted.

WITNESSING TO WHAT SHE SAW

The numerous alphabet agencies (and bureaucracies) that had been birthed to elevate the "forgotten man" did not bring a swift end to the Depression. Only mobilization for a global war, which put millions of Americans into uniform, and other millions, including women, into defense factories, would end the crippling economic distress. But as Franklin and his New Dealers worked to lift the nation's economy, Eleanor saw her role as bearing witness to the struggles of real Americans. Like an evangelist telling the tale of rescued souls, Eleanor testified to the suffering she saw, in hopes of inspiring action from those in power.

FDR would use this language of witness in his second inaugural address in 1937:

> In this nation I see tens of millions of its citizens—a substantial part of its whole population—who at this very moment are denied the greater part of what the very lowest standards of today call the necessities of life.
>
> I see millions of families trying to live on incomes so meager that the pall of family disaster hangs over them day by day.
>
> I see millions whose daily lives in city and on farm continue under conditions labeled indecent by a so-called polite society half a century ago.

I see millions denied education, recreation, and the opportunity to better their lot and the lot of their children.

I see millions lacking the means to buy the products of farm and factory and by their poverty denying work and productiveness to many other millions.

I see one-third of a nation ill-housed, ill-clad, ill-nourished.

Franklin saw these things on paper, or from afar, out the window of his train, but Eleanor saw them firsthand.

Early during Franklin's watch at the Navy Department, First Lady Ellen Wilson had invited cabinet wives to walk with her through the city's despicable slums. Mrs. Wilson died in August 1914, fighting for congressional legislation to clean up the squalor. Because little had changed in the slums and alleys since 1914, Eleanor resumed the walks but invited congressional wives to accompany her. Although Eleanor did not sleep with FDR, she appreciated the power of pillow talk and hoped that wives of the southern Democrats in Congress might be persuasive.

Lady Bird Johnson—a future First Lady—recalled these walks with Eleanor: "It was a learning experience, and it was interesting to see that she dared to do it, one, because it certainly wasn't a cup of tea and roses-and-lace sort of thing to do; two, she cared. And it was a learning experience just to see how dirty and grubby and, in a way, frightening and foreboding the area was." Those walks with Eleanor paid dividends in Lady Bird Johnson's efforts to beautify slum neighborhoods near the White House after she became First Lady in 1963.

Eleanor thought it essential for leaders to get out of the White House or Capitol "to assess conditions" firsthand. Eleanor traveled to let the public see her see them and to let individuals talk to her. Hence she refused Secret Service coverage. Individuals would not talk to her as freely with men in dark suits hovering. Eleanor also hoped that the journalists covering her travels—particularly photographers—would capture the conditions she witnessed. A picture was worth more than a thousand words. For example, Dorothea Lange's photograph capturing the hopelessness of a mother during the Depression, "Migrant Mother," became a haunting icon. How, Eleanor mused, can government help *that* woman?

Upon returning to Washington, sometimes over meals, Eleanor briefed the president on her findings before contacting appropriate government agencies. Assessments from the Missus, however, were seldom well received. "Bring back Mrs. Hoover. *Please,*" moaned bureaucrats in the rapidly expanding New Deal agencies who resented her intrusions and her follow-up calls or letters when she thought they had not acted.

Joseph P. Kennedy, who headed the federal Securities and Exchange Commission before he served as ambassador to Great Britain, in a blunt interview in the *Boston Sunday Globe* on November 10, 1940, conceded that while Eleanor was "a wonderful woman," "marvelously helpful," "full of sympathy," she "bothered us more on our jobs in Washington to take care of the poor little nobodies who hadn't any influence." Kennedy's eight words, "*the poor little nobodies who hadn't any influence,*" might as well have been printed in bold banner headlines! Commenting on his position in London, Kennedy griped, "She is always sending me a note to have some little Susie Glotz to tea at the [British] embassy." (*Glotz* was a slang word commonly applied to Jews.)

Eleanor knew Jesus' words, "Blessed are the eyes which see the things that ye see" (Luke 10:23).

Eleanor rejected the modus operandi of many bureaucrats: been there, seen that, on to the next stop on the schedule. At times, she held naked underweight babies on her lap with the same affection with which she held her own grandchildren. Too many young women she had met could be described as haggard or old before their time. She would not ignore injustices, hunger, poverty, deprivation, and discrimination—nor tolerate platitudes about the poor—she either observed firsthand on her travels or read about in the appeals among the mounds of mail she received at the White House. Letters from children particularly troubled her. Although Eleanor had sipped tea with queens, movie stars, justices, writers, she could be at home anywhere. One day a persistent reporter tracked her to an Appalachian coal miner's shanty far off the paved road. He found the First Lady sitting in the kitchen with the miner's wife, "discussing their household problems as though that Appalachian hut was no different from a Washington drawing room." Later that reporter observed Eleanor holding a naked, sick baby as the mother cooked supper or, more accurately, what would pass for supper. Many wives invited Eleanor to eat with the family or, at least, "have something." Valuing their hospitality, she would not injure their self-esteem by declining.

On one trip into Appalachia, Eleanor visited a cabin that had "seen better days." As Eleanor petted a young boy's white rabbit, an older child whispered, "He thinks we are not going to eat it, but we are." The boy bolted out the door, holding his rabbit. Eleanor could not forget the incident. Repeatedly, Eleanor encountered American children who did not know what it was to sit down at a table and eat meat or vegetables, not anything close to what her friends at Cornell considered a nourishing meal. Few children, or adults, ate until they were full. Too many children she saw could not attend school because they had no clothes to wear, some clad in rags in winter. Eleanor understood the dual long-term consequences of hunger and poverty on the minds and the souls of children. How could these children—*our children, God's children*—survive childhood to become productive adults?

One night Eleanor shared "the rabbit story" at a White House dinner. William C. Bullitt, a wealthy diplomat, mailed her a generous check with a note expressing his hope that his donation "might help to keep the rabbit alive."

Especially during the Christmas season, Eleanor's heart turned to Washington's neediest residents—some living close to the White House. On Christmas Eves, Eleanor slipped from family and festivities in the White House—even when Winston Churchill was a trying guest—and drove slowly through the alleys of the capital's slums, delivering Christmas trees, leading carol singing, and passing out small presents. Eleanor Roosevelt was the *only* Santa Claus some of those "alley" children saw. Older children, although not convinced that Santa Claus would come, *knew* that Mrs. Roosevelt would come! After distributing the gifts, she returned to the White House "with an added awareness of the inequality of our earthly blessings" (IYAM, August 1954).

"I WANT YOU TO WRITE ME"

One could write a lengthy book with stories of the "little people" who received Eleanor's personal attention. Soon after the Roosevelts moved into the White House in 1933, the *Women's Home Companion* asked Eleanor to submit an article on any topic. Eleanor, with Lorena Hickok's urging, reached out to readers: "But you must help me. I want you to tell me about the particular problems which puzzle or sadden you, but I also *want you to write me* about what has brought joy into your life, and how you are adjusting yourself to the new conditions in this amazing changing world."

This was no publicity stunt. The White House post office staff were overwhelmed by an avalanche of mail addressed to the First Lady. Mrs.

Roosevelt, believing that troubling times "required all citizens to share their insight and prudence regarding the country's political and economic situation," and not just Franklin's "brain trust," was delighted! *All* Americans—not just the nation's elite and politically privileged—had to share in economic recovery. Moreover, she reasoned, those who were experiencing poverty had insights bureaucrats should read.

By December 31, 1933, more than three hundred thousand pieces of mail had been received. Over the next dozen years, millions of letters, postcards, greeting cards, and telegrams would find their way to Eleanor's staff and, in some cases, onto her desk for reading, often after midnight. Individuals penned poignant thoughtful descriptions of their troubles, fears, and anxieties. Some requested jobs, food, or clothes—even hand-me-downs from the First Family's closets. Eleanor nightly placed selected letters in the president's reading basket.

Thousands of individuals were stunned when the First Lady wrote back—and certainly no form letter. Even when she could not offer specific help, Eleanor acknowledged the writer's concerns and steered the individual to a federal agency for assistance. Envelopes stamped "The White House" were proudly shown to family, neighbors, and friends; some were framed and hung on the wall not too far from FDR's picture.

Eleanor paid particular attention to letters from children. In February 1936, as she walked in the fresh snow in Lafayette Square, across from the White House, two young boys stopped her. The older boy gushed,

> Thank you for answering my Christmas letter. I am your neighbor, we live in the attic of that house diagonally across from the White House. We are German born but we admire the President because we think he is for "the little people," so I wanted to write you at Christmas time and was very happy to have your reply. (MD, February 10, 1936)

The boys informed her that they had taken pictures the day before on the White House lawn (security was significantly more relaxed in that era) and promised to send her a set. With Eleanor's "Auf Wiedersehen"—she spoke German fluently—the boys went back to playing in the snow. This interaction happened *because* Mrs. Roosevelt answered a letter to a child. Today it would be impossible for "little people" to live so close to the White House or to have this kind of access to its occupants.

REACHING A WIDER AUDIENCE

After Eleanor lamented the limitations of talking to political leaders about poverty and injustice, Lorena Hickok proposed two responses to reach beyond Eleanor's one-on-one appeals. The First Lady could hold press conferences—women-only press conferences—partially to help female reporters keep their jobs as newspapers slashed expenses. Initially, questions were nonpolitical; certainly, Eleanor's answers became political when misquoted or misinterpreted by critics. Emma Bugbee of the *New York Tribune* recalled one reporter cautioning the First Lady that an answer to a particular question might provoke critics. Eleanor laughed:

> Sometimes I say things which I thoroughly understand are likely to cause unfavorable comment in some quarters, and perhaps you newspaper women think I should keep them off the record. What you don't understand is that perhaps I am making these statements on purpose to arouse controversy and thereby get the topics talked about and so get people to thinking about them.

In late 1935, Hickok pitched Eleanor the idea of writing a syndicated newspaper column about daily life as First Lady; "daily life" would be a wide umbrella. Eleanor took her suggestion and submitted her first "My Day" column for publication on December 30, 1935. Neither woman could have imagined Eleanor writing almost six thousand columns—without missing a deadline or using a ghostwriter. (She did pause for four days following Franklin's death.) Eleanor raised topics in her columns that many Americans did not wish to think about. Many Americans would have preferred columns on respectable teas and elegant dinner parties the First Lady hosted, rather than her perspectives on public policy and social issues.

Through the "My Day" columns, Eleanor rallied support for administration policies and attracted tens of thousands of loyal readers. She drew large audiences through the airwaves as well.

Eleanor first spoke on radio broadcasts during the 1920s. Between FDR's election and inauguration, Mrs. Roosevelt, sponsored by Pond's Cold Cream, broadcast twelve programs on topics related to parenting and families. Speaking candidly, she commented on the failure of Prohibition to prepare young girls to drink responsibly, which angered the ladies from the Woman's Christian Temperance Union. Eleanor learned that what people *thought* she said ignited more criticism than what she actually said.

Given the volume of requests for financial assistance that the First Lady received from individuals and organizations, Eleanor decided to go back to radio, "get the money and take the gaff," since charities would benefit. Over the years, the First Lady's radio sponsors included a roofing company, Simmons Mattress, the American typewriter industry, and eventually Shelby Shoe. John T. Flynn, an American journalist who disliked both Roosevelts, calculated Eleanor's earnings from radio during her first eight years in the White House to be $450,000 ($7.343 million in 2016 dollars).

TAKING THE GAFF

Whether it was for the content of her articles and talks, the amount she was paid for them, or the fact that she was working at all, critics like Westbrook Pegler blasted her for meddling "in many matters which are very improper business for the wife of the President of the United States." Eleanor could have rebutted, "in matters *heretofore* thought improper." The American crisis required conversation, awareness, and action. No topic was inappropriate, and no topic failed to yield criticism from some corner.

Cousin Alice Roosevelt Longworth, who married into money, dismissed Eleanor as "a do-gooder," bristling at Eleanor's "overly noble" concern for the poor and the marginalized.

Meanwhile, another woman ripped the chatty, conversational style of "My Day." Why, the reader demanded, do you fill your column

> with inane chatter about your family affairs—words, words, words, which are of little interest to anyone and only once in a blue moon of any value whatsoever. Why do you consider those things interesting to intelligent people just because you happen to be the President's wife? Why waste your valuable time and space in the paper with something so worthless. (MD, January 26, 1937)

In 1941, Eleanor began writing "If You Ask Me," a monthly column for *Ladies' Home Journal.* John T. Flynn protested her compensation: "a dollar per word!" Other critics charged that only because of her name and address was she paid so "exorbitantly": $2,500 per month by

Ladies' Home Journal; later $3,000 by *McCall's,* when yearly income for an average American family was $1,368.

Christian conservatives exhausted themselves bewailing the example Eleanor was setting for wives and young girls. Critics' imaginations were tormented by potential consequences of social acceptance of Eleanor's views. Many believed that *any* working married woman was taking a job away from a man. A woman's place was in the home and, according to Scripture, submissive to her husband or father.

At the end of one speech, a governor demanded to know why she wasn't at home taking care of her children. Eleanor graciously informed the governor that her children were married and lived on their own.

Eleanor triggered criticism from individuals who preferred their First Ladies standing beside husbands, expressing no opinions, smiling, shaking hands firmly, and steadily pouring tea. Actually, Eleanor poured tea and welcomed guests at several thousand White House social functions between 1933 and 1945. Mrs. Nesbitt recorded in her diary after the 1937 inaugural that almost ten thousand people had been entertained at the White House, forty-five hundred in one three-day period. "It was a wonder to me the way Mrs. Roosevelt breezed through these affairs and left nearly every person feeling she had given them some part of her understanding that was special." After three back-to-back receptions, Nesbitt commented, Eleanor "looked just as fresh at the end as she had before." In 1939, some 4,729 individuals dined at the White House (including the king and queen of England); 323 individuals stayed overnight; 14,056 individuals were greeted by Eleanor at teas and receptions; and 1,320,300 toured the public areas of the White House.

Eleanor recognized the chauvinist thread in the criticism. "She and other women," she retorted, "had a right to engage in careers" and "to be compensated for their work." Eleanor could have cited her predecessor Lou Hoover, a professional geologist, who had said, "To make a [political] party whole there should be as many feminine as masculine minds." Mrs. Hoover insisted "even after marriage it is possible for a woman to have a career. Asked to comment on "the woman who spends all of her time taking care of her home," she was blunt: "I think she is lazy."

Mrs. Hoover spoke out, and no one protested. However, when Eleanor defended women working, critics snarled, "There she goes again! *That woman!*"

During the 1940 presidential campaign, Mrs. Wendell Willkie, wife of the Republican nominee, pointedly announced that if Mr. Willkie were elected president, she would be "staying at home" in the White House, words that, in today's vernacular, went viral. That statement was disingenuous since her husband lived with his mistress, Irita Van Doren, *New York Herald Tribune* book editor, a fact FDR kept in escrow just in case the Republicans campaigned "dirty."

Eleanor was often asked why she did not just stay by her husband's side, knit, and keep him company at 1600 Pennsylvania Avenue. Surely, the man was lonely. Actually, Eleanor knitted thousands of sweaters and garments for Red Cross refugee projects. In reality, Franklin *always* had people around him until bedtime, particularly Missy LeHand until her stroke and Harry Hopkins after 1940, when he lived just down the hall from the president's bedroom.

Eleanor's travel—forty thousand miles the first year and three hundred thousand miles during the first two terms—also attracted criticism. A headline in the *Washington Star*, "Mrs. Roosevelt Spends Night at White House," was embellished by popular radio comedians Jack Benny and Bob Hope; Benny joked that he wanted to borrow money from Mrs. Roosevelt because he would never be able to find her to repay it.

Critics never acknowledged that the First Lady often traveled on her own dime or that she sometimes sat up in coach all night rather than relaxing in a sleeper compartment (or, like predecessors, in a private railroad car loaned by a railroad or wealthy businessman). Or that she carried her own luggage. Or that by declining Secret Service protection, Eleanor saved taxpayers money.

Well, perhaps, but did one see Dolley Madison or Julia Grant gallivanting here and there? Noooo! Critics were annoyed not just that Eleanor traveled but also by where she traveled, whom she met, and what she said about what she had seen. Of course, Eleanor could not explain that she traveled because her husband could not travel easily due to his disability. Or that, given that day's communication systems, crises demanded that he remain close to the center of government.

One irate White House visitor blamed Eleanor for failing to supervise the White House maids. "Instead of tearing around the country, I think you should stay at home and personally see that the White House is clean. I soiled my gloves yesterday morning on the stair-railing. It is disgraceful." In fact, because there were some one million visitors to the White House, the banisters were wiped every fifteen minutes. Moreover, the chief usher, not the First Lady, was responsible for supervising housekeeping in the executive mansion. While Eleanor conceded that she had "an obligation to run the President's house" well, since it "belongs to the people of the United States," she speculated, "If I confined myself to giving parties, even in wartime, my critics would be few, I imagine, though one cannot be sure" (IYAM, November 1944).

A First Lady, Eleanor concluded, could avoid criticism only by being a Dresden china figure. She gradually embraced a perspective of "damned if you do, damned if you don't."

EARNING AND GIVING AWAY

Eleanor tried to defuse criticism by disclosing that she donated most of her income from writing, radio, and lectures to charities; in fact, news of her donations triggered an avalanche of requests from charities and individuals.

Eleanor's attitude toward charitable giving was shaped by her paternal grandfather's example. Theodore Roosevelt Sr. embraced a "muscular Christianity," finding the Christian believer's duty clear: "to do good, to use wealth and position to aid the less fortunate." Eleanor was taught to be guided by the Gospel of Matthew:

> Take heed that ye do not your alms before men, to be seen of them: otherwise ye have no reward of your Father which is in heaven.
>
> Therefore when thou doest thine alms, do not sound a trumpet before thee, as the hypocrites do in the synagogues and in the streets, that they may have glory of men. Verily I say unto you, They have their reward.
>
> But when thou doest alms, let not thy left hand know what thy right hand doeth: That thine alms may be in secret: and thy Father which seeth in secret himself shall reward thee openly. (Matt. 6:1–4)

As New Testament teachings motivated Theodore Senior's philanthropy, so Eleanor's giving: "Unto whomsoever much is given, of him shall be much required" (Luke 12:48). In a sense, her checkbooks—she kept as many five—were as essential to her spiritual life as her worn Book of Common Prayer or her father's New Testament. She honored the "thread" of responsibility for the poor established in the Bible and the Book of Common Prayer, particularly the thirty-eighth Article of

Religion, which Eleanor memorized during confirmation, "Every man ought, of such things as he possesseth, liberally to give alms to the poor, according to his ability"—a passage obviously predating inclusive language. This biblical question, "But whoso hath this world's good, and seeth his brother have need, and shutteth up his bowels of compassion from him, how dwelleth the love of God in him?" (1 John 3:17), resonated with Eleanor! She prayed, from time to time, from her prayer book:

> Almighty God, whose loving hand hath given us all that we possess;
> Grant us grace that we may honour thee with our substance, and remembering the account which we must one day give, may be faithful stewards of thy bounty; through Jesus Christ our Lord. *Amen.*

CAMPAIGNING FOR A THIRD TERM

By 1940, Franklin and Eleanor's time in the White House was entering a new era. While the United States was not yet at war, world politics was pulling it in that direction. Eleanor assumed that Franklin was ready—she was more than ready—to go home to Hyde Park. FDR, a grand master of manipulation, kept wife, party leaders, and aides in the dark about his plans. Criticism erupted when Franklin sought (or schemed, according to some critics) for the Democratic National Convention to draft him for a third term. Finally FDR informed James Farley (the head of the Democratic Party, who wanted the nomination himself) that "the precarious world situation made it imperative for him to seek another term.

In Eleanor's opinion, the Republican nominee, wealthy businessman Wendell Willkie, would be a disaster as president! He would roll back all the gains of the New Deal for the poor, for women, and for the young.

FDR won the nomination. Convention delegates, however, balked at rubber-stamping his choice, Henry Wallace, to replace the elderly Texas curmudgeon Jack Garner as vice president. After fistfights broke out on the convention floor, the president threatened: either the delegates nominated his choice or he would not run!

Franklin began receiving "Send Eleanor!" telephone calls and telegrams, the most persuasive from Frances Perkins, secretary of labor. Finally he asked Eleanor to fly to Chicago to address the delegates.

Thus, she became the first presidential wife to speak to a political convention. When Eleanor appeared at the podium, the bedlam stopped. She spoke without notes: "You cannot treat it as you would treat an ordinary nomination in an ordinary time. We people in the United States have got to realize today that we face a grave and serious situation." Eleanor persuaded delegates to accept Wallace. Given the chaotic volatility in Europe and Asia, it was no time to elect a political novice. Willkie and company would push the agendas of big business at the expense of "the little people." As a result of Eleanor's 499 words, Wallace squeaked out the nomination.

Republicans harangued a "tired" FDR for sending "the Missus" to do his work. Would he next send the Missus to deliver the State of the Union address? The GOP distributed millions of campaign buttons: "We don't want Eleanor either" and "Eleanor: Start packing. The Willkies are coming." Roosevelt was reelected by a closer margin—five million votes—than in 1932 or 1936.

A WORLD AND MARRIAGE UNDER STRAIN

Despite a third inaugural, 1941 would not be kind to the Roosevelts. Sara Roosevelt, eighty-six, who had influenced the family's finances and the adventures and misadventures of her grandchildren by subsidizing the First Family yearly to the tune of $100,000 ($1.72 million in 2016 dollars), was dying.

In early September 1941, Eleanor had come home to Val-Kill and dropped in to check on Sara at Springwood. Alarmed by her condition, Eleanor telephoned Franklin, insisting that he come to Hyde Park immediately. FDR demurred. Given the escalating tension since the Germans had fired on the USS *Greer* in international waters and his upcoming national radio address, he needed to remain in Washington. Eleanor demanded: "Franklin, *come* home!"

FDR arrived after midnight and sat by Sara's bedside, even after she drifted into a coma. On September 7, around noon, Sara died. Franklin was so devastated by his mother's death, Eleanor had to make the arrangements. She later recalled viewing Sara's corpse: "It is dreadful to have lived so close to someone . . . & to feel no deep affection or sense of loss." She quickly added, "It's hard on Franklin however."

In reflecting on Sara's death, cousin Daisy Suckley commented, "That big house" where he had always been "my boy," "without his mother seems awfully big and bare." Certainly, "his wife is a wonderful person, but she lacks the ability to give him the things his mother gave him. She is away so much, and when she is here she has so many people around—the splendid people who are trying to do good and improve the world."

Meanwhile, Eleanor's brother Hall was also in his last days. Eleanor had been hard-pressed to "feel much about Hall" since, she wrote Anna, "he's been drinking an average of at least 1 quart of gin a day"— despite having cirrhosis of the liver. Helplessly, for four days, Eleanor sat beside his bed in Walter Reed Hospital. She reflected:

> From the time I was a little girl—perhaps from the time when my father had first talked to me in the old 37th Street house after my mother's death—I had always wanted to take care of my little brothers. After Ellie died, I yearned over Hall, which didn't prevent me from being disagreeable to him very often when we were both small! As I grew up I felt a great responsibility for him, and thought about him a great deal, loved him deeply and longed to mean a great deal in his life. I think at his wedding I felt as though my own son and not my brother was being married.

Watching Hall die wore on Eleanor's soul. "My idea of hell, if I believed in it," she wrote to Joseph Lash, "would be to sit... and watch someone breathing hard, someone struggling for words when a gleam of consciousness returns & thinking 'this was once a little boy I played with & scolded, he could have been so much & this is what he is.'"

Hall's death at dawn on September 25 led to a rare emotional moment with Franklin. After caring for Hall's wife, Eleanor drove to the White House and walked directly into the president's bedroom. James, who witnessed the moment, recalled: "She went to father and said simply, 'Hall has died.' Father struggled to her side and put his arm around her. 'Sit down,' he said so tenderly I can still hear it. And he sank down beside her and hugged her and held her head to his chest. I do not think she cried. I think mother had forgotten how to cry."

In what was perhaps another effort to bridge their emotional abyss, Franklin suggested—Eleanor said "sprang on her" the idea—that she might take his mother's bedroom at Hyde Park, adjacent to his, for her own. No, she told Anna, "I just can't and I told him so."

When Eleanor proposed some redecorating, she learned that "the prospect of changing any of the rooms stirred deep anxiety" in Franklin, who, after reflection, "wanted to keep the house exactly" as it had been when his mother was alive. He finally agreed to Sara's wish that the room in which "my boy" had been born would be rearranged to look as it had in 1882. "Hyde Park," Eleanor lamented, "is now to be a shrine and it will still not be a home to me."

THE OUTBREAK OF WAR

On Sunday, December 7, 1941—the forty-ninth anniversary of her mother's death—the Japanese attacked the US naval base at Pearl Harbor, Hawaii. Some twenty-four hundred Americans died that day; incredible damage was inflicted on the Navy's Pacific Fleet. The First Lady, as the mother of four sons in uniform, soon confessed, "I can't help but worry about the boys."

The world remembers FDR's brief address to Congress and the nation on December 8, particularly the stirring oratory, "Yesterday, December 7, 1941, a day which will live in infamy . . ."

Actually, the first words from the White House after the attack came Sunday night, when the microphone in front of Eleanor went live. Although her radio program had been scheduled for that evening, Eleanor spoke to the chaos of the day:

> Ladies and gentlemen, I'm speaking to you at a very serious moment in our history. . . . For months now the knowledge that something of this kind might happen has been hanging over our heads and yet it was impossible to believe.

Resolutely she continued: "We know what we have to face and we know that we are ready to face it." Then she appealed to "the women in the country tonight," saying:

> I have a boy at sea on a destroyer, for all I know he may be on his way to the Pacific. . . . Many of you all over this country have boys in the service who will now be called upon to go into action. . . . You cannot escape a clutch of fear at your heart and yet I hope . . . you [will] rise above these fears.

Eleanor's words were heard in luxurious mansions in New York City, in shacks in Appalachia, on ranches in California and New Mexico. "Whatever is asked of us I am sure we can accomplish it. We are the free and unconquerable people of the United States of America."

Soon John Boettiger, the son-in-law Eleanor loved as a son, also joined the Army. Periodically, Eleanor received scathing letters about her sons and their rapid promotions as officers. One writer insinuated that the uniformed Roosevelts were serving "easy duty." "Would you please tell us if any of your sons in the service is in actual danger?" (IYAM, March 1942).

Eleanor, like most parents, did not know the precise whereabouts of her loved ones due to military censorship, and she seldom admitted her psychological and spiritual angst about the safety of her sons. She remained keenly cognizant that as First Lady she had no immunity to losing a son, or two, and becoming a Gold Star mother—a reality driven home after Harry Hopkins's eighteen-year-old son and two of her cousins—Kermit Roosevelt and Theodore Roosevelt Jr.—died in uniform.

Once war broke out, Eleanor's access to Franklin was curtailed significantly, some days to hardly more than memos dropped into a basket beside his bed. Franklin made no time to hear about her social programs; he had little time to listen to reports on her travels. Eleanor grieved as FDR abandoned his role as Doctor New Deal to transition to Doctor Win the War.

Still, Eleanor never wavered from her commitment to the country's "ill-fed, ill-housed" and to fighting all forms of discrimination. She never forgot Jesus' observation, "For ye have the poor always with you" (Matt. 26:11), nor did she fail to model Jesus' compassion for the marginalized. Maybe there would always be poor Americans, but the depths of poverty could be reduced and the cycle that kept many families in poverty could be broken. Eleanor feared that this war, like World War I, would line the pockets of wealthy businessmen; her task was to include the poor and the marginalized in the war mobilization.

When FDR weighed running for a fourth term in 1944, Eleanor, among others, raised concerns about his health. FDR had installed his daughter Anna to serve as gatekeeper; now Eleanor had to go through Anna to see the president—which stirred resentment. When FDR wanted all their grandchildren at the White House for Christmas 1944, Eleanor made it happen. FDR gave a brief address at his fourth inaugural which, to conserve his energy, had been moved from the Capitol to the White House. Eleanor stood in for him in the receiving lines.

CONCLUSION

What Eleanor most feared—that she would become a prisoner as First Lady—never happened. Rather, she defanged that fear for herself and for future First Ladies. It would not be inaccurate to consider her years of service as a tectonic shift, such that presidential spouses could be classified pre-Eleanor or post-Eleanor. For twelve years, the White House belonged as much to her and her countless guests as to FDR and his merry band of New Dealers. She breathed freedom into every dimension of serving as First Lady. The White House never changed her. She remained Eleanor.

Certainly, the relentless criticism stung—and Eleanor winced many times—but she lived out the truth of a spiritual sung by Mary Bethune's students

> I've been 'buked an' I've been scorned,
> I've been 'buked an' I've been scorned, children;
> I've been 'buked an' I've been scorned,
> I've been talked about sho's you' born.
> Ain' gwine lay my 'ligion down,
> Ain' gwine lay my 'ligion down, children;
> Ain' gwine lay my 'ligion down,
> Ain' gwine lay my 'ligion down.

Eleanor lived by her moral convictions, no matter what her detractors said, and though many despised her, countless other American women admired her and quoted her: "Well, Mrs. Roosevelt says . . ." Eleanor's poll numbers, at times, were better than Franklin's. Doris Kearns Goodwin observes, "In support of her belief that the position of first lady could be used for a power for good, she had committed herself to an astonishing range of activities," which won the "lasting gratitude of millions of citizens." No few young girls confessed, "When I grow up, I want to be like Mrs. Roosevelt." Eleanor tried to deflate the adulation by responding, "Almost any woman in the White House during these years . . . would have done what I have done."

7

Refugees and Regrets

Eleanor and the Jews

I do not know what we can do to save the Jews in Europe and find them homes, but I know we will be the sufferers if we let great wrongs occur without exerting ourselves to correct them.
                    —Eleanor Roosevelt (MD, August 13, 1943)

One day in 1947, Eleanor Roosevelt arrived at a Jewish resettlement area near Tel Aviv to see firsthand the living conditions of North African and Middle Eastern Jewish refugees. When the refugees first heard that Mrs. Roosevelt was coming for a visit, many scoffed: Why would she come here?

Refugees lined the road to the camp, singing, "The Queen of America *has* come." Sampling food prepared by the women, Eleanor complimented each cook and asked questions: "How do you find your life here? Do your children go to school? Do you get medical care?" The answers made Eleanor smile, celebrating the life Jewish survivors had found.

Back inside the car, however, Eleanor's smile disappeared. Ruth Gruber, her host, noticing the change, asked, "Is anything wrong?"

"I wish I had done more for the Jews," Eleanor answered.

Gruber, reaching for Eleanor's hand, dismissed that judgment. Eleanor had done everything she could, certainly more than most Americans and most Christians.

"I should have done more." Eleanor would not be dissuaded. That self-indictment would never dissipate.

EARLY JEWISH INTERACTIONS

Given the isolation of Eleanor's childhood, she probably knew few Jewish individuals; she may have overheard observations by family members reflecting the ingrained anti-Semitism of their social status. Blanche Wiesen Cook characterizes Eleanor's attitude toward Jewish people as "impersonal and casual, a frayed raiment of her generation, class, and culture which she wore thoughtlessly." Anti-Semitism was just part of the landscape when Protestants dominated American culture.

During his navy years, Franklin worked closely with Bernard Baruch, who chaired the War Industries Board, and the Roosevelts attended many social events the Jewish financier hosted. Peter Collier and David Horowitz suggest that her "parochial narrowness" was fueled by a "sense of inadequacy" in any social setting, while Franklin was the life of the party.

Before one party, someone overheard Eleanor complain, "I'd rather be hung than seen" at an event with "mostly Jews." Eleanor complained to Sara that she had found "the Jew party appalling. . . . I never wish to hear money, jewels, and . . . sables mentioned again." How did such a slur come from Eleanor's lips?

After meeting Felix Frankfurter, who would become FDR's confidante and a Supreme Court justice, she dismissed him as "an interesting little man but very Jew."

While Sara Roosevelt had strong opinions about Jews, Joseph Persico clarifies, "Certain Jews were acceptable, the 'Our Crowd' type," particularly Dorothy Schiff, who increasingly showed up at Hyde Park as Eleanor and Franklin's political involvement intensified.

While attending those parties, Eleanor would never have imagined that someday Baruch would become her benefactor and even propose marriage after Franklin died! In two decades, Baruch's generosity and influence would keep Arthurdale, Eleanor's West Virginia housing resettlement experiment, afloat despite blistering congressional criticism and sniping from FDR's staff. In 1938, she boasted about Baruch's latest check, "Mr. Baruch has given me 'carte blanche' and says that anything which I want I am to do with the money."

Eleanor's tolerance was stretched by Jewish neighbors Elinor and Henry Morgenthau, the only Jewish couple with whom the Roosevelts socialized. The Morgenthaus, as assimilated Jews, did not keep kosher or attend synagogue, and they celebrated Christmas. When New York's prestigious women's organization, the Colony Club, blackballed Elinor Morgenthau, Eleanor resigned.

After Franklin's paralysis, Eleanor invested more time in Democratic Party activities, interacting extensively with politically astute Jewish women. She admired their energy and ability to forge coalitions that elected pro-labor candidates and lobbied for better working conditions for women and children. Eleanor enjoyed stimulating conversations with many nonobservant Jews, who, Michelle Mart noted, sought "to blend into the American landscape."

Jewish women mentored Eleanor's activism in the Women's Trade Union League. At one fund-raiser, Eleanor met Rose Schneiderman, the organization's energetic president. When Eleanor questioned why women should join unions, the fiery labor leader delivered an on-the-spot tutorial: women, some with children, worked six nine- or ten-hour days for, perhaps, three dollars per week. Women had no job security, and employers were unwilling to train them for higher-paying jobs. Eleanor recognized that Schneiderman held perspectives that Marie Souvestre had taught.

A friendship developed between Eleanor and Belle Moskowitz, a Democratic political operative and an influential Jewish social worker at a settlement house for Jewish immigrants. Eleanor and Belle joined forces in the Women's Division of the Democratic Party of New York working for Al Smith, an Irish Catholic politician. After Smith was elected governor of New York in 1922, Moskowitz became the governor's gatekeeper and Eleanor's friend in Albany.

In the inner circle of the Women's City Club, Eleanor and Belle influenced politically active women, many of whom were Jewish. Eleanor admired Belle's organizational genius. When Smith ran for president in 1928, Moskowitz headed publicity and Eleanor worked under her as director of women's activities—ironically, not for FDR in his uphill race for governor!

Working alongside Jewish women, Eleanor's stereotypes about Jews were challenged and true friendships formed.

EARLY AWARENESS OF GERMAN CHAOS

Adolf Hitler became chancellor of Germany on January 30, 1933, just thirty-five days before the Roosevelts moved into the White House, and he soon began constricting the rights of Jewish citizens. Both Roosevelts had visited Germany several times and spoke German. The German economy had been savaged by the Allied-imposed reparations following World War I. Hitler blamed Jews for Germany's distress, ignoring the reality that Jews had been the yeast of German intelligentsia for several hundred years.

Some assumed Hitler's power was temporary; others dismissed his policies as the latest resurgence of anti-Semitism; some Jews left Germany intending to return after the Nazis had flamed out. Many American Jews ignored reports in the *American Jewish Year Book* chronicling deteriorating conditions in Germany.

Rabbi Stephen S. Wise, who enjoyed access to FDR through Eleanor, with whom he often shared lecture platforms, organized rallies to protest Nazi hostilities until leading rabbis pressured him to stop. Wise's hysteria, they protested, was counterproductive: "That's over *there*. Jews are safe *here*!"

During Eleanor's first summer in the White House, four leaders in the women's rights movement—Jane Addams, Lillian Wald, Carrie Chapman Catt, and Alice Hamilton—came bearing haunting details of rapidly deteriorating Jewish life in Germany. Although Eleanor arranged for Hamilton, the first woman to serve on the Harvard University faculty, to talk to FDR, the administration faced more immediate priorities. In December 1933, Eleanor received a heart-wrenching letter from Maria Meyer Wachman, a German Jewish exile in London:

> Having the fullest confidence in your kind understanding for the matter . . . I herewith beg you to help us, us Jewish people from Germany. If you would tell the American women and men *the crime that is done by not helping us*, I do believe—in spite of all—they will hear and listen and—finally admit this fact, if you would tell them and challenge their conscience.
>
> As a poor human being, I appeal to you as an American woman and mother, high placed in life. . . . Can you really stand by and watch this? . . . I should like to have your word, you will do something.

Eleanor replied, "Unfortunately, in my present position I am obliged to leave all contacts with foreign governments in the hands of my husband and his advisers."

Blanche Wiesen Cook, Eleanor's definitive biographer, finds the First Lady's response chilling. "There is," she reports, "no comparably curt reply on any domestic subject in her entire correspondence."

On a range of issues during the Roosevelt years, Eleanor tested public opinion that influenced FDR's policies. Presidential aide Rexford Tugwell, after repeatedly witnessing the First Lady confront FDR on a variety of issues, commented that no one would ever forget hearing her say, "Franklin, I think you should ..." or "Franklin, *surely* you will not. . . ." But on this issue, Eleanor was cautious. Cook acknowledges the political tightrope that FDR navigated, which relied on "the enormous German and Catholic vote" and solidarity with "Southern Democrats who dominated Congress." The United States had its own anti-Semitism; almost a quarter of Americans polled identified Jews as "a menace to America."

Cook unequivocally declares: "ER had full and immediate knowledge" of the Nazi hatred of Jews. She must have, given Wachman's letter in 1933, Albert and Elsa Einstein's visit to the White House in January 1934, and a League of Nations appeal that Eleanor cited in September 25, 1934. In a radio broadcast sponsored by Simmons Mattress, Eleanor commented on the deepening crisis:

> From Geneva comes a plea from James G. McDonald [League of Nations] high commissioner for refugees from Germany, telling the sad story of the exodus from Germany not only of Jews but of non-Jewish people as well. He appeals for help in rehabilitating these people in the countries in which they are now settling.

In late January 1934, when Albert Einstein and his wife were overnight guests of the Roosevelts, the two couples conversed in German. Einstein pleaded for admitting more refugees, particularly from the scientific community, and forcefully warned FDR and Eleanor of Germany's insatiable ambition and of anti-Semitic attitudes within the US State Department.

By 1936, the Nazis had confiscated property, art, jewelry, bank accounts, and businesses, which robbed Jews of financial resources needed to immigrate. William J. vanden Heuvel reports that in 1936, a presidential election year, the United States admitted twice as many Jewish refugees as the rest of the world combined—a slim start, considering the masses wanting to flee Germany. Lest we judge the Roosevelts too harshly, vanden Heuvel cautions, "It is critical to our understanding of these years to remember that at the time no one inside or outside of Germany anticipated that the Nazi persecution would lead to the Holocaust."

NATIONAL RETICENCE

Some Americans supported Hitler's actions. German Americans who believed their homeland had been humiliated by Wilson's peace treaty in 1918 applauded the growing resurgence of German Aryan confidence. In American cities with large German American populations, organizations such as the German American Bund and the Friends of

New Germany recruited and mobilized members, distributed propaganda, conducted raucous rallies, and organized large, loud parades.

Among anti-New Dealers, anti-Semites like Senator Huey Long and Senator Theodore Bilbo praised the Nazis' race purification effort; the Rev. Gerald L. K. Smith and Father Charles E. Coughlin, joined by a chorus of second-string bigots, ranted against both Roosevelts. Millions listened to Coughlin's Sunday night radio tirades disguised as sermons. Coughlin praised the Nazis for confronting "Jewish-sponsored Communism" which, he charged, Roosevelt and his many Jewish aides were ignoring.

Other Americans with no desire to fight in another war "over there," such as aviator Charles Lindbergh, embraced isolationism. Whatever was unfolding in Germany—a sovereign nation—was not America's concern! Many Americans preferred not to know about the Third Reich's atrocities, and newspapers cooperated with that desire. Laurel Leff documented the rarity of articles on the plight of German Jews in the *New York Times*—paradoxically, owned by a Jewish family, the Sulzbergers. In some twelve hundred editorial columns in the *Times*, Arthur Krock, a Jewish member of the editorial board, never mentioned the persecution of Jews. The *Times* syndicated articles to 525 newspapers—including most major metropolitan papers. Many newspaper editors concluded that if the *Times* did not cover the oppression of Jews, the harassment was inconsequential.

Even within Jewish denominations, arguments erupted over an appropriate response to Hitler. Some assimilated Jews pleaded: "Do nothing that attracts attention to us!" The Jewish denominations (Orthodox, Conservative, Reform) as well as secularists like the editor of the *New York Times* and the Morgenthaus were anything but cohesive. Moreover, individuals competed to be *the* voice of American Judaism; debates raged in Jewish communities far from the power concentrations of New York City, Boston, Philadelphia, and Washington.

Creating a unified plan for rescuing Jewish refugees proved impossible because of power struggles among leaders of Jewish organizations and their financial backers. For example, Kurt Peiser, director of Philadelphia's Federation of Jewish Charities, warned Gilbert Kraus, who was attempting to facilitate the immigration of two hundred Jewish children from Germany, "to cease and scrap this plan at once!" "If you continue with this plan," Peiser threatened, "we will be obliged to take all necessary steps to prevent it." Kraus ignored Peiser and at great risk brought fifty Jewish children to the United States.

Anti-Semitism appealed to Americans across social, religious, political, and economic categories; to many it identified a scapegoat and explained economic chaos. Although Jews, most of whom lived in urban areas, made up only 3.6 percent of the US population in 1937, they were widely resented for their perceived influence and business acumen. Jonathan Sarna reports that 120 American organizations agitated anti-Jewish hatred. Henry Ford, according to historian Hasia Diner, regularly published articles in his newspaper, the *Dearborn Independent*, "that would refer to Jews in every possible context as at the root of America and the world's ills. Strikes: It was the Jews. Any kind of financial scandal? The Jews. Agricultural depression? The Jews. So 'the Jew,' in a way, became the symbol of a world that was being manipulated and controlled."

The electorate's discomfort with Jewish bankers, financiers, and private lenders impacted presidential appointments. Initially, Franklin had declined to appoint Eleanor's friend Henry Morgenthau to head the US Treasury Department. Seeking Senate confirmation was thought too risky until Roosevelt concluded he needed cabinet officers who, without questioning, would implement his policies. After appointing Morgenthau in 1935, the president balked at nominating a Jew to be assistant secretary. Two Jews at the head of the nation's monetary system would ignite backlash at home and agitate Hitler's propaganda machine.

Joseph P. Kennedy Sr., the US ambassador to the Court of St. James in Great Britain from December 1937 through November 1940, blamed Jews for bringing wrath down on their own heads. Kennedy harangued movie producers and directors in Hollywood to tone down their products for export to avoid offending German audiences. Some of the producers and directors who caved in were Jewish. Would Americans, Kennedy demanded, sacrifice their sons to "defend Jews"? Clearly he, the father of two sons of military age (and another fast approaching it), was *not* willing!

ELEANOR ON HITLER

After the German army invaded Poland on September 1, 1939, England and France declared war. Eleanor closely monitored the escalating discrimination against Jews. Initially, the Nazis had oppressed *German* Jews. Now, she feared, the "beast" intended to eradicate Jews in neighboring countries.

Despite her reticence in the early 1930s, Eleanor realized Nazi atrocities would become America's concern long before most Americans did. Too many Americans, she charged, like those active in the America First Committee and the American Liberty League, preferred not to know what was happening or let charismatic personalities do their thinking. Eleanor bewailed the "stark tragedies" being visited on people who, in the opinion of too many Americans, "count for little in history."

"It is important," she insisted, for "every one of us, to understand what happens to the individual forced to live under such circumstances and to those other individuals, who through force and fear, rule people in such a manner. If we lack this knowledge, we cannot understand what is happening in Europe today" (MD, March 7, 1940).

In 1939, Eleanor exchanged candid letters with Carola von Schaffer-Bernstein, an Allenswood classmate who lived in Berlin. Eleanor read in Carola's letters support for the Nazi agenda. Eleanor expressed concern not only for Jews but also for Catholics and liberal German Protestants threatened by Hitler's National Reich Church, courageous individuals like Lutheran theologian and pastor Dietrich Bonhoeffer. "We do not hate the German people," Eleanor assured Carola:

> There is an inability here to understand how people of spirit can be terrified by one man and his storm troops to the point of countenancing the kind of horrors which seem to have come on in Germany not only where the Jews are concerned. . . . I hope that our country will not have to go to war, but no country can exist free and unoppressed while a man like Hitler remains in power.

When Carola discredited Eleanor's charges as hearsay, Eleanor wrote back, "I have actually seen many of the people who have reached this country from concentration camps."

Eleanor closed the letter, "You who believe in God must find it very difficult to follow a man who apparently thinks he is as great as any god."

Because Eleanor spoke German, nothing in Hitler's incendiary tirades was lost in translation. As Eleanor listened to Hitler's radio "performances," she concluded that the führer believed himself a god—as did many Germans; others rationalized that he was doing "God's work." Moreover, many Germans believed that Hitler was "the defender of Christian values." Meanwhile, Hitler had allowed the SS, his Nazi security force, to kill priests at will, particularly in Poland. Hitler made a boastful threat, "Once we hold the power, Christianity will be overcome and the Deutsche Kirche established. Yes, the German Church, without a pope and without the Bible—and Luther, if he could be with us, would give us his blessing."

What Hitler was hawking, Eleanor found blasphemous, unchristian, and a violation of the commandment against taking God's name in vain. In Eleanor's thinking, this commandment prohibited more than cursing. One took God's name in vain by calling God's blessings on human or national enterprises that clearly violated God's nature, Scripture, and human decency. How could anyone who orchestrated or condoned virulent, inhumane hatred and violence against any group be Christian? How, Eleanor fumed, could Germans—in the land of Luther—be so gullible as to swallow Hitler's proclamation: "I have regarded myself as called upon by Providence to serve my own people alone and to deliver them from their frightful misery." On November 8, 1939, after surviving a bombing in a place where he had just spoken—because he had ended early—Hitler proclaimed his escape "a miracle" and "a sure sign" that Providence favored his mission.

Eleanor scoffed at Hitler's egocentric prophecy: "Napoleon failed in conquering the world, but I will succeed." She warned, "No man can count forever on being so completely dominated by his dream of power" that Almighty God will ignore him indefinitely—a truth Eleanor thought was demonstrated in the biblical narrative of God using Moses to challenge the abusive Pharaoh. From her understanding of God's justice, Eleanor protested, "One can only pray that it will dawn upon Hitler that the Lord is not patient forever and that he who puts other people to death by the sword is often meted out the same fate" (MD, December 5, 1942).

In a speech in April 1922, Hitler had called himself "a Christian" and claimed Jesus as "Lord and Savior." But by 1936, he said, "I myself am a heathen to the core." Eleanor would not have contradicted him. "Not to believe in the dignity and worth of every human being," Eleanor wrote, "is neither a Christian attitude, nor since real democratic ideals are based on the Christian attitude is it a true conception of democracy."

Hitler institutionalized anti-Semitism by promising a pure Aryan race. He boasted, "In standing guard against the Jew I am defending the handiwork of the Lord." Eleanor knew that such hatred and violence toward any people was in no way affiliated with the Lord's work. Echoing Jesus' parable of the Good Samaritan, she had an inclusive definition of the word *neighbor*. "Our neighbors, of course, do not include only the people whom we know; they include, also, all those who live anywhere within the range of our knowledge."

In 1940, as Europeans fought, Eleanor lamented in *The Moral Basis of Democracy* that "the great majority of people accept religious dogmas handed to them by their parents without very much feeling of having a personal obligation to clarify their creed for themselves." She raised a trilogy of questions, calling on her American readers to recall their religious commitments: What do I believe? How do I intend to live? What am I doing for my neighbors? Surely, if she could make Americans aware of the horrors happening to marginalized "little people" in Europe—Jews, trade unionists, Gypsies, handicapped people, homosexuals—they would reject isolationism. Thinking Christians, Eleanor reasoned, would see through the rhetoric and hysteria marketed by the Liberty League and the America First proponents—particularly her cousin Theodore Roosevelt Jr., a committed pacifist, who had informed her, "A country always loses by a war."

THE REFUGEE CRISIS

FDR inherited restrictive immigration quotas established by Republican Presidents Harding and Coolidge, quotas Congress rigorously monitored. President Hoover had mandated that no immigrant who "might" become a public charge could immigrate to the United States. Business owners and union leaders railed against raising quotas because, sooner or later, the immigrants would steal American jobs. A *Fortune* poll in April 1939 reported that 83 percent opposed admitting refugees beyond "the established immigration quotas."

Kristallnacht—the Nazi rampage against Jews on November 9, 1938, in retaliation for the death of Ernest von Rath, a German diplomat in Paris, by a sixteen-year-old Polish Jew resulted in the destruction of 267 synagogues, the plundering of seventy-five hundred Jewish-owned businesses and shops, the deaths of ninety-one Jews, and the arrests of more than thirty thousand Jews—a thousand of whom would die in Nazi hands in the next few months—complicated FDR's position. After the Nazis brazenly imposed an "atonement fine" of one billion marks on Jews for the property damage Nazi thugs wreaked, Roosevelt recalled Ambassador Hugh Wilson and severed diplomatic relations with Germany; the United States was the only nation to do so.

Still, the position of Congress on refugees and immigrants, particularly Jewish refugees, could be summarized as "Hell, no!" Eleanor's concerns were misinterpreted, thwarted, ignored, and ridiculed on the floor of the Senate and House of Representatives. Politics and economics first.

Eleanor, outraged by Kristallnacht, expressed her dismay in "My Day": "I cannot somehow believe that under any circumstances in any country it can be good for human nature to deal cruelly and oppressively with any group of people" (MD, November 15, 1938).

Many find FDR's legacy irreparably tarnished by his failure to accommodate Jewish passengers aboard the SS *St. Louis*, which had sailed in May 1939 from Hamburg, Germany, with 939 Jewish passengers, including 400 women and children. These passengers had paid—bribed—the Cuban government for permits to immigrate. When the *St. Louis* arrived in Cuban waters, disembarkation was denied. Cuban president Federico Laredo Brú, citing high unemployment in Cuba, claimed Jewish refugees would threaten economic recovery. Forty thousand demonstrators—funded by Joseph Goebbels, the German minister of propaganda—marched through Havana streets in a boisterous "spontaneous protest" against the refugees. Laredo Brú, after attempting to extort more money from the Jewish passengers, ordered the ship to leave Cuban waters and pocketed their deposits.

With Gustav Schroeder, a compassionate man, at the helm, the *St. Louis* steamed slowly up the Atlantic coast seeking a port of refuge; Schroeder stalled to give FDR ample time to intervene. American Jewish families cabled, telegraphed, and telephoned the US State Department, the Oval Office, members of Congress, and Eleanor, pleading for help. When a proposal surfaced that Jewish passengers disembark in the Virgin Islands, State Department officials convinced FDR that spies "might be" embedded among the passengers. As the ship sailed back to Europe, the Nazis propagandized: Even the Americans do not want more Jews! While the number of passengers who were ultimately part of Hitler's "final solution" is uncertain, 288 passengers, or 31 percent, were given refuge by England. The others received shelter in Belgium, Holland, or France, which, tragically, in short time were overrun by the Nazis.

Eleanor confronted Franklin and members of his administration over their timidity on Jewish refugees. She regretted failing to pressure Franklin more forcefully to admit these refugees. James Roosevelt identified this as his mother's "deepest regret at the end of her life." At the bottom of one memo, Eleanor scrawled, "FDR, Can't something be done?" which led to yet another "Now, Eleanor . . ." confrontation.

The barrier to doing something was a stone's throw from the White House. At the State Department, top officials colluded to circumvent any softening of policy toward Jewish refugees. Secretary of State Cordell Hull's wife was one-fourth Jewish! Undersecretary Breckenridge Long, Roosevelt's Harvard classmate and a to-the-bone anti-Semite, wielded jurisdiction over refugee issues. Blanche Wiesen Cook is straightforward: "Breckenridge Long . . . dedicated himself to keeping refugees out of America."

In one tense exchange about Long's actions, Eleanor pushed FDR: "Franklin, you *know* he's a fascist!"

"I've told you, Eleanor," Franklin snapped, "you must not say that." Eleanor went for the last word. "Well, maybe I shouldn't say it, but he is!" FDR could not refute her. Long and his underlings crafted dense bureaucratic language and administrative hurdles that resulted in the deaths of tens of thousands of Jews.

Stephen Pressman damns Franklin Roosevelt's political callousness and silence on this issue: "Saving Jewish lives—particularly those of innocent children—may well have appealed to FDR's humanitarian instincts. But it did not square up with his broader political agenda" with a presidential election a year away. Given nine million unemployed Americans—17 percent of the American workforce—*anything* that threatened jobs trumped compassion. When Eleanor's close friend, Rep. Caroline O'Day of New York, wrote to the president asking for his views, FDR scribbled on her letter, "File No Action FDR."

Many recognized Eleanor as the conscience in the White House. Her efforts were recognized by Albert Einstein, who flattered her in a letter, "You always stand for the right and humaneness even when it is hard." He confessed to know of no one else who might help Jewish refugees. "The State Department . . . makes it all but impossible to give refuge in America to many worthy persons who are the victims of Fascist cruelty in Europe." Einstein, himself a refugee, charged that FDR's State Department was "erecting a wall of bureaucratic measures" supposedly "to protect America against subversive, dangerous elements." Professor Einstein urged Eleanor to investigate. "If then you become convinced that a truly grave injustice" is unfolding, "I know that you will find it possible to bring the matter to the attention of your heavily burdened husband" and to readers who would, in turn, pressure members of Congress. Eleanor wrote across the bottom of the letter that she would raise the issue with FDR. And she did.

A year after the ill-fated SS *St. Louis* was turned away, Jewish passengers on the SS *Quanza*, a Portuguese ship, were denied admission to Mexico. En route back to Germany, the ship refueled in Norfolk, Virginia. Jewish organizations and individuals besieged Eleanor to intervene. She fought for intervention until FDR approved all the passengers for entry.

NOT EVEN THE CHILDREN

Even before the war, the United States had resisted taking even the most vulnerable refugees—children. Mary Ann Glendon thought Eleanor's emotional loss and loneliness as an orphan "helped to fuel her passionate commitment to those she regarded as disadvantaged" and those whom Jesus called "the least of these," such as refugee children.

In 1939, Eleanor breached the congressional legislative process, a rarity for presidential wives, to push the admission of twenty thousand German Jewish children, all under age fourteen. The *Washington Post* covered her move on page 1 on Valentine's Day, under the headline "First Lady Backs Move to Open U.S. to 20,000 Exiles," sidestepping the trigger word, *refugees*. Eleanor proposed admitting ten thousand in 1939 and ten thousand in 1940. She plotted strategy with her friend Judge Justine W. Polier, daughter of Rabbi Stephen Wise, following coaching from FDR: "Get two people from opposite parties in the House and Senate and have them jointly get agreement on the legislation."

Democratic Senator Robert Wagner and Republican Congresswoman Edith Rogers, Eleanor's friends, introduced the legislation on February 9, 1939, cognizant that two previous quota-raising bills introduced by Jewish members of the House had died in committee. "I should prefer to let in 20,000 old Jews who would not multiply," William R. Castle Jr., former undersecretary of state, informed Rogers.

Laura Delano Houghteling, FDR's cousin, should have been more discreet: "Twenty thousand charming children," she snarled in opposition to Eleanor's efforts, "would all too soon grow into twenty thousand ugly adults." The irony? Houghteling's husband was FDR's commissioner of immigration!

The Wagner-Rogers Bill stirred raucous bigotry during hearings. Agnes Waters, "representing" World War I widows, testified: "Why should we give preference . . . to these potential Communists" who eventually might attempt to topple the US government? Would her children, who she claimed were descendants of a signer of the Constitution, be deprived of their rights by an army of so-called innocent children, each of whom would grow up to be a potential "leader of a revolt against the American government"?

John Thomas Taylor, director of the legislative committee of the American Legion, testified that while veterans had concern about persecution, resources "directed to the children of our own country would do more good." If the German children were admitted, Secretary Hull fumed, how long before Eleanor and her "do-gooders" would be back, asking to admit child refugees from Spain and China?

Helen Hayes, a prominent actress, and Dorothy Thompson, a journalist expelled from Germany for negative reporting, supported the proposal and appealed to members to imagine the courage required of mothers to give up their children to strangers. Hayes pleaded: "I beg you to let them in." Former First Lady Grace Coolidge made headlines by announcing that she and friends would accept twenty-five of the children into their homes in Vermont.

Senator Robert Rice Reynolds (D-NC) volunteered to be drum major for the "nos." On a national radio broadcast he howled, "Shall we first take care of our own children, our citizens, our country, or shall we bestow our charity on children imported from abroad?" He dismissed the claim that Americans were willing to provide homes. "If homes are available . . . Americanism demands that needy American children also be adopted into these homes." Anticipating criticism for hard-heartedness, Reynolds postured, "My heart beats in sympathy for those unfortunate children across the seas. But my love and duty belongs firstly to our children here at home." Those words, from a Democrat and a Christian, pierced Eleanor's heart.

In 1940, Eleanor helped launch the International Rescue Committee to support relaxed immigration quotas to admit refugee intellectuals, scientists, political leaders, and labor leaders. Resistance was fierce, despite the increasing number of eyewitness accounts to the atrocities happening "over there." Time was running out.

THE SITUATION GROWS MORE DIRE

On October 26, 1941, Mrs. Roosevelt, on her radio program, *Over Our Coffee Cups,* reported breaking news from Germany demonstrating how utterly without mercy or regard for human life is the German führer. How, otherwise, can we explain the reports of sending numberless Jewish people from Berlin and other cities, at an hour's notice, packed like cattle into trains, with their destination either Poland or some part of occupied Russia? . . . And the punishment for acts of rebellion against German rule in any country becomes more severe every day.

On September 4, 1942, Eleanor read a copy of a telegram from Isaac and Recha Sternbuch, representing the Agudath Israel World Organization in Switzerland, reporting the deaths of some one hundred thousand Jews in the Warsaw ghetto. Such mind-boggling reports stoked memories of propaganda about atrocities during World War I; not surprisingly, some in Eleanor's circle voiced skepticism. The Germans, a civilized people, *could not* have behaved so inhumanely! However, in July 1942, British Prime Minister Winston Churchill had cabled a message read to a Jewish rally in Madison Square Garden: the Nazis had already killed more than a million Jews!

Eleanor summarized Churchill's remarks on Jewish suffering under Nazi rule for "My Day" readers: "Starvation and horror live with them day by day. I wonder more and more at the Nazi psychology when I read descriptions of what happens to people in the occupied countries under Nazi control" (MD, September 25, 1942). The same column reported conditions in the Ravensbrück Women's Preventive Detention Camp in Poland, a death camp that would become widely known because of one Dutch Protestant survivor, Corrie ten Boom:

People are regarded as ill only when they drop. Prisoners have to go barefoot in streets sprinkled with coarse gravel. In consequence prisoners get sore and festered heels, but they have to go on walking barefoot. No food is provided during the examination period so, if they bring none of their own, they go hungry until they are finally assigned to barracks.

Rabbi Wise, desperate for FDR's intervention, pleaded with Secretary Morgenthau to do *something*. Henry Morgenthau III reported that his father had cautioned, "Please, Stephen, don't give me the gory details." The more graphic Wise became, the paler Morgenthau grew. Finally, the secretary cried out, "I cannot take any more!"

By 1943, eyewitness reports circulated in the top government echelons as a result of the courageous Jan Karski, who had infiltrated and escaped from the Belzec concentration camp. Justice Felix Frankfurter said his brain could not believe Karski's account.

The curious could have read brief articles about the Jews' predicament on back pages of the *New York Times*. On December 5, 1942, Eleanor reported her horror after reading a short article, which she insisted should have appeared on page 1: "In Poland . . . more than two-thirds of the Jewish population had been massacred"—two million men, women, and children! Recognizing the atrocities as a military, political, and *spiritual* issue, Eleanor lamented: "There seems to be little use in voicing a protest, but somehow one cannot keep still when such horrors are going on" (MD, December 5, 1942).

Fourteen months into the war, the Gallup organization polled Americans: "It is said that 2 million Jews have been killed in Europe since the war began. Do you think that is true or just a rumor?" Only 48 percent accepted the report as fact.

ELEANOR'S LATENT PREJUDICE

When someone is as unambiguously hateful as Hitler, it is tempting to whitewash all those opposed to him as unequivocally virtuous, all those concerned for the Jews as having righteously shed the anti-Semitism of their culture. I was quite disturbed to find, among Eleanor's papers, evidence of lingering personal prejudice. In her prewar correspondence with Carola von Schaffer-Bernstein, the Allenswood classmate unconvinced of Hitler's threat, Eleanor equivocated: "I realize quite well that there may be a need for curtailing the ascendency of the Jewish people, but it seems to me it might have been done in a more humane way by a ruler who had intelligence and decency."

There may be a need for curtailing the ascendency of Jews?

How could these words flow from the same woman who declared it unchristian "not to believe in the dignity and worth of every human being"? It seems that, despite her convictions and even friendships with Jewish individuals, Eleanor still shared some of the culture's perception that Jews were too powerful, too influential in finance and politics. Her resentment of the sable-wearing, jewel-flaunting women she socialized with during the Roosevelts' first stint in Washington must have lingered somewhere under the surface.

In this way, Eleanor was like many other Americans of the day. And yet her choice to be guided instead by her belief in the God-given worth of all peoples, regardless of creed or race, set her apart. Navigating between her own latent bias against and simultaneous conviction to help the persecuted Jewish people may have given her a unique position from which to compel her fellow Americans to act.

In a 1943 "My Day" column, Eleanor described a conversation she had with a representative of a group committed to rescuing Jews. After summarizing the hardships European Jews had experienced, Eleanor noted:

> The Jews are like all the other people of the world. There are able people among them, there are courageous people among them, there are people of extraordinary intellectual ability along many lines. There are people of extraordinary integrity and people of great beauty and great charm.
>
> On the other hand, largely because of environment and economic condition, there are people among them who cringe, who are dishonest, who try to take advantage of their neighbors, who are aggressive and unattractive.
>
> In other words, they are a cross section of the human race, just as is every other nationality and every other religious group. But good or bad, they have suffered in Europe as has no other group. (MD, August 13, 1943)

Pointing out the flaws of victims, particularly with such slurs as "aggressive and unattractive," seems in poor taste, at least to our modern sensibilities. She remarks in the same column that when a group is hated, they have the right to survival and self-improvement, to "try to change the things within [them] that brought it about." In a 1941 *Ladies' Home Journal* article, Eleanor counseled American Jews—including close friends—to "go about their own lives" without being "too aggressive, too ingratiating, or too flattering," but she also urged readers to "try to forget that the people with whom we associate belong to any particular race or to any particular religion" (IYAM, December 1941). Her 1943 "My Day" column suggests that she was herself "trying to forget" her own prejudices as she compelled readers that no matter their personal opinions about Jewish people, they must nonetheless take action in the face of great suffering. As the magazine column goes on to say:

> The same thing might happen to any other group, if enough people ganged up against it and decided on persecution. It seems to me that it is the part of common sense for the world as a whole to protest in its own interest against wholesale persecution, because none of us by ourselves would be strong enough to stand against a big enough

group which decided to treat us in the same way. We may have our individual likes and dislikes, but this is a question which far transcends prejudices or inclinations. (IYAM, December 1941)

Eleanor's argument reminds one of the poem based on speeches by German pastor Martin Niemöller: "First they came for the Socialists, and I did not speak out—because I was not a Socialist. . . ." Each line names another persecuted group for whom Niemöller, who was eventually sent to a concentration camp for his faith-based opposition to Hitler, did not speak out. The poem ends, "Then they came for me—and there was no one left to speak for me."

One cannot know to what extent Eleanor wrestled with her latent prejudices. Periodically, Eleanor read haunting words from Psalm 139 in her well-worn Book of Common Prayer:

> Search me, O God, and know my heart;
>   try me and know my thoughts.
> And see if there be any wicked way in me.

Perhaps she was ashamed to have such instincts toward a group of people of whom she counted many as friends. At some point in her adult life, she began ending her day by praying a prayer that included these two phrases: "Open our eyes to simple beauty all around us and our hearts to the loveliness men hide from others because we do not try to understand them" and "Save us from ourselves and show us a vision of a world made new."

Eleanor's values compelled her to love all people, and, as she reminded her readers, our commitment to justice and compassion must transcend our inclinations toward prejudice.

CRITICISM AND GUILT

The paradox of latent prejudice in a tireless activist seems fitting for a woman reviled by some for her sympathy toward the Jews and by others for her failure to do more. Anti-Semites charged that the Roosevelts must either be Jewish, have "Jewish blood," or be controlled by Jews. Critics branded the New Deal "the Jew Deal." On February 20, 1939, Fritz Kuhn, the enraged leader of the German American Bund, a Nazi movement, screamed at more than twenty thousand Nazi supporters packed into Madison Square Garden, "All Jews are enemies of the

United States!" The crowd thunderously roared in agreement. "Do you know," he demanded, "FDR's *real* name? Franklin Rosenfeld!" The audience jumped up in sustained applause. Thousands repeated that line. In 1940 Cousin Alice outraged many by saying the president's real name was "Fuhrer, Duce, Roosevelt." She declared that she would rather vote for Hitler! FDR banned her from White House events.

Haters pointed to Eleanor's friendships with Jewish individuals and demanded to know if a majority of her friends were Jewish. Eventually Eleanor responded:

> I never have thought of classifying my friends whether by race, religion or even color, so I have not the faintest idea whether they are Jew or Gentile in the majority. I have only a few very close and intimate friends, and these are of different nationalities and religions. (IYAM, July 1955)

In fact, Eleanor's best friend, Elinor Morgenthau, was a Jew. Joseph Lash was the son of Jewish immigrants from Russia. Lash introduced her to Jewish physician David Gurewitsch, whom she deeply loved and with whom (along with Mrs. Gurewitsch) she even jointly owned her last home.

Historians and biographers remain divided about assigning guilt to FDR on Jewish issues. The indictment in the *Encyclopedia of the Holocaust* stings: "Although he probably could have done more than any other leader . . . to save the Jews of Europe, many historians believe that he did not try hard enough." I see no need for *probably*. Not until 1944 did Henry Morgenthau muster enough chutzpah to confront FDR with evidence that the president's State Department was responsible for the deaths of "my people, the Jews." By the time FDR created the War Refugee Board, European Jewry had suffered beyond comprehension. Jay Winik blasts FDR's leadership: too little, too late! Winik, among other biographers and historians, charges that FDR could have bombed Nazi concentration camps or railroad tracks leading to them. Repeatedly FDR stated that—based on information supplied by the US Army Air Forces—he could not because Jewish prisoners would be killed and the Nazis would use those deaths for propaganda. Besides, the Nazis would quickly rebuild the tracks.

FDR defenders have spun explanations: Roosevelt was "distracted by the war," was slowed by health problems and fatigue—he died before the war ended, in April 1945—or could not, like many Americans, comprehend the scale of the murdering.

The sheer numbers of the dead—six million Jews, one million Gypsies, and thousands of homosexuals—reverberate down history's corridors. Imagine the contributions those dead *could* have made to the postwar world. How many Albert Einsteins and Marlene Dietrichs, Thomas Manns and Hermann Hesses, Hannah Arendts and Béla Bartóks died in Buchenwald, Dachau, Treblinka, and Bergen-Belsen? Conrad Black charges that FDR and the Congress missed an incredible opportunity to "enrich the human talent pool of the nation." As the Jerusalem Talmud declares: "And whoever saved a life, it is considered as if he saved an entire world."

One could use Eleanor's confession, "I should have done more," to indict her. But the truth is: Franklin, Congress, and the entire country should have done more. Only Congress could change immigration law! People of faith should have done more! Eleanor channeled her regret into an unyielding commitment to the establishment of Israel and enhancing the quality of life for Jews wherever they lived.

POSTWAR CHAOS

Many readers may assume that following the defeat of the Nazis, Jews were safe. Hardly. Many displaced persons who returned home found themselves in unstable, unsafe conditions. German Jews released from Russian-controlled camps were not provided ration cards for food. And living conditions were deplorable.

The Allies egregiously, as historian Leonard Dinnerstein documented, put ex-Nazis in charge of the displaced person camps. Thus survivors found themselves again "prisoners with armed guards surrounding the centers." Jews continued to die, only on a smaller scale. On February 1, 1946, the *Manchester Guardian* printed four headlines that chilled readers:

> Jews Still in Flight from Poland
>
> Driven Abroad by Fear
>
> Political Gangs Out to Terrorize Them
>
> Campaign of Murder and Robbery

In 1946, as Eleanor celebrated with family and friends at a Fourth of July picnic, thirty Jews were murdered in Poland. Some twenty-five hundred Jews were killed in Poland in 1945 *after* the war. Instability, deprivation, and violence forced many Jews to flee again. More troublesome was the fate of Jews in Russian-occupied nations: Poland, Czechoslovakia, Hungary, and more than half of Germany.

The sheer number of refugees and the widespread devastation of homes and businesses, the instability of postwar governments, and legal issues between former and current property owners complicated resettlement. Between May and September 1945, the military repatriated several million refugees. However, another 1.5 million, predominately Jews, fearing discrimination, refused to return to what was left of their homes and neighborhoods. Russians denounced many refugees as quislings or traitors who must return to face punishment for allegedly collaborating with the Nazis. Eleanor pointedly disagreed!

Rooting out entrenched anti-Semitism became a postwar challenge, even in the United States. As Americans began using GI Bill benefits to buy homes and create suburbia, covenants in contracts blocked the sale of real estate to Jews and Negroes. Many social clubs denied membership to Jews; elite universities and even some state universities imposed quotas to restrict enrollment of Jewish students. The founding of Brandeis University as a Jewish institution of higher learning in 1948 thrilled Eleanor. She served as a trustee, fund-raiser, and lecturer but declined to be called "professor" because she had no earned degrees. To attract attention to Brandeis, for several years she broadcast her weekly television show from campus.

TRUMAN APPOINTS ELEANOR TO UN DELEGATION

President Harry Truman knew he needed Eleanor Roosevelt's support for the fledgling United Nations. Many Americans, including Eleanor and her sons, thought the Missourian woefully unprepared for the presidency. Truman appointed Eleanor as a delegate to the United Nations, over her initial objections—and objections from the other American delegates. The alpha males on the delegation maneuvered to assign Eleanor to Committee Three—the Committee on Humanitarian, Social and Cultural Concerns—to keep her out of the limelight. She could do little harm on that committee, they reasoned, because the Russians would not agree to anything supporting human rights.

Once members of Committee Three elected Eleanor chair, she threw herself into learning the nuances of diplomacy and navigating ideological landmines. In that position, while midwifing the drafting of the Universal

Declaration of Human Rights, Eleanor endured through long, tedious debates. She patiently bore the relentless barrage of anti-American rhetoric and Russian stall tactics. She negotiated skillfully behind the scenes by inviting delegates to her apartment or home for less formal conversations.

Eleanor worked to craft a preamble that would be a beachhead for religious freedom. While she did not get everything she wanted, Eleanor got more than many diplomats had thought possible. Article 2 of the declaration states:

> Everyone is entitled to all the rights and freedoms set forth in this Declaration, without distinction of any kind, such as race, colour, sex, language, religion, political or other opinion, national or social origin, property, birth or other status.

Eleanor lobbied for an expansive "freedom of residence" through brutal deliberations. Eventually, the Universal Declaration of Human Rights passed, with these guarantees:

> Everyone has the right to freedom of movement and residence within the borders of each state. (art. 13.1)
>
> Everyone has the right to leave any country, including his own, and to return to his country. (art. 13.2).
>
> Everyone has the right to seek and to enjoy in other countries asylum from persecution. (art. 14.1)

Any declaration of human rights, Eleanor insisted as chair, must be unequivocal: "No one shall be arbitrarily deprived of his nationality nor denied the right to change his nationality" (art. 15.2). *No one!* Despite Russia's belligerent protests against such generosity, Eleanor refused to budge and thereby saved additional tens of thousands of Jewish lives.

Eleanor's status as Franklin Roosevelt's widow did not go unnoticed at the United Nations. But Eleanor was driven by a haunting awareness that her husband had done so little to rescue Jews.

VISITING THE CAMPS

What other American woman waded through mud in the displaced-person camps in Europe after the war? Not just once, but repeatedly during her service at the United Nations. Who else informed Americans that "at least fifty of these poor creatures" were dying in postwar camps every day? Who else cared about two hundred fifty thousand in the *she'erit ha-pletah*—the surviving remnant—who waited for years in displaced-person camps, held behind barbed-wire fences, guarded by former Nazis?

Three encounters in a refugee camp in Zeilsheim, near Frankfurt, Germany, on February 15, 1946, haunted and energized Eleanor. After her arrival, Jews escorted Eleanor to see the stone monument they had built on a small hill in the center of the camp: "To the Memory of All Jews Who Died" in Germany. Jewish collective resilience and an unquenchable longing for a homeland touched her. Eleanor commented on these survivors, "Though every face I saw seemed to represent a story more tragic than the last, these people faced the future resolutely," as had generations of Jews before them.

One such face in Zeilsheim was a ten-year-old boy who, interpreters explained, had walked into the camp one day holding the hand of his six-year-old brother. He did not know his name, where he was from, his parents' names, or what had happened to them. Only God knew the horror the boy had witnessed! Eleanor must have thought back to the years she had cared for her younger brother, Hall.

Then the boy sang "A Song of Freedom" "so touchingly that no one listening could speak." Finally Eleanor asked interpreters, what would happen to these boys? No one could answer her.

Eleanor met a young woman with a baby. Surely, Eleanor assumed from their physical condition, both would die soon. When Eleanor asked the camp superintendent to do something to save both lives, he promised to try. Years later, Eleanor was reunited with the mother and daughter in Israel, delighted that both had thrived.

A third encounter that day forever haunted Eleanor. Through the mud, an elderly woman trudged toward Eleanor. Dropping to her knees in the mud, she wrapped her arms around Eleanor's legs although Eleanor tried to lift her up.

"Israel," the woman pleaded, over and over again. "Israel! Israel!"

"As I looked," Eleanor recalled, "at her weather-beaten face and heard her old voice, I knew for the first time what that small land meant to so many, many people." Eleanor "could not speak." She later asked "My Day" readers, "What could one say at the end of a life which had brought her such complete despair?" (MD, February 16, 1946). Eleanor never forgot the passion in the woman's plea.

Before leaving Germany, Eleanor had a tense encounter with Carola von Schaffer-Bernstein, her Allenswood classmate, who lived nearby. Eleanor saw that the war had not stolen Carola's beauty. While times were tough, Carola's family was hardly destitute. The classmates talked around the subject of the German inhumanity toward Jews, although they had addressed the issue in correspondence. Finally, as time neared to leave for the airport, Eleanor lamented the war's consequences on the "little people" she had met that day.

"It was everybody's fault," Carola responded. "We are all to blame. None of us has lived up to the teachings of Christ." Eleanor suspected Carola was spiritualizing the issue to avoid acknowledging the ugly reality of personal culpability. Oh no, Eleanor countered, it was more than not "living up" to Jesus' teachings. German Christians had ignored their responsibility to protest the inhuman carnage and the idolatry of Hitler as a leader. German Christians had chosen not to see the Jew— any Jew—as a neighbor. She stared at Carola.

"You have always been a very religious person. How is it possible that one can be so devoted to the principles of the church yet not protest the mistreatment of the Jews?"

Carola shrugged, "Sometimes, it is wiser not to look over the hill." Eleanor did not ask if Carola or anyone in her family had been members of the Nazi Party or had profited from the Nazis' theft of property, money, jewelry, land, and art.

The two women had nothing further to say. Eleanor realized the friendship had no future. Marie Souvestre had drilled into her students that one's duty was to come to the aid of the underdog. By failing to do so, Carola had dishonored Souvestre. Eleanor left the room.

In February 1946, a German reporter asked Eleanor if she thought "the whole German nation was responsible for the war." Eleanor responded cautiously but firmly: "All the people of Germany have to accept responsibility for having tolerated a leadership which first brought such misery to groups of people within their own nation and later created world chaos" (MD, February 16, 1946). *All* included a particular person: Carola.

On the flight home to New York, an elderly woman's plea, "Israel! *Israel!*" echoed in Eleanor's heart. She became an outspoken advocate for a Jewish state even if Arabs would be displaced.

ISRAEL

Eleanor argued at the United Nations that *everyone* had a right to live where she or he wanted to live, including—perhaps especially—Jews. Eleanor lobbied for a Jewish homeland. As she experienced her own upheaval as a widow, she identified with tens of thousands of widows who wanted new lives.

Eleanor lived by a simple mantra: She had not done enough for Jews before and during the war. Well, by God's grace, she would *now*! The Jews were going to have a homeland! Eleanor's commitment sparked a firestorm of opposition within the State Department. State Department professionals who had opposed Jewish refugee resettlement during the war now aggressively fought a homeland for the Jews. Eleanor recognized the crux of their opposition: oil. For postwar prosperity, America would need Arab oil. Lots of Arab oil.

Palestine, under British mandate since 1922, *could have* offered safety to thousands of European Jews during the war. Instead, Eleanor knew the British government belligerently limited immigration to reduce conflict with the Arabs and, more importantly, to keep oil flowing to their ports. In 1939, just before the outbreak of the war, eighty-three thousand Jews lived in Palestine; Palestine seemed the only "society on earth" willing to accept Jews. The British, however, limited Jewish immigration to seventy-five thousand spread over the following five years, ensuring that Jews would never make up more than one-third of the population. That diplomats repeatedly reassured anxious Arabs that there would be *no* Jewish state irritated Eleanor! Her focus was on what was right rather than what was geopolitically expedient, i.e., access to Arab oil!

When Harry Truman urged British Prime Minister Clement Attlee to admit one hundred thousand Jews to Palestine, Attlee growled, "Take them yourself." British Foreign Secretary Ernest Bevin snarled that Americans wanted more Jews to go to Palestine because the Americans "did not want too many of them in New York." A year after the war's end, Eleanor urged Americans to step forward to accept refugees. "It would be quite possible to absorb far more than our share of displaced people in Europe" (MD, June 22, 1946). What she did not say was: do it as atonement for our timidity before and during the war and to live up to the words on the base of the Statue of Liberty, "Give me your tired, your poor, your huddled masses yearning to breathe free."

The United States, despite Eleanor's lobbying, never took the high road on postwar refugee issues. The United States would not accept refugees but insisted that other nations take in refugees. The exception to American timidity was the temporary Fort Oswego Emergency Refugee Shelter at Oswego, New York. After the Allies liberated Italy in 1944, some 875 Jews were transported to the United States, aware that they could not remain after war's end. On arrival, these refugees were shocked to find themselves housed behind wire fences at an abandoned military base.

Originally, the refugees were to be "adopted" or sponsored by local families and social service agencies. That idea was nixed by FDR, the attorney general, and the War Refugee Bureau. Providing refugees jobs was illegal and might stir congressional ire. The impasse attracted Eleanor's attention.

So Eleanor Roosevelt and Elinor Morgenthau, wife of the secretary of the treasury, visited Fort Oswego on September 22, 1944. Eleanor's annoyance rose as she toured the camp. Why were these refugees behind barbed-wire fences? Why were these individuals not being prepared for postwar life? When camp officials offered bureaucratic jargon, she rolled her eyes. More than half of these refugees had relatives in the United States and could have lived with them. Fourteen refugees had sons serving in the US military!

Touring the camp infirmary, Eleanor paused to talk to David Levy, a college-age refugee, and quizzed him about conditions in the camp. Levy expressed his desire to continue college. Eleanor turned to Joseph Smart, the administrator.

"I believe I was told all the young people are in school?" Regulations prevented that, Smart explained. On learning that college-age refugees were spending their days doing nothing, Eleanor was not amused! Americans, the bureaucrat added, would not tolerate refugees being educated at taxpayers' expense. These refugees, Eleanor pointedly noted, were *already* supported on taxpayers' expense.

Levy, deeply moved by her interest, extended his hand to the First Lady. "I have the feeling your coming here today was *beshert*—destiny—like the hand of God." Levy's boldness would impact the lives of many refugees! Before she left the camp, Eleanor addressed the refugees, "My visit to this shelter has been one of the most wonderful days I have ever spent."

Needless to say, camp policies evolved expediently through the tag-team persuasive skills of Eleanor and Elinor. Early one cold morning in January 1945, the first day of the semester, a bus stopped at the camp's main gate. Eleven refugees boarded and rode to the state teachers college in Oswego to start classes and, more importantly, futures.

At war's end, bureaucrats began planning to send the refugees back. Back to *what?* Eleanor demanded. The refugees, she was informed, *knew* when they came that they had to go back. No, argued Eleanor, sending these refugees back to the chaos in Europe would be inhumane.

Eleanor and Elinor lobbied for governmental "obstacles and regulations" to be waived. On December 22, 1945, President Harry Truman gave the refugees an early holiday gift: an executive order permanently admitting 853 refugees and acknowledging the US citizenship of twenty-three babies who had been born in the camp.

Four students from that group eventually attended Harvard Medical School. One, Alexander Margulis, became a world-renowned oncological radiologist who chaired the Radiology Department at the University of California at San Francisco from 1963 to 1989. In that post, Dr. Margulis helped fund the development of computerized axial tomography, the CAT scan. Whatever money the government expended on tuition and expenses for him proved a wise investment. Over his career he attracted outstanding radiologists to UCSF, including Dr. Charles Higgins, the husband of one of the strongest cheerleaders of this book, Dr. Sally Higgins.

For Levy, Margulis, and many others, Eleanor made a difference. Eleanor showed up. Eleanor asked questions. Eleanor worked to make their future a reality.

8

Children of God

Eleanor and Civil Rights

Whether in praise or criticism, millions view Eleanor Roosevelt as one of the major reasons for the change in status of colored people . . . during the last quarter century.

—Carl T. Rowan

One warm March day in 1941, after attending a meeting of the Julius Rosenwald Fund at the Tuskegee Institute in Alabama, Eleanor made time to visit the young African American pilots training nearby. Although many politicians and military leaders did not, or would not, believe that these men could be competent pilots, the First Lady bristled at such ignorance.

The flying instruction Eleanor had taken and her friendship with aviator Amelia Earhart facilitated her conversation with the pilots; she affirmed their skills and patriotism. Words, however, were not enough to trump the prejudice these men experienced due to the entrenched racism in the US Army Air Forces, particularly on southern bases. Eleanor, who had often quoted from James 2:26, "Faith without works is dead," knew a photograph of her chatting with pilots was not enough. Something more was needed. But what? A smile spread across her face.

"I've always heard the colored can't fly an airplane," Eleanor said to chief flight instructor Charles Alfred "Chief" Anderson. "Oh, yes they can, Mrs. Roosevelt," he replied defensively.

"I'm going to find out for sure. I'm going to take a flight with you." Anderson was not certain he had heard her clearly. She wanted to go up in a plane with an African American pilot? That was illegal in Alabama! But who could say no to Eleanor? Wearing a dress and hat and carrying her purse, with the help of instructor Adolph J. Moret Jr. she climbed into the open cockpit of the Piper J-3 Cub and strapped herself in the rear seat. She waved to airmen as the plane taxied toward the runway. Several groaned: *If anything goes wrong. . . .*

The flight, though lasting less than an hour, provided ample time for reporters and photographers to gather. If Eleanor trusted a Tuskegee Airman, why couldn't others? As she climbed out of the cockpit she chuckled, "Well, you can fly all right."

Racists went ballistic. Did the president know, one irate White House caller demanded, what the First Lady was "up to"? Yes, he answered, she's attending a board meeting. When informed she was flying in a small plane, FDR replied that "the Missus" loves to fly. The caller cut him short, informing him that she was flying with a black pilot.

Well, FDR responded, she is in good hands. When reporters asked about the flight, FDR made clear that the country's defense would need the efforts of all Americans. *All!*

Southern newspaper accounts of the incidents drew attention to the Tuskegee Airmen. The picture of Eleanor and Captain Anderson that inflamed Southerners appealed to open-minded Americans. Since Mrs. Roosevelt trusts the Tuskegee pilots, we should too!

The Tuskegee Airmen, technically the 332nd Fighter Group and the 477th Bombardment Group, distinguished themselves as bomber escorts. More than once when a Tuskegee Airman experienced racism or a threat, personal or toward his career, Eleanor received a phone call. Immediately, Mrs. R. "got on it," going right up the chain of command until the issue was addressed, reversed, or remedied.

The head of the Army Air Forces in Europe, Maj. Gen. Frank O'Driscoll Hunter, no advocate for black pilots or fan of Eleanor, fumed about the First Lady throughout the war. He mockingly explained the chain of command: "General [Hap] Arnold got his orders from General [George] Marshall and he got his from Secretary of War Stimson, and he got his from Mrs. Roosevelt."

Eleanor, as a trustee of the foundation that administered the estate of Julius Rosenwald, one-quarter owner of Sears, Roebuck and Company, persuaded the foundation to loan Tuskegee Institute $175,000 to build a new airfield to enhance training opportunities. Southerners derided the airmen as "Eleanor Roosevelt's niggers."

TWISTING THE BIBLE TO SUPPORT SEGREGATION

Eleanor was widely lambasted for being prejudiced against the South, particularly because of her unyielding opposition to segregation. On

more than one occasion she was dismissed as a "damn nigger-lover."
Eleanor reminded readers and audiences that she had "southern blood"
from her paternal grandmother Bulloch of Roswell, Georgia. Nevertheless, Eleanor's encounters with southern Christians were unsettling
given the entrenched prejudice against African Americans, Jews, and
Catholics—prejudice that Franklin ignored for political expediency.

Eleanor could not understand how church-going, Bible-toting
Southerners who professed such allegiance to the word of God could
abuse biblical texts to deny African Americans—God's beloved children—their constitutional rights, such as voting, particularly after their
heroic service in World War I. How could Southerners deny children
comprehensive educational opportunity? How could they think that
God Almighty favored racial segregation? How, Eleanor wondered,
could Southerners recite the Lord's Prayer—"thy kingdom come, thy
will be done, on earth as it is in heaven"? Would heaven be segregated
so that Southerners would not feel uncomfortable? To Eleanor, nothing in the biblical message affirmed such intolerance:

> Nothing should ever keep us from advocating, however for all races
> that come together as citizens in our land, or that we meet through-
> out the world, equal respect and equal opportunity. Only in this
> way can we live side by side in peace and goodwill. Our desire must
> be for equal justice and we know, no matter to what sects and reli-
> gions we belong, that most of us acknowledge that God made us all.
> (MD, July 29, 1943)

Taylor Branch, the distinguished historian of civil rights, makes clear
that unreasonable biblical interpretation fueled opposition to black and
white children attending schools together. William Carter, an outraged
citizen, wrote to Eleanor protesting that "God, whom we all revere,"
opposed integration:

> Desegregation is against the Bible. I find my scripture for this
> in Genesis 9:27, where God did segregate and separate the three
> sons of Noah, sending one out to be a servant while the other two
> remained in the Tabernacle. I say that God has given the word, his
> Bible. It ain't right for men to end the curse that He's placed upon
> any human flesh.

Elected officials likewise argued that segregation was God's mandate. Senator Absalom Willis Robertson of Virginia, father of televan-
gelist Pat Robertson, echoed the belief of many southern Christians
that segregation was the way God Almighty intended the races to live

in harmony. Robertson informed one Senate colleague seeking his vote, on some mild civil rights legislation, "I'd sure like to help the colored, but the Bible says I can't."

Senator James O. Eastland of Mississippi vigorously defended segregation on the floor of the US Senate on May 27, 1954:

> The Southern institution of racial segregation or racial separation . . . promotes racial harmony. It permits each race to follow its own pursuits, and its own civilization. Segregation is not discrimination. . . . Mr. President, it is the law of nature, *it is the law of God*, that every race has both the right and the duty to perpetuate itself. All free men have the right to associate exclusively with members of their own race, free from governmental interference, if they so desire. (emphasis added)

Eleanor closely reread the senator's remarks to make certain she had not misunderstood. Segregation is "the law of God"? How absurd! Jesus' life was the model of inclusion to anyone who read the Gospels, Eleanor insisted. Christians, she declared, do not collude to deny constitutional rights to fellow citizens.

Eleanor called out Eastland in a "My Day" column:

> We talk of brotherhood; we say that democracy means an appreciation of the importance of the human personality and of the rights of individual human beings; we say that democracy is inspired by Christianity as exemplified in the teachings of Christ.
>
> Then we allow people such as Senator Eastland to quote the Bible and the life of Christ as justification for doctrines entirely opposed to the whole spirit of Christianity, or ethics, or human brotherhood. (MD, April 27, 1957)

Christians, Eleanor believed, were called to midwife social change. Had not Paul, in the early church, rebuked Peter for his prejudice toward Gentiles? Eleanor groaned that it was easier to sponsor "Brotherhood Week" and exchange platitudes about race than to make brotherhood reality "from sea to shining sea." Christians must remember the apostle Paul's warning, "For we wrestle not against flesh and blood, but against principalities, against powers, against the rulers of the darkness of this world, against spiritual wickedness in high places" (Eph. 6:12). "High places," in Eleanor's thinking, included courthouses, statehouses, *and* high-steepled churches across the South, as well as the offices of southern Democratic committee chairs in the House and

Senate, and the office of Alaska's territorial governor (who did not want African American troops stationed in his territory).

While some Americans did not want to deny equality to any child of God, they were unwilling to risk the hard work to make equality reality. On Sunday mornings in stained-glass sanctuaries and concrete-block churches across this nation, white Americans pretended that they were not beneficiaries of entrenched institutionalized racism. Oh, they sang, "In Christ There Is No East or West" and from time to time dropped money into offering plates to send white missionaries to the Dark Continent, but they ignored darkness within the shadow of their steeples.

Americans had waited too long to demonstrate to the world the majesty of the Declaration of Independence's "all men are created equal." Eleanor reiterated until her last breath the constitutional rights bestowed at birth or naturalization on *every* American: "Equality before the law; equality of education; equality to hold a job according to his ability; equality of participation through the ballot in the government."

Eleanor argued in 1942 that, given the number of African Americans serving in the military, "I do not see how we can fight this war and deny these rights to any citizen in our land." Moreover, "it seems trite to say to the Negro, you must have patience, when he has had patience so long; you must not expect miracles overnight, when he can look back to the years of slavery and see how many nights he has waited for justice."

Repeatedly she reaffirmed her longing for segregation's demise. In May 1956, Eleanor wrote pointedly:

> One hundred years is a long time to wait. Our Negro citizens have been patient beyond belief. The question that so many of us have been asked over and over again, "Do you believe the Negro is capable of development as the white man?" should be answered once and for all with, "I do believe that, given the same opportunity with discrimination removed, the Negro is as capable of achieving any standard of success." (MD, May 5, 1956)

SEEING SEGREGATION FIRSTHAND

Eleanor, raised in the aristocratic social circles of the Roosevelts, had little firsthand interaction with African Americans—other than maids, butlers, yard workers, or stable hands—until she became politically active in the 1920s. Certainly, she had heard family stories about Martha

Bulloch Roosevelt, her paternal grandmother from Georgia. Although she resided in New York City during the Civil War, *that* Mrs. Roosevelt had been unapologetically Confederate. Eleanor, at some point, may have pondered the possibility that she had unacknowledged kin fathered by Bulloch males during the years of slavery.

Segregation in Warm Springs, Georgia, disturbed Eleanor, particularly at the polio center, where she noticed only white patients. This discomfort, in some part, explained why she seldom visited Franklin there. How could he ignore such blatant segregation? Obviously, the same way he overlooked Prohibition. Eleanor knew why: political expediency. Georgians would help FDR secure the 1932 presidential nomination.

The ownership of Warm Springs evolved into a national foundation headed by Basil O'Connor, FDR's law partner. After hearing O'Connor boast that "no victim of infantile paralysis, regardless of age, race, creed or color, shall go without care for lack of money," Eleanor asked: "Where are the Negro patients?" When Eleanor persisted, she was informed, "Blacks were widely believed to be 'less susceptible' than whites to polio, and therefore less in need of care." Eleanor, visiting polio patients at Tuskegee, discovered the rates were about the same. Admitting black patients would have riled the locals and would have made some white patients and their families pursue treatment elsewhere.

Because of what she had seen in her extensive travel as First Lady, some three hundred thousand miles, Eleanor insisted African Americans were "the poorest of the poor," in some cases not even on the local, state, or federal governments' radar, let alone recipients of aid.

Eleanor's forays deep into Dixie exposed her to the racism of federal program administrators, particularly in the Subsistence Homesteads Division, which systemically ignored black farmers. Eleanor never wavered: the New Deal had to be *everyone's* New Deal!

Eleanor pressured—as only she could pressure—Donald Richberg, of the National Recovery Administration, to investigate race-based differentials in compensation in southern industries receiving New Deal funding.

Details in thousands of letters sent in response to her invitation, "Write me," in a 1933 magazine article, horrified Eleanor. Many African American families, particularly sharecroppers, reported being destitute and "left out" of government assistance; some reported being threatened for seeking assistance. Eleanor forwarded letters to friendly administrators, particularly Aubrey Williams and Ellen Woodward, asking for investigation of the claims. Armed with documentation, she demanded federal administrators explain why African Americans were being excluded.

In 1933, Eleanor immediately terminated the all-white White House staff and hired black replacements. Eleanor's decision provided African American staff with good salaries and benefits in jobs that would be passed down through families. Eleanor provided not just jobs but economic futures! Critics might point out that FDR had ordered a 25 percent reduction in operational costs for the White House; Eleanor could pay black workers less than white workers. In talking with the new staff, she learned of the discrimination they experienced beyond the White House grounds.

Lillian Parks, after years working in the family residence as White House seamstress, assigned broader consequences to Eleanor's hiring policy. "The Roosevelt White House was the catalyst for the whole civil rights movement that would eventually open all front doors," alluding to Eleanor's practice of receiving African American guests at the White House's *front* door rather than at the service door, as in previous administrations!

Eleanor's decision to hire "colored help" irked Sara Roosevelt enough to confront her daughter-in-law. This time, Eleanor rebuffed her: "You run your house and I'll run mine."

On occasion, staff shook their heads while watching Eleanor hurry down the sidewalk to walk Mary McLeod Bethune to and *through* the front door and, in time, greet Dr. Bethune with a kiss on the cheek. It was one thing for Dr. Bethune, a college president and head of Negro Affairs in the National Youth Administration, to walk in the front door, yet a much different thing for every black guest to be welcomed through the front door.

One afternoon jaws dropped and tongues wagged. After visiting a depressing reformatory for African American girls, the First Lady invited the inmates to a garden party at the White House! When Steve Early, FDR's press secretary and a staunch segregationist demanded the event be canceled—apparently he had never heard Jesus' words about entertaining strangers—the president sent Early to "talk to the Missus."

Early returned. The president inquired, "Did you persuade Eleanor to change her mind?" Early muttered no. FDR grinned, "Steve, if you couldn't do it, how could I?" The inmates came, had a wonderful time, and in the words of one attendee, "Nothing terrible occurred—not even very bad repercussions in the press." And years later, elderly black women asked great-grandchildren, "Have I ever told you about the time I went to a garden party at the White House? *I* was invited by Mrs. Roosevelt." Through hospitality, Eleanor repeatedly demonstrated that the White House belonged to all Americans.

ELEANOR'S BLACK FRIENDS

Franklin Roosevelt could not match Eleanor's roster of close African American friends: Mary McLeod Bethune, Rosa Parks, Adam Clayton Powell, Ralph Bunche, Walter White, Harry Belafonte, Thurgood Marshall, Pauli Murray, and many others. While segregationists used photos of Eleanor with African American friends against her, black newspaper publishers ran the same pictures to demonstrate that she was not the stereotypical white "all-talk" northern liberal. In 1953, her eyebrow-raising article for *Ebony* magazine titled "Some of My Best Friends Are Negro" created a stir.

Eleanor became a friend to civil rights activist Pauli Murray as a result of the firebrand's letters protesting that FDR and his New Dealers were "doing too little" for African Americans. Initially, Eleanor chided Murray for being "too critical." Name a president, Eleanor retorted, who had done as much as FDR had.

The relationship evolved through dueling typewriters and Eleanor's invitation to come to her New York City apartment for the first of many spirited conversations over tea. Slowly, the two strong-willed Episcopalians grew to respect, trust, and love each other. By 1940, Murray had enlisted Mrs. Roosevelt in a campaign promoting National Sharecroppers Week and in organizing the National Committee to Abolish the Poll Tax, a southern tactic that kept African Americans from voting. Many southern blacks could neither pay the tax nor pass the convoluted literacy examinations that were required before they could register to vote. Across the South, African Americans could not vote, could not vote easily, or realized voting "might be the last thing I do." African Americans who were able to vote had deserted Mr. Lincoln's party to vote Democratic in 1936—a shift that Republicans could not ignore. Pundits, of course, linked Eleanor's activism with keeping those votes in the Democratic column in 1940. In national politics, "Negro politician" was an oxymoron except for Congressmen Oscar De Priest, from Chicago, and the Rev. Adam Clayton Powell Jr., from

Harlem, Eleanor's friend with whom she, on occasion, shared speaking platforms. The only ongoing direct interaction FDR had with African Americans was with his valets LeRoy Jones, Irvin McDuffie, and Arthur Perryman, plus a few White House maids, like Lillian Parks. Only his wife's constant prodding pushed FDR closer to acknowledging the injustice many African Americans experienced daily.

Near the end of Mrs. Roosevelt's life, she and Pauli Murray served together on President Kennedy's Commission on the Status of Women. Eleanor's service as chair, although she was ill, drew media attention to the commission's work, but she died before the final report was released. Murray, who drafted much of the document, not only dedicated the panel's finding to her mentor, friend, and hero but released the report on Eleanor's birthday.

THE FIGHT TO STOP LYNCHING

FDR and his top aides were paranoid about antagonizing southern committee chairs in Congress, the majority of whom, from the one-party South, were Protestant Democrats elected and reelected in "whites-only" primaries. The District of Columbia was a fiefdom ruled over by southern members of Congress. Had they, Eleanor wondered, not read the Declaration of Independence, which her ancestor had signed? Had they never thought about how dark-skinned foreign visitors personally experienced Washington's racism?

Tensions intensified between the First Couple after Eleanor endorsed the Costigan-Wagner anti-lynching bill in 1935. FDR dissembled when pressed for support by activist (and friend of Eleanor) Walter White, saying, "I've got to get legislation passed by Congress to save America. . . . If I come out for the anti-lynching bill now, they [the southern chairs] will block every bill I ask Congress to pass to keep America from collapsing." Six last six words jolted White, "I just can't take that risk."

More than forty-seven hundred Americans—predominately black—were lynched during Eleanor's lifetime; few of the perpetrators had ever been punished. In 1933, twenty-four African Americans were dragged from jails and hanged; seventeen would be lynched during the first three years of World War II. Many were sadistically tortured before being killed. A "spectacle lynching" drew large crowds, including children, some of whom posed for pictures with the corpse. Postcards of hangings sold well. According to Carol Anderson, an Emory University historian, plans for a lynching were announced in churches, and spectators could buy discounted train tickets to attend! Southerners blocked antilynching legislation, railing that lynching was essential to preserve the purity of white women from defilement by African American "brutes."

Eleanor publicly, repeatedly declared that any lynching violated an American's constitutional right to due process and was a stench in the nostrils of God! Eleanor would not cede any ground on racial issues to her husband, his aides, his cabinet, or southern politicians. Racism, Eleanor believed, could be eliminated if Christians would lead.

In 1934, Eleanor and Walter White joined forces to aggressively push legislation making it a federal crime for three or more individuals to collude to injure, taunt, or kill anyone in police custody. Too many blacks, Eleanor knew, never got a full night in jail, let alone a trial "by a jury of their peers." Southern jailers, sheriffs, and police colluded with or were themselves members of the Ku Klux Klan.

FDR was "unavailable" to talk to White. Frustrated, White enlisted Eleanor's help. She went to Franklin, angering some of his aides who resented her intrusion on their turf and, more significantly, the heat she drew to racial issues.

Finally, in May 1934, through Eleanor's prodding, FDR and White met. FDR, after telling jokes and stories—his technique to eat up the time allotted for interviews—finally pushed White: You would not want to work against the good of "your people," would you? White stood his ground, persistently deflating FDR's arguments, even at one point interrupting the president! An irritated Roosevelt snapped: "Somebody's been priming you. Was it my wife?"

Due to Southerners' manipulation of procedural tactics in Congress, no antilynching legislation could reach the Senate floor.

On October 26, 1934, a mob lynched Claude Neal, a black man who had "confessed" to killing a young white woman, Lola Cannady. Neal was not immediately hanged but first tormented for ten hours after being kidnapped from a jail in Brewton, Alabama, where he had been moved from Florida for safety. The kidnappers crossed the state line to transport Neal to a tree about four miles from the deceased woman's Florida farm.

Neal was stripped. His genitals were cut off, and he was forced to eat them. He was repeatedly stabbed; his fingers and toes were sliced off and thrown into the crowd for souvenirs. Laughing men burned Neal's skin with red-hot irons. Several times he dangled until he choked and then was cut down so that more individuals could brag that they had taken part. After his heart stopped beating, tormentors dragged his corpse behind an automobile for four miles!

A cheering mob, including women and young children—estimates ranged from three thousand to seven thousand people—celebrated as if attending a sporting event. Finally, Neal's nude body was hung from a tree on the lawn of the Jackson County Courthouse in Marianna, Florida.

Any American, but particularly any Christian, Eleanor declared, should find this so-called southern justice unconscionable. Where were the local and state authorities? David Sholtz, Florida's governor, outraged Eleanor by claiming that no one had requested assistance from him.

US Attorney General Homer Cummings angered Eleanor by explaining that he could not have intervened because no federal law prohibited lynching. Had not, Eleanor pushed back, Mr. Neal been kidnapped and driven across the state line? Then enforce the 1932 Lindbergh Law that made transporting a *kidnapped* individual across state lines a federal crime. But according to J. Edgar Hoover, director of the Bureau of Investigation, the Lindbergh Law did not apply because there had been no demand for ransom.

When Walter White asked Eleanor to speak at a rally in Carnegie Hall protesting Neal's murder, FDR vetoed her appearance. Eleanor told her friend Lenora Hickok, "I feel like a skunk not to do more on the lynching thing openly." White, angered by the president's timidity, resigned from a federal advisory council. FDR loved to brag that he had appointed almost one hundred African Americans to posts in his administration. Yes, White retorted, mostly to "advisory" panels.

CRITICS, RUMORS, AND ALLEGATIONS

The road to social change is not pretty or easy. Those who pave the way, who speak out and act out as Eleanor did, become targets for hatred, criticism, and violence. Allida Black reports eleven assassination attempts on Eleanor before 1940.

Senator Theodore Bilbo, Democrat of Mississippi, an ordained Southern Baptist preacher, loathed the First Lady. As the ranking racist in the Senate, Bilbo supported the New Deal only to bring home the bacon to impoverished Mississippi. However, he drew the line with Eleanor and her "pro-nigra" activities. In denouncing the antilynching legislation she promoted, Bilbo defamed the bill's advocates as "uppity" African Americans and northern agitators who, he thundered in stem-winding oratory, threatened Anglo-Saxon civilization and would "open the floodgates of hell in the South." He predicted:

> Raping, mobbing, lynching, race riots, and crime will be increased a thousandfold; and upon your garments and the garments of those who are responsible for the passage of the measure will be the blood of the raped and outraged daughters of Dixie, as well as the blood of the perpetrators of these crimes that the red-blooded Anglo-Saxon white Southern men will not tolerate.

So Bilbo, often lubricated with southern libations, proposed an alternative in 1938: Deport *all* black people back to Africa! That would be the most expedient way to preserve white supremacy and end hostility. On May 24, 1938, the reverend-senator, boasting that African Americans had "no better friend that I am," claimed to possess the signatures of 2.5 million African Americans *wanting* to populate a new country to be created in Africa, "Greater Liberia." He assured critics his ideas represented the wishes "of the Almighty that the Negroes may be transferred back to the land of their forefathers."

Bilbo's foolishness had no chance of serious consideration, but Mississippi voters cheered Bilbo because he put Eleanor and "her kind" in their place. Moreover, he stewed, why was she visiting black colleges across the south? His conclusion? Stirring up unrest and anarchy. Even though Eleanor dismissed his ideas as "stupid," Bilbo mused, "I might entertain the proposition of crowning Eleanor queen of Greater Liberia."

African Americans believed the First Lady—*their* First Lady—"walked the talk" in raising awareness for their welfare. Cynics charged that the Roosevelts were only being kind to attract African American voters in 1936 or 1940. One popular ditty had FDR instructing Eleanor:

> You kiss the niggers
> I'll hug the Jews
> We'll live in the White House
> As long as we choose.

Anxious white Southerners began exchanging tales of clandestine Eleanor Clubs composed of "uppity" African American women making pacts not to work in white homes, not to enter residences through the back door, and to assault white women on sidewalks. These clubs were somehow linked to Eleanor's agitation for better-paying jobs for African Americans, particularly in federally sponsored programs and, eventually, in defense industries.

Rumors metamorphosed into "fact," then alarm. J. Edgar Hoover, a racist Eleanor-hater, at an enormous expenditure of tax dollars dispatched FBI field agents across the South to investigate. They found nothing. Well, Hoover speculated, Eleanor must have "black blood," otherwise, why would she be so concerned with the alleged plight of Negro domestics?

The White House received thousands of letters asking if the mixed-blood allegations were true. Eleanor responded to one writer's question: "As far as I know, I have no African American blood; but I suppose if any of us could trace our ancestry back far enough we would find that in the tribes from which we are all originally descended, all kinds of blood is mixed."

THE MARIAN ANDERSON CONCERT

After Marian Anderson, an African American concert artist, sang at a White House social event in February 1937, Eleanor commented in "My Day" that she had "rarely heard a more beautiful and moving voice or a more finished artist" (MD, February 21, 1937). Both Mrs. Roosevelts, Eleanor and Sara, resigned as members of the Daughters of the American Revolution (DAR) when that organization canceled a contract with promoters for Anderson to perform on Easter Sunday 1939 in the DAR's three-thousand-seat Constitution Hall, the largest auditorium in Washington.

Stunned by the negative publicity, DAR leaders explained the cancellation was due to "shadowy rules and regulations," certainly not racism! Then, Eleanor suggested, schedule another date. The DAR declined. Challenging denials and what the DAR president-general dismissed as misinformation, Eleanor demanded to know how an American artist who had sung to great acclaim in all the great European concert halls could not be allowed to sing in this historic venue.

More than four hundred newspapers published the news, many including Eleanor's resignation letter: "I feel obliged to send in to you my resignation. You had an opportunity to lead in an enlightened way and it seems to me that your organization has failed." After Eleanor telegraphed the Marian Anderson Citizens Committee, "I regret exceedingly that Washington is to be deprived of hearing Marian Anderson," someone leaked her telegram to the *New York Times*. The hubbub intensified. Many believed that the DAR had acted to prevent blacks and whites from sitting together during the concert.

While many people supported Eleanor, others thought she should have remained a member and worked for change. While she might have been "a little too far ahead of the thinking of the majority" of DAR members, Eleanor conceded, remaining a member "implies approval" of the cancellation (MD, February 27, 1939).

Harold Ickes, secretary of the interior, and Eleanor put their heads together. What if Anderson sang outdoors? What location with symbolic meaning might be available? FDR, asked to authorize the use of the Lincoln Memorial, snapped, "I don't care if she sings from the top of the Washington Monument as long as she sings." Eleanor persuaded radio station owners to broadcast the concert live. An Easter concert, she suggested, offered a meaningful way to end Holy Week. She urged the National Association for the Advancement of Colored People (NAACP) to take advantage of the coverage.

On Easter afternoon 1939, seventy-five thousand Americans jammed the open space in front of Lincoln's gaze; whites mingled with blacks. Marian Anderson walked majestically to the microphone and began singing "My Country 'Tis of Thee." The irony of segregation in this "sweet land of liberty" resonated across the venue.

Eleanor, however, was not there. Conscious that her presence would distract attention from Anderson, she listened by radio in Hyde Park. Because no hotel in the District of Columbia would rent Anderson a room, Eleanor arranged for the singer to dress for the concert at the White House. With Eleanor's help, Marian Anderson "had gone from being a little-known concert singer to an icon who reminded Americans not just of the evils of segregation but of their capacity to do better." Months later, Eleanor invited Anderson to sing for the visiting king and queen of England.

WAR AND EQUALITY

As America rearmed in the late 1930s and early 1940s, African Americans were not encouraged to volunteer for military service. Military brass stereotyped African Americans as "incompetent and lazy." Hence, a high percentage of African Americans in uniform were assigned to low-status jobs as cooks, stewards, janitors, or dock workers. Paradoxically, black men itched to defend the country that denied them full equality.

The Selective Training and Service Act of 1940 forbade mingling black and white draftees, legislation denounced by the NAACP, which said, "A Jim Crow Army cannot fight for a free world." In July 1942, Dwight Eisenhower, the supreme Allied commander, issued a cleverly crafted order, "It is the desire of Headquarters that discrimination against the Negro troops be sedulously avoided." African American soldiers knew, however, that it was a long way from Eisenhower's headquarters to barracks, tents, and trenches on southern military installations. The racism turned brutal, sometimes deadly, when black soldiers were given leave to go off base. African Americans, particularly from northern states, were angered by mistreatment and harassment when wearing a US military uniform. To some, wearing the uniform implied that the black soldier was equal to a white.

As Hitler's nightmare in Europe escalated, Eleanor's outspokenness on economic and social conditions of African Americans stirred opposition and reflection. What good was a democracy, she opined in 1940, if *any* citizen was denied constitutional rights? "We have never been willing to face this problem," she wrote, "to line it up with the basic, underlying beliefs in Democracy." Racial injustice and prejudice anywhere blemished American values everywhere! "No one can honestly claim that . . . either the Indians or the Negroes of this country are free." By denying minorities full equality, Eleanor declared, "we do not completely practice the Democratic way of life" or a "Christ-like way of living." Her words sent detractors into apoplexy.

Eleanor's travels heightened her awareness of discrimination. Clearly, the military enforced dual standards in training, housing, recreation, and assignment of troops. African Americans had limited opportunities for socializing off base because of segregated bus systems and the antagonism of citizens in nearby towns. Eleanor barraged Gen. George Marshall's office with so many "passionate missives" on rectifying these injustices that Marshall assigned two staff members to process them.

Soldiers and sailors wrote home about the discrimination; mothers appealed to Eleanor to do something for their sons. Mrs. Roosevelt confronted Claude Swanson, secretary of the navy: would he explain why 95 percent of African Americans wearing a navy uniform worked in kitchens or did custodial work? Eleanor dismissed his lame answers: "Well, that's just the way things have been" and "Negroes are not comfortable around water." Navy publicists crafted a talking point: sailors needed food—particularly in battle—therefore, as cooks, African Americans *were* directly involved in the war!

Eleanor aggressively pursued reports of injustice that reached her desk. Racism, she knew, did not start with drill sergeants and chief petty officers but at the top of the chain of command. Had not Secretary of War Henry L. Stimson publicly stated that African Americans "were less capable of handling modern weapons" and, based on his experience in World War I, African Americans could not become competent as officers because "leadership is not imbedded in the Negro race yet"? Stimson blatantly failed to acknowledge the promotion of Col. Benjamin O. Davis, at the nudging of Eleanor and others, to be the army's first African American brigadier general. Despite his rank, Davis could not eat in the War Department's whites-only cafeteria.

Eleanor "enlightened" Assistant Secretary of War John McCloy about de facto equality: "These colored boys lie side by side in the hospitals in the southwest Pacific with the white boys and somehow it is harder for me to believe that they should not be treated on an equal basis. . . . They get killed just the same as the white boys."

Equal sacrifice, African Americans reasoned—and Eleanor concurred—should translate into equal opportunity! Eleanor insisted that African Americans should be eligible for all military training programs.

UNREST AT HOME

Likewise, she insisted, *everyone* deserved equal access to good jobs, wages, and perks at home. Thousands of African Americans migrated north and west for jobs in war industries, particularly in Detroit and Los Angeles. By 1945, some 1.2 million African Americans had fled the south, creating enormous labor shortages in the region. Michael Bess reports a typical experience: an African American woman quit her $3.50-a-week job as a domestic, moved to California, and began working as a riveter for Lockheed, soon earning $48 a week.

Reports of African American workers beaten by angry white bigots in the workplace were unsettling. In June 1943, twenty-five thousand workers walked off their jobs at a Packard plant because *three* black workers received promotions. At one rally, a speaker drew cheers when he declared, "I'd rather see Hitler and Hirohito win the war than work beside a nigger on the assembly line!" In Detroit, the United Auto

Workers union instituted a zero-tolerance policy: If white and black workers did not want to work side by side, they could find another job! Slowly, as blacks and whites worked side by side to defeat "the enemy," David Kennedy concludes, socialization and shared-goal commitment "sanded away stereotypes that [had] ossified under segregation."

Detroit earned the designation "the arsenal of democracy." If blacks worked in defense industries, Eleanor insisted, they had the right to live in government housing for workers. Klan members in Detroit disagreed and swore to keep African Americans, war or no, "in their place." For some two hundred thousand African Americans, "their place" was Paradise Valley, a sixty-block area that was certainly no paradise!

When black families moved into Detroit's new Sojourner Truth Housing Project, violence erupted. On June 20, 1943, mobs attacked individuals. In a thirty-six-hour period, thirty-three people were killed—twenty-five of them African Americans; seventeen were shot by police and more than seven hundred injured as the result of fighting between citizens, white and black. Of the thirteen hundred arrested, 85 percent were African American. Calm was restored only after FDR sent in six thousand federal troops to patrol the streets; the troops stayed for six months.

Needing a scapegoat, southern newspapers and politicians, even a few of FDR's aides, blamed Eleanor's "agitating" for the racial unrest. One editorial indicted her, "It is blood on your hands, Mrs. Eleanor Roosevelt. More than any other person, you are morally responsible for those race riots in Detroit." Jeff Davis of Memphis blasted Eleanor: "You have been personally proclaiming and practicing social equality at the White House and wherever you go" and a riot resulted! "Your unwise talks and actions" inflamed racial unrest far beyond Detroit. Davis demanded, "Why don't you stay home and quit talking and writing on everything under the sun?"

FDR, his aides, and Democratic Party leaders, anxious about the 1944 election, began to sweat: Would the riot and unrest elsewhere depress the critical African American vote in northern cities?

Concluding the "Negro situation was too hot," FDR dispatched Eleanor to the Pacific, according to press releases, "to visit the troops." Wearing a Red Cross uniform—which angered critics—and traveling alone, Eleanor saw segregated housing, segregated mess halls, segregated recreation halls, and segregated hospital tents. Even segregated blood plasma!

Racists went ballistic upon seeing newspaper pictures of the First Lady holding the hands of wounded African American soldiers! However, in other homes, those pictures were cut out of the paper, framed, and hung on walls or pressed into family Bibles. "This," hundreds of African American parents told friends, "is Mrs. Roosevelt with *my son!*"

Eleanor's island-hopping through the Pacific theater of operations, despite opposition by the military brass, particularly Gen. Douglas MacArthur, turned into a public relations grand slam. Although she lost more than thirty pounds on the trip, her energy seemed boundless.

One particularly hot day as Eleanor walked into a tent filled with African American soldiers, she paused and listened to one soldier's bitter rant about the treatment he had received as a GI. Noticing the ice-cream cone he was enjoying, Eleanor stepped forward and asked if she could "have a taste." Before he could answer, she took the cone from his hand and took a bite. Then she handed back his cone. "That is good ice cream."

None of the soldiers could believe what they had seen: the First Lady taking a bite from a black man's ice-cream cone. Who would believe them if they wrote home about it? Racists and segregationists, had they heard of the incident, would never have believed Eleanor would have "stooped that low." Calvin Johnson, the astonished soldier, later wrote, "Mrs. Roosevelt made me feel like a man again, I will never forget her."

Some Southerners expressed relief when FDR died in April 1945. Now "that woman" would be out of the White House! Surely Harry Truman, from Missouri, would be more sensitive to southern concerns. Surely Bess Truman would not be gallivanting about with black soldiers and friends, sticking her nose where it did not belong!

Ironically, FDR's death freed the widow Roosevelt to become more involved in seeking justice and racial equality and to speak her mind! She was no longer *Mrs. Franklin D. Roosevelt.* She would be just Eleanor! In a press conference aboard ship as she sailed to Europe in January 1946 to begin her work at the United Nations, she told reporters and critics, "For the first time in my life I can just say what I want. For your information it is wonderful to be free."

WHEN THE WAR IS OVER

Eleanor expected that the war would initiate enormous political, social, and spiritual shifts. On radio, in her columns and lectures, over meals with leaders, she warned that democracy might wax or wane, in light of how Americans facilitated full opportunity for *all* Americans in a postwar economy. When benefits were provided to veterans, Eleanor insisted, *all* veterans must have equal access.

Critics quickly discovered that Eleanor's influence would continue. Nudged by her friend Walter White, she urged President Truman to establish a permanent Fair Employment Practices Commission to address widespread postwar economic injustice, experienced most egregiously across the south. She persuaded him to address the annual conference of the NAACP—the first US president to do so.

Southerners wanted to believe that race relations would revert to prewar standards. Theodore Bilbo and others of his ilk were too blinded by racism to perceive that FDR's agenda—to win the war—had permanently challenged if not reframed "attitudes outside of the South toward public racism."

Nora Bayes's popular song from World War I, "How Ya Gonna Keep 'em Down on the Farm (After They've Seen Paree)?" now characterized southern paranoia. Black men who had fought the Nazis, Italians, or Japanese were not coming home to put up with the entrenched racism of the past. One black GI angrily swore an oath: "I spent four years in the Army to free a bunch of Dutchmen and Frenchmen, and I'm hanged if I'm going to let the Alabama versions of the Germans kick me around when I get home. No siree-bob! I went into the Army a nigger; I'm comin' out a *man!*"

Many speculated on where violence would break out next. Birmingham? Memphis? Atlanta?

In February 1946, racial tensions erupted in Columbia, Tennessee, a town of eight thousand people south of Nashville. James Stephenson, a black navy veteran, had accompanied his mother to the Castner-Knott Department Store to pick up a repaired radio. When Mrs. Stephenson disputed the cost, the clerk became verbally abusive. James Stephenson intervened. A scuffle broke out, and the clerk fell through a plate glass window. Both Stephensons were arrested, jailed, and released after paying a $50 fine. James, however, was arrested again after the clerk's father charged that Stephenson had intended to murder his son. African Americans began to fear a lynching.

That night, four police officers walked into the African American business district and were killed in an ambush. Governor Jim Nance McCord ordered the Tennessee Highway Patrol into Columbia. Patrolmen fired randomly into homes and stores, stole cash and valuables, and confiscated weapons. One hundred African Americans were arrested and then denied bail and an opportunity to speak with an attorney.

On February 28, jailers claimed that prisoners had grabbed their weapons and began shooting. A white jailer, "acting in self-defense," he said, shot two prisoners dead and wounded another. To no one's surprise, an all-white jury refused to convict the police officers; however, twenty-five African Americans were tried for shooting at police officers.

Thurgood Marshall, the future Supreme Court justice, launched an intense investigation as attorney for the NAACP. Eleanor cochaired the National Committee for Justice in Columbia, Tennessee, to draw attention to the debacle and raise funds for the defense.

Marshall, believing the incident merited national conversation, asked his friend Eleanor to chair a new committee to investigate the violence. Eleanor focused on *what* started the riot rather than *who* started it, but she failed to persuade the US Justice Department to scrutinize the case put forward by white local officials.

DESEGREGATION AND THE DEMOCRATIC PARTY

On July 28, 1948, in a presidential election year, President Truman, when he realized Congress would never pass legislation to desegregate the army, signed Executive Order 9981, banning discrimination in the military. Eleanor had supported the president's vision of a desegregated military. Weeks later, segregationists led by Governor Strom Thurmond of South Carolina stormed out of the Democratic National Convention in reaction to the strong civil rights plank in the party platform. Thurmond blustered that there were not enough soldiers in the army to force integration on the south.

Weeks later, the so-called Dixiecrats nominated Thurmond to mount a third-party campaign against Truman. This, Eleanor feared, sealed Truman's defeat. Thurmond knew he could not win the election, but he could strip southern electoral votes from Truman, to push the election into the House of Representatives. Only 350 "Give 'em hell, Harry!" speeches on the whistle-stop campaign circuit and the large turnout of black voters in northern states secured his election. On one spectacular afternoon, October 29, 1948, Truman addressed sixty-five thousand people in Harlem. The crowd went quiet after thunderously welcoming the candidate to the podium. Philleo Nash, who had shaped six revisions of the speech, watched the audience nervously. Eleanor Roosevelt, sitting in the audience, noticed the shift in the mood of the crowd. Nash recalled, "Almost everybody in the crowd was praying, either with his head down or actually was kneeling. . . . They were praying for the

President, and they were praying for their own civil rights." A political rally had metamorphosed for many into "a religious occasion."

While southern senators like Willis Robertson of Virginia insisted that "separate but equal" worked, Eleanor, after visiting hundreds of African American schools across the South, dismissed the phrase as ridiculous. Any southern county or city school for whites was far superior to facilities for African Americans. Eleanor, as a former teacher, judged southern schools to be separate *and definitely unequal.* Eleanor was incensed that African American schools lacked basic resources, such as up-to-date textbooks, blackboards, attractive playgrounds, libraries, supplies, and toilets; moreover, she found African American teachers' compensation scandalous.

In 1954, the US Supreme Court unanimously ruled in *Brown v. Board of Education of Topeka* that "separate but equal" schools were unconstitutional. That decision produced a political tsunami! By so ruling, the court decreed that "liberty and justice for all" were more than words in the Pledge of Allegiance. No longer would prejudicial traditions douse the dreams of Americans like Eleanor's friend Pauli Murray, an African American who had been denied admission to graduate school at the University of North Carolina, then one of the most progressive universities in the South. Education, Eleanor believed, was an essential element in the "holy trinity" of commitments: equal education, housing, and employment. She celebrated the *Brown* ruling, while southern Democrats dug in to fight implementation for years.

Eleanor admired the courage of the nine African American students who enrolled at Little Rock Central High School in Arkansas in September 1957. However, the venom of white women, presumably Christians, who taunted those students horrified Eleanor:

> I think what most of us remember most vividly . . . is the pictures we saw in our newspapers, pictures which gave us a tremendous shock when we realized what ugliness and degradation mass fear could bring out of human beings.
>
> Grown women wanted to kill one poor little nine-year-old girl, one of the children going into the Little Rock school. The cold fact is hard to believe that anywhere in our country women would be screaming for the death of a child because she was going into a white school.

Southerners feared the federal government would force local school boards to implement the ruling. Eleanor, although describing herself as a "tired old woman," could not turn down invitations to speak in support of the decision. Her presence attracted media attention and donors' dollars and challenged some Christians to think more responsibly and act justly.

Paul Butler, chair of the Democratic National Committee, fearing that racial issues would again split the party, appointed Eleanor to chair platform committee hearings on civil rights. Southern delegates arrived at the 1956 Democratic National Convention ready to brawl! From long experience chairing UN committees with unruly Russians, Eleanor moderated vigorous debate but pointedly reminded delegates that the issue had been settled by the Supreme Court. Democrats, she insisted, had an incredible responsibility to implement that mandate in Detroit, Michigan; Round Top, Texas; and Landry, South Carolina. Voters, if educated, Eleanor insisted, would respond positively to the changes, particularly with supportive preaching from clergy.

She helped craft a platform plank condemning the use of force in integrating schools and reaffirming the Supreme Court's position as the nation's third but equal branch of government. With Eleanor's nudging and behind-the-scenes persuasion, the plank passed in committee by one vote. On the convention floor, Eleanor lobbied vigorously for its adoption.

As chair, Eleanor invited a then little-known black minister to open a committee session with prayer. Then she asked that pastor to testify about his work in Montgomery, Alabama. He testified: "In seeking a strong civil rights plank we are not seeking to defeat or humiliate the white man, but to help him as well as ourselves. The festering sore of segregation debilitates the white man as well as the Negro." Thus, Eleanor introduced to the national press and Democratic delegates the courageous Rev. Dr. Martin Luther King Jr., pastor of Dexter Avenue Baptist Church in Montgomery.

COURAGE AND COMMUNISM

Critics had long assailed the Highlander School in Grundy County, Tennessee, as "a communist front" for its commitment to racial justice. Anyone attending the school's workshops, southern racists insisted, was either "a damn communist" or a "fellow traveler." In June 1958, when Highlander announced that Eleanor would speak, the KKK boasted that she would never deliver the lecture "even if," according to FBI files, "they had to blow the place up."

In those days, former First Ladies did not have Secret Service protection. FBI agents informed Eleanor of a credible threat and urged her to cancel. Eleanor thanked the agents for their concern but proceeded to Nashville, where Septima Clark, a black activist, met her with a car. As the two women drove south through the night, both were aware of the danger. (A local historian claims that Eleanor placed a loaded revolver on the front seat—a gun she knew how to use!) Nothing and nobody, not even ill-mannered southern hoodlums, would prevent her from speaking. Indeed, she spoke the next morning at Highlander.

Eleanor waved aside as "nonsense" allegations that Highlander was a hotbed of communism. Southerners, she groaned, jumped to brand good individuals such as Martin Luther King Jr., James Bevel, John Lewis, and Rosa Parks as communists because they had attended or taught a Highlander workshop. Joseph Lash commented that these attacks "upon Eleanor for her racial views were more savage, systematic, and unrelenting than any she had ever encountered."

Eleanor's friend, theologian Richard Niebuhr, thought courage to be "the primary test of prophesy" and spiritual vitality. Because Eleanor spoke and wrote frequently and poignantly about civil rights, newspapers chose not to run particular columns by her on race or severely edited them; other newspapers, particularly those owned by Republicans, dropped her column. Months before she died, Eleanor reviewed her writing career: "I have learned over and over to my cost, one needs only to be outspoken about the unfair treatment of the African American to be labeled 'Communist.'" Yet, speaking out was "the only honorable and civilized course for a citizen of the United States" *and* for a citizen of God's kingdom! Eleanor only regretted that the loss of income reduced her charitable giving.

Eleanor wrote thousands of letters in response to individuals who challenged her sanity or wisdom or who blasted her "do-gooding" for the African American. "You must remember," she reminded A. A. Tiscornia in 1950, "that there are more people who are not white in this world than there are white." She repeatedly explained, following the passage of the United Nations Universal Declaration of Human Rights, that *everyone* had a responsibility to oppose racial injustice. In a speech to the Americans for Democratic Action in 1950, Eleanor "laid it on the line."

We have to make sure . . . that we have civil rights in this country. There was a time when we could look on that question as a purely domestic one—that we could take all the time we wanted to educate ourselves to solve the problem. It isn't any longer a domestic question—it's an international question. It is perhaps the question which may decide whether democracy or communism wins out in the world.

Eleanor knew that individuals—and nations—were watching how the United States dealt with racial injustice. Only a few Americans got up every morning and went to a UN meeting or session aware that if the Russians, Ukrainians, or Poles were recognized to speak, they would once again lambaste the United States for its racism and violence against African Americans. Repeatedly, Eleanor endured Andrei Vyshinsky's or Alexei Pavlov's long-winded tirades detailing injustice in the South and the behaviors of the Klan. For Eleanor the allegations were like listening to a stuck needle on a phonograph record. When Eleanor tired of the rhetoric, she interjected that "while the United States is not perfect," conditions in the South "are decidedly improving year by year." Would the Russians allow conditions in their country to be examined by UN representatives and American reporters?

Slowly perhaps, but changing.

COMMITTED TO THE END

Though hampered by illness in the early 1960s, Eleanor continued to speak out on civil rights. She opened her mind, her heart, her time, her address book, and her checkbook to support the civil rights movement. Through her speeches, newspaper columns, and magazine articles, Eleanor attempted to stretch readers' thinking on race.

Had Eleanor been healthy, she might well have traveled south to ride the buses and march beside the young folks and link arms with Episcopal clerics, Jewish rabbis, and Catholic nuns marching for racial justice. She was appalled by the beating and arrests of the courageous Freedom Riders in Alabama and Mississippi in 1961—more than four hundred were jailed and one of their buses was burned. Some northern liberals groused that the riders were "going too far, too fast" or "just agitatin'." Southerners denounced the Freedom Riders as northern agitators or, worse, damned communists!

Eleanor declared her admiration for the group, saying: "Never has a tinier minority done more for the liberation of a whole person than these few youngsters."

Allida Black reports that Eleanor "was so incensed by the violence" against civil rights activists that she left her sickbed to chair the Commission of Inquiry into the Administration of Justice in the Freedom Struggle hearings. The panel examined the conduct of federal judges who tried civil rights activists across the South. Eleanor named names. Her anger at the judicial conduct of Mississippi Judge Ellis sent her to the Oval Office for regress. She wanted to see some of the "bold leadership" John Kennedy had promised during the election of 1960 when she campaigned for him. She, as chair, urged the media to pay closer attention to the violence.

In hearings, when officials of the Kennedy administration pressed the Commission of Inquiry to go into executive session, thereby denying the media and the public access to the facts, Eleanor angrily snapped, "I did not come here to equivocate, [but] to get at the truth." She later characterized the hearings as "one of the most difficult experiences I have ever been through." She confessed in her last book, "I found it difficult—and intolerably painful—to accept the fact that [these] things could happen here in these United States. This was the kind of thing the Nazis had done to the Jews of Germany."

The testimony of racist behaviors she heard convinced her that the nation needed moral renewal. She longed for a day when "whites only" signs would be branded not only un-American but unchristian! Eleanor would have appreciated the wording of Galatians 3:28 in the Weymouth New Testament: "In Him the distinctions between Jew and Gentile, slave and free man, male and female, disappear; you are all one in Christ Jesus." She longed for the disappearance of all the distinctions between African American and Caucasian, powerless and powerful, rich and poor. How, she wondered, could churchgoing, Bible-reading folks not commit themselves to seeing it become reality? Why did they not hear this message from the pulpits of the churches they attended?

Given the state of racial inequality at the time of her death in 1962, could she have imagined a January day in 2009 when an African American man would raise his right hand and swear the oath of office she had heard Franklin swear four times? Or All Saints' Day in November 2015, when her Episcopal Church would consecrate Michael Curry, a black southern bishop, to be presiding bishop of the denomination?

In an interview in 1987, Supreme Court justice Thurgood Marshall contrasted the Roosevelt attitudes toward civil rights. He blasted FDR: "He was [not] worth a damn so far as Negroes were concerned." Well, the interviewer followed up, what about Mrs. Roosevelt? Eleanor, Marshall assured the reporter, *never* failed to come through.

9

One Nation under God

Eleanor and Religious Diversity

> I would like to make it clear once and for all that I believe in the right
> of any human being to worship God according to his conviction, and I
> would not want to see this right taken away from anyone.
> — Eleanor Roosevelt (MD, July 8, 1949)

In October 1952, Mrs. Roosevelt enthusiastically endorsed National
Bible Week, whose organizing committee urged Americans—"us all,"
in Eleanor's words—to pray and meditate on Scripture. The committee hoped that the effort would "plant in the hearts of everyone a belief
and faith in God and a thankfulness for our American way of life"
(MD, October 8, 1952) in response to growing anxiety about Communist infiltration in American government and society.

It was this same juxtaposition with so-called godless communism
that motivated President Eisenhower and Congress to add the phrase
"under God" to the Pledge of Allegiance in 1954 and make the national
motto "In God We Trust" two years later. The God referenced in
such civil affirmations was as nonsectarian as the deity had ever been
in America's history. Though the term is common today, the idea of
Protestants, Catholics, and Jews sharing a common "Judeo-Christian"
tradition dates back only as far as the Roosevelt administration, when
Franklin framed the brewing global conflict as a confrontation between
"religion" and "irreligion." The United States' battles, both hot and
cold, against fascism and then communism had the ironic effect of
tempering relations between religious sects in the United States as
entrenched anti-Judaism and anti-Catholicism were, to an extent, overcome by opposition to a greater, external enemy.

The idea that Judeo-Christian values were essential to being an
American made church attendance, mealtime prayers, and attention

to the Bible not just marks of religiosity but also signs of patriotism. But the former First Lady would never succumb to a self-righteous or superficial definition of either her Christian faith or her commitment to democracy. Eleanor's sensitivity to ecumenism, pluralism, and the separation of church and state made a powerful—and controversial— statement in the face of so many who would conflate Christianity and Americanism.

CHRIST WAS NOT A CAPITALIST

Eleanor affirmed the popular notion of America as a "Christian coun- try," but to her this was not a justification for circling the wagons in exclusion or nativism. The context of her assertion that "the basis of our democratic life lies in Christian religion" (MD, February 16, 1951) was an appeal for Americans not to give in to the fear that Senator Joseph McCarthy and other conservatives were mongering. Eleanor was horrified by McCarthy's crusade to expose communist sympathiz- ers in the US government, particularly through distortions and lies. She found his bullying unchristian and morally repugnant. McCarthy, Eleanor pointed out, mocked the commandment "Thou shalt not bear false witness against thy neighbour" (Exod. 20:16). Surely McCar- thy, a Catholic, could recall that according to Jesus, all people are our neighbors.

During the hysteria of the McCarthy era, as Americans were branded communists, fellow travelers, or pinkos—their livelihoods ended, their reputations shredded, or their political careers stopped, as happened to Rep. Helen Gahagan Douglas, Eleanor's close friend— Eleanor questioned if the self-appointed patriot vigilantes had read the New Testament (MD, February 8, 1949). Defending one University of Washington professor, Eleanor minced no words:

> Our main danger at the present time lies in the tendency to label Communist all opinions that are new and, therefore, strange and considered somewhat radical. There have been a number of people recently who have been accused of Communist tendencies. Yet, what they said was no more Communistic than some of the teach- ings of Jesus Christ. (MD, February 8, 1949)

In response to readers' backlash over those comments, Elea- nor pointed to the description in Acts of the experience of the early

Christians: "And all that believed were together, and had all things common" (Acts 2:44). Imagine *no* private ownership. Moreover, the early Christians had "sold their possessions and goods, and parted [gave] them to all men, as every man had need" (v. 45). As a result, there were no financially needy individuals in that early church. Those words, Eleanor enjoyed pointing out, were from the Bible, *not* Karl Marx!

Eleanor struggled to be civil after learning that a member of the textbook committee of the Indiana State Board of Education had recommended that the tales of Robin Hood be banned from school and public libraries. Robin stole from the rich and gave to the poor—he redistributed wealth—an action some Hoosiers believed was a basic tenet of communism. After noting that her children and grandchildren, and the underprivileged boys of Wiltwyck School, found great delight in such tales, she discounted such narrow thinking and challenged her readers' assumptions about Christianity's presumed capitalist bias:

> I seem to remember in a book that many of us revere . . . a story about the young man who asked the Master how he could be saved and that the answer was, "Give all your worldly goods to the poor." Is that story looked on as Communist today? (MD, November 21, 1953)

Eleanor rolled her eyes on learning that this same official also wanted stories of Quakers expunged from Hoosier curriculum because Quakers were pacifists. Well, Eleanor noted, "If Robin Hood and the Quakers are to be classed as Communist influences, we are living in a topsy turvy world!" How long before Jesus will be banned in Indiana? she may have wondered.

Eleanor's Jesus would not be domesticated into a flag-waving apologist for the American Way. She asked Americans who prized capitalism and consumerism, especially the private ownership of land and personal property, why Jesus had never accumulated many possessions. Why did Jesus' friends bury him in a borrowed tomb? Jesus thought that confidence in money was a barrier to spiritual growth. Eleanor agreed. Jesus' response to the *rich* young ruler was radical: "Go and sell that thou hast, and give to the poor, and thou shalt have treasure in heaven: and come and follow me" (Matt. 19:21). Eleanor would have had difficulty with many today who sanctify American capitalism at the expense of the marginalized and the poor, and the wealthy advocates of the prosperity gospel, as well as those who preach a gospel of intolerance and dismiss tolerance as political correctness.

ECUMENICAL ELEANOR

Eleanor believed that devotion to Jesus Christ should make us more inclusive, not less. In her 1940 book, *The Moral Basis of Democracy*, Eleanor argued that "differences in religious belief are inherent in the spirit of true Democracy." The evolution of thirteen colonies—the Anglicans of South Carolina and Virginia, the Baptists of Rhode Island, the Puritans in Massachusetts, the Catholics of Maryland—into the *United* States took argument, reasoning, and tolerance. Eleanor explained, "Because so many beliefs flourished side by side" in those early days, "we were forced to accept the fact that 'a belief' was important, but 'what belief' was important only to the individual concerned." Thus, a century and a half later, she argued, "We must acknowledge that the life of Christ was based on principles which are necessary to the development of a Democratic state."

The principles of which Eleanor spoke, of course, were not capitalism and dogmatism, but tolerance and care for the well-being of all, in essence, answering that ancient question, "Am I my brother's keeper?" Not that this was an easy task. One recalls the latent anti-Semitism Eleanor consciously confronted in order to work for the good of Jewish refugees during and after World War II. In the 1920s, Eleanor abandoned layers of anti-Catholic prejudice while working in the campaigns of Alfred Smith, an Irish Catholic, for governor of New York and for president in 1924 and 1928. Because of virulent attacks alleging that Smith would be controlled by the pope and supported ending Prohibition, Smith lost the Democratic presidential nomination in 1924 and (after securing the nomination in 1928 with FDR's help) lost to Herbert Hoover in a landslide. The Ku Klux Klan, a political force in the late 1920s across the South and in Indiana, grew in popularity as it demonstrated against Smith, fanning strong prejudice against Catholics—particularly immigrants—as well as Jews and Negroes. The rabid prejudice and crassness of campaign materials targeting Smith's religion incensed Eleanor.

As many Americans embraced ecumenism in the 1950s, Protestant, Catholic, and Jew began to enjoy near-equal status in the US religious landscape (though John F. Kennedy received a degree of the same treatment as a Catholic presidential candidate that Al Smith had thirty years prior). The National Council of Churches of Christ formally organized in 1950 as a partnership of many Christian denominations, and the organization's United Church Women sponsored and grew the World Day of Prayer, a decades-old observance that Eleanor repeatedly championed. This annual observance called people "all over the world" to pray collectively on a particular day for peace, understanding, and goodwill. In calling attention to the event in 1944, Eleanor expressed delight that "the day will be observed in 10,000 places in the United States and in over 50 countries around the world." Women who spoke many languages and identified with many religions prayed "for a world in which justice and right shall prevail" (MD, February 24, 1944).

By 1956 the World Day of Prayer's global initiative had expanded to 134 countries, and Eleanor celebrated the wide variety of faithful voices featured, including Christians of various ethnic origins. That year the official service came from the Cook Training School for Indian Christian Leaders, Phoenix, Arizona. In her "My Day" column, she highlighted portions of a prayer composed by Chief Yellow Lark, a prayer remarkably similar to the one she prayed at day's end over the last decades of her life:

> O, Great Spirit, Whose voice I hear in the winds, and Whose breath gives life to all the world, hear me. I come before You, one of Your many children. I am small and weak. I need Your strength and wisdom.
>
> Let me walk in beauty and make my eyes ever behold the red and purple sunset. Make my hands respect the things You have made, my ears sharp to hear Your voice. Make me wise, so that I may know the things You have taught my people, the lesson You have hidden in every leaf and rock.
>
> I seek strength not to be superior to my brothers, but to be able to fight my greatest enemy—myself. Make me ever ready to come to You with clean hands and straight eyes, so when life fades as a fading sunset, my spirit may come to You without shame. (MD, February 10, 1956)

Promoting the 1958 World Day of Prayer, Eleanor pointed to a prayer composed by Australian aborigine Christians:

> Most High Father God, may Your love go into all parts of the earth, and may the people of all nations learn to know your great truths and goodness through Jesus Christ, and so be able to teach their children that only through Him can the peoples of the world have true happiness and lasting peace. (MD, February 6, 1958)

Opening herself up to experiencing diverse manifestations of Christianity helped Eleanor appreciate even those people with whom the United States was most at odds in her later years.

Before visiting the Soviet Union, Eleanor assumed that Lenin's dogma had replaced religion. Homage to Lenin, she mused, mimicked the veneration of saints in Christianity. One Sunday morning in Leningrad, Eleanor, skeptical of her Russian hosts' explanations of religious freedom, slipped from her hotel to find a church service. After entering the church, Eleanor was distracted—given her lifelong experience of formal Episcopal ritual—by "people wandering in and out" of a prayer service. Persistent, she climbed two flights of stairs and walked into what she called "a full service" with beautiful singing. Eleanor paused to watch elderly Russians kneeling to pray at "every icon on the stairs" (MD, October 17, 1957). Such discipline impressed Eleanor, given her growing difficulty kneeling during the Eucharist; eventually, at St. James' in Hyde Park, the bread and wine had to be served to her as she sat in her pew.

GOD BEYOND CHRISTIANITY

Through her interaction with UN delegates, Eleanor came to appreciate prayer in other religions and spiritual traditions. She realized that ending a prayer with "through Christ Jesus, our Lord" or "in Jesus' name" could raise a barrier to dialogue. As she aged, Eleanor's prayers included rather than excluded. "I think I believe that the Lord looks upon all His children with compassion and allows them to approach Him in many ways," she concluded.

Eleanor insisted that other religions offered reservoirs of wisdom worthy of exploration for knowledge and for the nourishment of the soul. While for most Americans, "our lessons have come to us from the life of Christ," she wrote, "great numbers of people take theirs from the teachings of Mohammet or Budda [sic] or some other prophet, but in almost every case these are the teachers and the one God gives up to the opportunity to follow His plan" (MD, December 25, 1951).

She read and had respect for the sacred literature of other world religions, discovering that different sacred texts contained striking similarities. Eleanor called attention to the work of the American Biblical Encyclopedia Society to make the Torah Shelemah, a compilation of nine centuries of commentary on the Torah, available in English for the first time. This multivolume resource, she insisted, would assist scholars and laypeople to gain a "better understanding" of Jewish teachings. "It is only," Eleanor noted, "as we understand the beliefs and the religious laws by which others live that we will understand some of their spiritual motivations." Moreover, "I have read with great interest some of the books on the Hindu and Moslem religions that have been given to me in the past few years and they help very much in the understanding of the peoples of the countries where these are the principal religions" (MD, October 8, 1952).

Because UN delegates represented a rich diversity of religious, ethnic, and political beliefs, including atheism, the organization instituted a moment of silence to open its sessions. After *Look* magazine published a photograph taken during the opening moment of silence, Christian fundamentalists howled! Why no prayer at the United Nations? If the US Congress opened with prayer, why not the United Nations? Did not the United Nations depend on the generosity of God-fearing American taxpayers?

Eleanor repeatedly explained that silence is a form of prayer, pointing to the long Quaker tradition and appealing to the Hebrew prophet Habakkuk: "The LORD is in his holy temple: let all the earth keep silence before him" (Hab. 2:20). Though the United Nations was not a religious temple, it *was* a gathering committed to peace on earth. Eleanor reminded critics that delegates—such as those in this particular photograph—practiced many religions, others *no* religion. Some religions had strict rules about prayer practices, such as forbidding women to pray with men, but all delegates could stand together to silently pray or meditate.

Explanations failed to satisfy fundamentalist Christians who demanded to know what "the godless communists" were "meditating" about. Eleanor speculated, "If you have no religion I suppose during that moment" of silence "such attitudes of mind . . . may help you to greater efficiency" (MD, November 8, 1951). By way of example, she disclosed that after Russia attempted to call a vote to eject the Chinese Nationalists from the UN General Assembly, a moment of silent prayer and meditation altered the atmosphere and deflated the Russians' parliamentary grandstanding.

One writer harangued her about her tolerance of the UN's pluralism: "I have yet to hear you mention His name. Why? Cannot God's name be mentioned at the United Nations?" Scores of letters to the editor in American newspapers raised similar questions. Eleanor "took a lot of heat" over the fact that "God" was not found in UN documents. Eleanor refuted one critic:

This lady cannot have listened to me very often, since I have mentioned God's name many times in connection with the efforts made throughout the world for peace. Let me assure you that God's presence is keenly felt in the U.N. But different religions worship God under different names and in different ways with different customs.

. . . I doubt very much if anyone serving in the U.N. ever goes to a meeting without a prayer in his heart. Although God is not mentioned in the U.N. meetings as "God," you must not think He is not present there. He is present under different names, and we must respect each other's religions. (MD, July 28, 1952)

Though the United States was growing more open-minded to varieties of Christianity and Judaism, Eleanor found that most people still did not embrace the tolerance of *all* religions that she felt was so essential in a democratic society.

BATTLING THE ARCHBISHOP

In their desire to highlight America's devotion to God, many Americans failed—in Eleanor's day as today—to comprehend the First Amendment's two-pronged implications for religious freedom: "Congress shall make no law respecting an establishment of religion, or prohibiting the free exercise thereof." First Amendment debates often played out in the arena of education.

In 1949, Eleanor's opposition to public funding for Catholic schools—which she considered a violation of the so-called establishment clause preventing government endorsement, in words or in dollars, of any particular religious group—created an ugly slugfest. Throughout the summer, Eleanor waged a war of words with one of America's most prominent Catholics, Francis Joseph Cardinal Spellman, the archbishop of New York City. His Eminence was "the principal American Catholic spokesperson" and, for all practical purposes, "the American Pope." Given the size of the Irish Catholic vote in New York, Spellman wielded enormous power over the Democratic Party. Protestants were suspicious of Spellman for "his politicking, close ties to the government, and refusal to recognize the separation of Church and State," and according to syndicated columnist Murray Kempton, "everybody was a little afraid of him," particularly New York Democratic politicians.

The Catholic Church, given its burgeoning postwar parochial

school system with nearly three million students, particularly in suburban parishes, needed funds. Archbishop Spellman built or remodeled 370 Catholic elementary and secondary schools in New York at a cost of over $500 million. To subsidize parochial schools as Spellman requested would siphon billions of dollars from equally fast-growing public schools, which were essential to building a thriving democracy, Eleanor believed, by educating immigrants and the poor.

The cardinal loathed Mrs. Roosevelt because, John Cooney explained, "she personified everything that Spellman detested." Eleanor's support for birth control "grossly offended" the cardinal. Mrs. Roosevelt's views and public stature, he charged, tempted Catholic women to stray from the church's teachings against contraception. Dismissing her as a "flaccid liberal who lets emotions obscure reason," Spellman agreed with his friend J. Edgar Hoover that Eleanor was probably "a Communist dupe."

Tired of the cardinal's ecclesiastical bullying, Eleanor tackled the issue head-on in her June 23 "My Day" column, and a few more in July in which she responded to Spellman's unconstitutional proposal and its supposed justification as well as the arguments of Catholic readers who wrote to her.

Eleanor schooled her readers on the significance of separation of church and state:

> Many years ago it was decided that the public schools of our country should be entirely separated from any kind of denominational control, and these are the only schools that are free, tax-supported schools. . . . To change these traditions by changing our traditional attitude toward public education would be harmful, I think, to our whole attitude of tolerance in the religious area. (MD, June 23, 1949)

Spellman had argued that, by using nuns and brothers as teachers—and by paying low salaries to lay teachers—Catholics lowered federal, state, and local expenditures because fewer students had to be educated by taxpayers. Federal funding, he preached at every opportunity, was only fair because Catholics paid property taxes!

Eleanor quickly reminded the cardinal and the many readers who accused her of anti-Catholic prejudice that "while there probably are more Catholic parochial schools that would be benefitted if the taxpayers' money went to private schools," Protestant and Jewish schools would also benefit. "All of the people whose children attend these schools are taxpayers as well as the members of the Catholic Church" (MD, July 8, 1949). All the Roosevelt children had attended private schools, and Eleanor paid hefty taxes.

To critics who snarled that the "liberal" Mrs. Roosevelt did not want children to have religious education (a foolish allegation clearly refuted by her writings), she responded:

> I think there should be a great effort made to stress that education is not purely for material purposes, but is directed toward moral and spiritual aims and that religion plays a distinct part in achieving these ends. . . . But no school, private or public, can give any child a complete religious education. That must be done in the home, through the family and in the church. (MD, July 8, 1949)

Cardinal Spellman, unaccustomed to being challenged by a woman or a Protestant, stewed over strategy for almost a month. His Eminence took Eleanor's writing—given how widely she was read—as a personal attack. His staff prepared three drafts of a letter: moderate, firm, and tough. The cardinal took the tough draft and made it incendiary! On July 23, 1949, Spellman released an open letter to be published in parochial and select private newspapers across New York charging that Mrs. Roosevelt had "deliberately" misinterpreted his intentions and character. In a moment best described as ecclesiastical insanity (some blamed the hot weather), Spellman denounced Eleanor as a Protestant, a person, and—perhaps most hurtfully—as a mother. Immediately, Protestants voiced outrage that "some cardinal" dared imply that Eleanor Roosevelt was an "unfit mother," a legal term attached to a mother who had lost custody of her children. Protestant fundamentalists, long suspicious of the Catholic hierarchy and Eleanor, nevertheless waded in to support their "sister in Christ." Priests quoted Spellman in homilies and parish newsletters, as did Protestant ministers in their pulpits. The pastoral letter was read and reread around the world, particularly stirring angst among Vatican bureaucrats.

Some nine thousand letters (90 percent supporting Eleanor's position) overwhelmed the Hyde Park Post Office, many from Catholics embarrassed by Spellman's hysterics. Eleanor expressed appreciation for all the support she had received: "Anyone accustomed to hearing from the public knows that those who disagree usually write in far greater numbers than those who agree. In this case, however, the reverse seems to be true." Perhaps with some amusement, she commented, "I feel sure that the usual pattern will establish itself shortly" (MD, July 27, 1949).

PRAYER IN SCHOOLS

During the dustup with Cardinal Spellman, Eleanor felt it necessary to clarify that she was not suggesting that schools—even public schools—be purged of religion. Twice in July 1949 she affirmed the concept of a nonsectarian prayer, "which all children of all denominations could say in the public schools," and even declared that it "ought to be possible to read certain verses from the Bible every day. It probably would do children no harm to learn to know some of the writings of other great religious leaders who have led other great religious movements" (MD, July 8 and 15, 1949).

That last proposal—of teaching the Christian Bible alongside the sacred writings of other world religions— did not sit well with many of the same people who would support prayer in public schools, but constitutionally it would be far more feasible. Eleanor likely realized even at that time how difficult it would be to devise a truly nonsectarian prayer, particularly one drafted by bureaucrats and politicians, and by the last year of her life the courts agreed.

In 1962, prayer in schools emerged as a political hot potato following a US Supreme Court decision striking down the use of a prescribed written prayer devised by the New York State Board of Regents for all state-funded schools. Five decades later one still hears the rants, "They have taken prayer out of the public schools!" and outspoken critics still blame the Supreme Court for all sorts of maladies in contemporary society. The nation's governors piously decried the decision as "the final straw" of excessive federal intrusion. Immediately they proposed a prayer-in-school amendment to the First Amendment of the US Constitution.

While Eleanor labeled the New York prayer "innocuous," the regents' mandate troubled her. She supported the Supreme Court's ruling, noting that any individual could still pray in public school—especially before math tests. In her mind, however, it was a huge leap from *could* pray to *must* pray. Eleanor blasted political opportunists, newspapers, and radio for sensationalizing the issue:

Someone reported to me that he had heard a man on the radio in tears saying that he never thought he would live to see the day when God would be outlawed from our schools. Another told me that a Southern woman wrote to her daughter in New England, saying that she was horrified to find that the Supreme Court was controlled by the Communists and, of course, the Communists were controlled by the Eastern European Jews. (MD, July 5, 1962)

That last phrase led Eleanor to bemoan that, as far as America had come in the last few decades, "one can still find astounding beliefs about the Roman Catholics and the Jews," as well as "about what communism is and how much influence it may have in our country. And the emotional reaction to a Supreme Court decision, such as we are witnessing, seems to me to be the product of an unwillingness to read with care what is actually said and an unwillingness to look at the Constitution and reread the First Amendment" (MD, July 5, 1962).

A CHANGING AMERICAN FAITHSCAPE

One can only speculate on how Eleanor would respond to the plethora of faith expressions, religions, and spiritualities that make up the contemporary American religious landscape. Diana Eck of Harvard Divinity School insists that America is now "the most religiously diverse nation in the world," due to Lyndon Johnson's immigration reform in 1965 that dismantled the quota system and expanded immigration from Asia and Mexico.

Today, Buddhists, Muslims, and Hindus live in communities of all sizes—and serve in the US House of Representatives and in state legislatures and in the US military; there is generous variety within each religion. Eleanor was a loud advocate for immigration and acceptance of refugees, particularly children. In the five decades since her death, the diversification of the American religious scene has been swift. Immigrants brought their faith constructs with them; some modified dogma and practice to fit into the American spiritual sensibilities.

While a significant majority of Americans identify as Christians, the tremendous diversity and more broadly pluralistic mentality of today's culture would not have threatened Eleanor. While she believed that "the most revolutionary doctrine in the world was the way of life preached by Christ," still, "almost any other religion, if you lived up to the ideals of the founders, would lead you to what might be termed a revolutionary way of living." The value of a faith is measured in how one lives. Eleanor never wavered from her position in that first book, *It's Up to the Women*, published in 1933: Believers "must show by their own way of living what are the fruits of their faith," and "the reason that Christ was such a potent preacher and teacher was because He lived what he preached."

Eleanor, I believe, would have celebrated with Thomas Moore, a leading thinker in contemporary American spirituality, that given the changes in culture, "the new spirituality is a many-storied one, in which we can honor tales and share images from many traditions, even as we retain allegiance to our own." Eleanor could have quoted Jesus' words, "In my Father's house are many mansions" (John 14:2) or "And other sheep I have, which are not of this fold: them also I must bring, and they shall hear my voice; and there shall be one fold, and one shepherd" (John 10:16). Eleanor commented on overlapping threads of religious truth:

> If we believe that where men of pure heart do their work in the world, it results in the developing gradually of a pattern which is part of a master plan, then we must believe that those things which have tended to draw nations closer together to bring us more inter-communication in thought and in physical contact, must be used to develop the kind of human beings and that way of life which the great spiritual teachers of the world have preached in different parts of the world. (MD, December 25, 1951)

How might Eleanor, as an Episcopalian, respond to the tensions within the American Episcopal Church and the worldwide Anglican Communion? Certainly, she would applaud the growing inclusivity of her church, particularly the growing ranks of female priests, deacons, and bishops and the inclusion of LGBTQI congregants. After all, Mrs. Roosevelt mentored Dr. Pauli Murray, an attorney and civil rights activist who became the first ordained African American lesbian Episcopal priest. I think Eleanor would have been delighted that the previous presiding bishop of the Episcopal Church in the United States of America, Katharine Jefferts Schori, is a woman, a theologian, *and* an oceanographer and pilot.

How would Eleanor, as a New Yorker, respond—and she definitely would have an opinion—to the tempest over a proposal to build an Islamic community center two blocks from ground zero in New York City? Certainly, she would be pleased by the election in 2008 and reelection in 2012 of a mixed-race president—although outraged by birthers insisting that Barack Obama was a foreign-born Muslim, first because of the prejudice implicit in doubting the word and legitimacy of a nonwhite person, and second because of the insinuation that Muslims are not suitable leaders of this country. Christian or Muslim, Eleanor would only want to know whether a leader's faith translates into care for the world, for people who are marginalized, and for people who are poor.

Eleanor would be pleased by today's vast network of interfaith organizations and programs promoting religious diversity, understanding, and cooperation, and yet I imagine she would lament that her fellow Americans, proud as we are of our freedom and our religions, still do not seem to fully understand what our democracy means. In her final year, she called out the hypocrisy of our supposedly moral democracy's racial inequality with a roll call of cities that had experienced racial turmoil:

> The United States is the world's show window of the democratic processes in action. We know, too well, what people see when they look in that window. They see Little Rock and Baton Rouge and New Orleans. They see Albany, Georgia. They see the deep-rooted prejudice, the stubborn ignorance of large groups of our citizens, which have led to injustice, inequality, and, sometimes, even brutality.

To Eleanor, both one's Christianity and one's democracy should lead to greater tolerance. If that is not the case, Americans may not be much better off than those who struggled under "godless communism." For Americans today, her warning must be pondered in light of the rapid speed of global communication. News of an incident sparked by hatred or intolerance in Dallas or Minneapolis, Ferguson or Baltimore, San Bernardino or Orlando is transmitted in split seconds, reinforcing a reputation for prejudice and violence the nation would rather shed. Eleanor wondered in 1933 what could happen in every community "if everybody, who had anything beyond her own needs would really take the trouble to be the kind of neighbor the Good Samaritan was." If we could, like the Good Samaritan, love our neighbors, both black and white, Catholic and Muslim, capitalist and communist, we would be far closer, in Eleanor's eyes, to embodying the faith and democratic principles American Christians hold so dear.

10

Her Final Years

I don't want to end up simply having visited this world.

—Mary Oliver

The 1960 Democratic National Convention was not on Eleanor's summer schedule; instead, she planned to tour Europe with some of her grandchildren. Four years earlier, as keynoter on the opening night of the convention, the grande dame, speaking without notes, had brought cheering delegates out of their seats and into the aisles for a loud spontaneous demonstration. Newscaster Edward R. Murrow called her effort "the greatest convention speech I ever heard."

Eleanor changed her mind in 1960 after endorsing Adlai Stevenson for a third nomination. She flew to Los Angeles to serve as "drum major" for him and to slow down the John Kennedy bandwagon. She could accept Kennedy, perhaps, as the vice presidential candidate, but he was too unseasoned for the presidency. She was suspicious of Joe Kennedy's bankrolling his son's campaign, and saw JFK as a conservative who did not support the liberalism of her progressive wing of the Democratic Party. His timidity in the Senate on civil rights issues, particularly the watered-down 1957 Civil Rights Act, showed a lack of the moral conviction she would have expected from a Catholic. More disgusting was Kennedy's silence on the vicious tactics of Wisconsin senator Joseph McCarthy, also a Catholic and recipient of Joseph P. Kennedy's generous checks.

Arriving in Los Angeles, the seventy-six-year-old hit the ground replicating "almost 100 percent the frenzied activity" she had expended for Stevenson in 1956. She pitched Stevenson to eleven state delegations and made fervent appeals wherever she found delegates. And yet Eleanor was trampled in the stampede for the dashing young Kennedy. Her heart broke as he neared the magic number of delegates for the nomination. Anna Rosenberg, another delegate, spotted Eleanor with tears streaming down her face.

"People loved her but disregarded her message," Joseph Lash summarized.

In the pandemonium on the convention floor, she had an epiphany: Her day had passed. The future belonged to the young Kennedys, their agenda, and their zealous backers. Oh yes, she had called for "young voices" to emerge in the Democratic Party, but these youngsters were unwilling to wait their turn.

The next day Eleanor, "angry and disheartened," flew home. Why hang around? The Democratic Party had moved on. Elliott Roosevelt summarized his mother's last Democratic convention: The influence she had exercised as a public figure . . . counted for nothing now in the party she had served all her adult life. Her pleas had gone unheard. She had put her heart and soul into a fight for Stevenson, and she had lost.

While traveling with her grandchildren that summer, she remembered the delightful days when she and Marie Souvestre had traveled the Continent. She remembered some of the days she and Franklin had honeymooned in the same locales. How could a half century have sped by? The trip offered moments to ponder her future: How much time did she have left? What was worth fighting for?

A VIBRANT WIDOWHOOD

In 1945, many assumed that Eleanor would fade from public sight like previous First Ladies. When Henry Morgenthau reported that he had been to the White House and no one recognized him—the former secretary of the treasury—Eleanor smiled. Had he never read the words in Exodus 1:8, "Now there arose up a new king over Egypt, which knew not Joseph"? "Don't you know," she asked, "if you are out of the limelight three days they will forget you?" Before he could respond, she added, "They will forget me too." Her words may have been more an acknowledgment of her own status than an attempt to make her friend feel better.

Anna Eleanor Roosevelt flourished after she left the White House at age sixty-one—old by the life expectancy of the post–World War II era.

Just as she had reinvented the role of First Lady, she reshaped the role of the former First Lady.

Retirement had never been in Eleanor's lexicon, although at one point she thought her later years might be spent with Lorena Hickok. In those first post–White House years, she scripted a meaningful life as Eleanor rather than as the Widow Roosevelt. *Time* summarized her experience after the White House:

> In the seven years since she has become the world's most famous widow, Mrs. Roosevelt has hardly been still a moment: kind, literal, awesomely helpful and endlessly patient, she has trotted up & down the stairways of the world, year after year—straightening its curtains, eyeing its plumbing, and occasionally admonishing the landlords of those political slums behind the Iron Curtain, in sharp but hopeful tones.

As a child, Eleanor had been scarred by two negative models of aging: her grandmother Hall and her great-grandmother Ludlow. In old age Ludlow terrorized the family with her demands; she even frightened Eleanor's grandmother! Those bad memories influenced Eleanor's drive to age productively without making intrusive demands on her children.

At times, Eleanor Roosevelt conceded that her body was beginning to rebel against her appointment book. Once Eleanor had had little use for luggage that was not packed for the next adventure, whether five hundred or five thousand miles away. Travel these days seemed more draining. But travel meant usefulness. The great fear that menaced her spirit, embedded by her mother, was of uselessness.

SHE REFUSED TO SLOW DOWN

On a busy, overscheduled April day in 1960, as Eleanor headed to her hairdresser, she stepped off a sidewalk and cut between two cars to cross the street. In a split second, a taxi driver backed into her and knocked her down. When the driver got out and saw Mrs. Roosevelt on the ground, his anguish erupted. As he helped her stand, she ordered him to get back in the taxi and to drive away. Quickly, she urged, before a crowd gathered! When he asked if she was injured, she firmly told him: Leave! She realized the potential harm that could come to this young man; he might be arrested, lose his job and his future. What was a little pain, she reasoned, to a seventy-five-year-old so that a young man's life was not harmed?

Eleanor hobbled to a cancer benefit, came home to greet two dozen children and their chaperones, and *then* summoned her physician. Dr. David Gurewitsch taped up her leg and gave her a cane. That night at a large gathering at the Waldorf-Astoria, she apologized to her audience for having to sit while speaking. She told an inquisitive *New York Times* reporter she had been "too busy to think much about the injury." The next day, after X-rays, she reluctantly agreed to stay off her feet for a week. A week! Eleanor ignored pleas from family and friends to "slow down" just as she had ignored the racists' and segregationists' calls to "shut the hell up"! The simmering inequalities in the postwar world challenged her faith, mind, spirit, checkbook, *and* calendar. She brokered practical, realistic innovations and deflated what politicians packaged as solutions. Eleanor's questions, observations, and convictions still made politicians and bureaucrats squirm. Through her travels, columns, letters, articles, and lectures—and through countless one-on-one conversations—she called attention to close-to-boiling hot spots where injustice percolated.

Illness or fatigue would disappoint people and complicate her schedule. Despite her age, she kept a pace that exhausted younger activists.

One snippet from her December 1960 schedule—at age seventy-six—captures her pace: "I got home from Boston last night & Maureen [Corr] & I leave at 7 a.m. tomorrow for Ogden Utah then L.A., Palm Springs, L.A. again & home on Friday a.m. Next week end to Boston."

The Roosevelt children fretted over her workload. Her fascination with aviation and advocacy for the airline industry enabled her globe-trotting because flying increased the number of speaking invitations she could accept. Eleanor realized that slowing down would mean less money to donate to charities and also a loss in fund-raising for the agencies she supported. For many Americans, Eleanor's name on a fund-raising letterhead (as a speaker, board member, or advisory board member) was enough to open a checkbook. If she were not personally and financially invested, she reasoned, recipients of appeals for money would be less inclined to donate.

In August 1962, age seventy-seven, she kept a promise to Congressman William Ryan, a Democrat, to campaign for him in New York City. Although Ryan attempted to excuse her participation due to her recent illness and the foul weather, the veteran campaigner showed up and climbed ladders onto sound trucks so that the crowd could see her. When someone offered an umbrella, she waved it away. At one stop, after a group of children presented a bouquet of flowers, Eleanor whispered to Ryan, "You see, I had to come. They expected me." During the last summer of her life, she spoke at dozens of political rallies—on one occasion coming directly from her doctor's office. The size of the crowd never mattered to her, but the issues did.

THE SPIRIT BEHIND ELEANOR'S SCHEDULE

Her motivation to keep going was the same as it ever was, embodied in the prayer of Francis of Assisi, "Lord, make me an instrument of thy peace"—words she had framed on her bedroom wall. Eleanor's life was prayer in action. Joan Chittister, addressing the dual nature of prayer, asked, "If we thank God for the good that comes to us but do nothing to bring that same good to others, what is the use of prayer?" Eleanor would have heartily agreed. Chittister insisted, in words which could describe Eleanor, that an individual

who learns to pray with the heart of God has no patience for injustice anywhere. They see with the prophet's eye. They break down national boundaries. They transcend gender roles. They have no sense of color or caste, of wealthy or poor. They see only humanity in all its glory, all its pain.

When Eleanor closed her day praying, "Save us from ourselves and show us a vision of a world made new," she knew the world of which she spoke. Through her travels, columns, articles, interviews, lectures, and conversations, she called attention to injustice and inhumane conditions that diminished beloved children of God.

Eleanor had concluded that she could not persuade others to be merciful unless she had seen conditions firsthand. In 1961, she wrote, "My interest or sympathy or indignation is not aroused by an abstract cause but by the plight of a single person whom I have seen with my own eyes."

As Cornelius Gallagher would eulogize on the floor of the US House of Representatives: Eleanor reached "into the dark corners of this globe to comfort the depressed, to ease the pain of the suffering." She challenged individuals who responded timidly or patronized needy humans.

Even in her final years, Eleanor functioned like a John the Baptist "preparing the way" for the civil rights movement and, in time, the women's movement and gay equality movement. Eleanor never wavered from her conviction that equality and economic opportunity were first *spiritual* issues, a theme that would resound in the speeches and writings of her friend Martin Luther King Jr. and in courageous individuals, black and white, who prayed and sang, then marched and picketed and, in some cases, died across the South. As she kept watch over change in the South, she encouraged the young activist-preacher King. Eleanor and her friend Harry Belafonte raised large amounts of cash to support King's work.

On her seventy-seventh birthday, Eleanor conceded,

> I know I should slow down, but I think I have a good deal of my uncle Theodore in me, because I could not, at any age, be content to take my place in a corner by the fireside and simply look on. Life was meant to be lived. Curiosity must be kept alive. . . . One must never, for whatever reason, turn [her] back on life.

Elliott pleaded with his mother, "Restrict your activities to what you feel you really want to do," promising, "If you do, I am sure that you will be able to perform many useful services in the years ahead." Eleanor, aware of her doctor's diagnosis, realized she had no "years ahead."

SPIRITUALITY AND SENSING DEATH'S BREATH

In a life narrative punctuated by so many deaths—and persistent death threats against her—how could Eleanor enjoy life sitting on the sidelines, waiting for the end?

Many elders fear oblivion or nothingness, a reality captured in the haunting phrase, "Who will remember me after I am gone?" Many religions' tenets about the afterlife ease this fear. Eleanor, as a lifelong Episcopalian, was cognizant of her church's teachings on resurrection. As a child, she had memorized Jesus' words:

> Let not your heart be troubled: ye believe in God, believe also in me. In my Father's house are many mansions: if it were not so, I would have told you. I go to prepare a place for you. And if I go and prepare a place for you, I will come again, and receive you unto myself; that where I am, there ye may be also. (John 14:1–3)

Eleanor repeatedly explained, "I have tried . . . not to worry about the future"—immediate or eternal—"or what was going to happen."

Thoughts on her own aging were influenced by grieving the deaths of family and friends, particularly the tragic death of her granddaughter Sally Roosevelt, age twelve, following a fall from a horse in 1960. The day after Sally's death, Eleanor wrote, "There is no explanation for tragedies as we feel them in the loss of a young life, but we must believe there is a reason which wisdom beyond our own can understand" (MD, August 16, 1960).

Eleanor had to have wondered: Why Sally? Why not me?

Eleanor grieved when political leaders and diplomats whom she knew died, especially those who were co-investors in the dream for "a world made new." She grieved the death in 1961 of UN Secretary-General Dag Hammarskjöld in a plane crash in Africa, where he was trying to settle a dispute with Congo secessionists. After Pope Pius XII died in October 1958, Eleanor commented, well aware that some of her readers were less than enamored with the papacy and/or with Pius XII, "The loss of any good man, no matter what his religion, is a loss to the whole world, for there are not too many others who can exert a beneficial influence and give strength to the forces of virtues" (MD, October 13, 1958).

Eleanor gave a moving tribute at her friend Elinor Morgenthau's funeral and included it in her column:

It is always a shock when someone who you thought of as a vital living force ceases to be part of this world and moves on to whatever awaits us in the future. . . . There is great satisfaction to anyone who loved her in looking back on the full accomplishment of her life and yet there is also a deep regret that it was not her destiny to carry it on for a longer period. . . . When the bell tolls for any soul that has had a real interest in his fellow men and worked for their well-being, then I think the bell tolls for the loss that is the loss of all humanity. (MD, September 23, 1949)

Eleanor closed her column in a beautiful benediction for her Jewish friend: "We know that a loving God will say to her: 'Well done, thou good and faithful servant. Rest in peace.'"

THINKING AND WRITING ABOUT DEATH

Long before Eleanor understood the nuances of the words, she read the liturgies of the Book of Common Prayer in daily morning and evening prayers that her grandmother Hall conducted. Thus, long before

her own death approached, she knew the words from Evening Prayer,
"Make us ever mindful of the time when we shall lie down in the dust;
and grant us grace always to live in such a state, that we may never be
afraid to die."

The Book of Common Prayer offered comfort to Eleanor at important junctures in her life through its prayers for the sick, the dying, and
the dead. Eleanor overheard some variations of those prayers during
her mother's illness and dying and as the first Franklin D. Roosevelt
Jr. died.

During her illness, Eleanor may have read in her own spine-cracked
prayer book

> GOD . . . Make us, we beseech thee, deeply sensible of the short-
> ness and uncertainty of human life; and let thy Holy Spirit lead us
> in holiness and righteousness, all the days of our lives: that, when we
> shall have served thee in our generation, we may be gathered unto
> our fathers.

Given Eleanor's lifelong longing for her father—at one point asking
the Rev. William Turner Levy if she would see her father again—the
words "that . . . we may be gathered unto our fathers" must have resonated in her soul.

Eleanor, as she aged, increasingly addressed dying and death in
her writing, sometimes in response to a reader's letter or the deaths
of friends, even in recommendations of books. In 1958, she recommended to readers Gaetano Salvemini, an Italian historian. "I think
[his insights] have a quality which many of us approaching death might
like to bear in mind." Eleanor concurred with his observation, "I do
not understand why people are afraid of death. One should let people
know of such a way to die, so people should not be afraid." Salvemini,
Eleanor thought, offered the "right" approach by being ready for death
"because he had lived and loved and been loved" (MD, February 12,
1958).

Mrs. Roosevelt often recited death-themed poetry she had memorized as a child or adolescent, particularly William Cullen Bryant's
"Thanatopsis":

> So live, that when thy summons comes to join
> The innumerable caravan which moves
> To that mysterious realm where each shall take
> His chamber in the silent halls of death,

Thou go not, like the quarry-slave at night,
Scourged by his dungeon; but, sustain'd and soothed
By an unfaltering trust, approach thy grave,
Like one who wraps the drapery of his couch
About him, and lies down to pleasant dreams.

Death in Eleanor's day and social circles was an inappropriate topic for polite conversation over tea or dinner; heaven was a given. Because of her openness in speaking and writing about religious themes, Eleanor received letters with deep questions that others would have forwarded to clergy. When one reader asked what dying might be like, Eleanor acknowledged that she was curious to know "when one passes from life to death." She told Edward R. Murrow, "There must be some 'going on.' How exactly that happens I've never been able to decide. There is a future—that I'm sure of. But how? I don't know."

Eleanor was open to questions about her understanding of eternity, heaven, and hell, but of course she had never pushed the notion of personal salvation, that is, "being saved." Eleanor's understanding reflected the thinking of many Americans who attended mainline churches. Her responses to readers' questions often troubled the waters for conservative Christians and led to letters from people who felt compelled to straighten her out theologically lest she lead readers astray. After one radio interview in which Eleanor allegedly revealed that she did not believe in hell, angry Christians wrote to President Truman demanding that she be fired as a delegate to the United Nations. E. W. Vogel, from Kansas City, wrote to Truman:

> In a recent radio broadcast Mrs. Roosevelt openly admitted she does not believe in god or a hearafter [sic]. This is a god fearing country and a God loving people. And to have such a person in authority in the United Nations is a disgrace to all of us. and [sic] a credit to Communism and Stalin.
>
> It is your duty to have her removed—and at once.

Truman, a strong believer in hell who was known to direct people there on occasion, ignored the letters.

Eleanor had spent considerable time thinking about the afterlife; anyone who had experienced as many deaths as she had during a lifetime had to have pondered it; moreover, in the era before miracle medicines, procedures, and technologies, untimely death was a common intrusion. Eleanor passed on invitations to debate biblical interpretations.

"You know," she responded, "I'm really too busy. I'm interested in what's going to happen, but I'm too busy to worry about it. I'll find out soon enough."

One prepared for eternity with the Creator, she reasoned, by participating in building a just world for all of God's children, whether down the street, across the country, or beyond an ocean. At her funeral, the Rev. Gordon Kidd summarized his parishioner's faith:

> Christ's teaching on the brotherhood of man was no mere pious sentiment with Mrs. Roosevelt. It governed her relationships with all people. She was too honest and too civilized to spurn any person because of the accident of race or religion. She was a follower after the truth, and the truth which she found made her free, and others free as well.

TROUBLING SIGNS

Early in 1961, Eleanor began feeling fatigued, which surprised friends, because she had never complained of aches or pains. Some chided her, "Well, no wonder! Look at your schedule." Others urged her to sit back and take it easy. Chatting with her friend David Lilienthal, she acknowledged having observed negative aspects of aging among friends and was determined not to get self-absorbed when the inevitable irritations of older age came; no long commentaries on aches and treatments and prescriptions for her. Aches and pains could be anticipated, she conceded, but "if you pay much attention to them, the first thing you know you're an invalid," like her great-grandmother Ludlow.

So when Dr. David Gurewitsch, her personal physician, wanted her to see a hematologist, a blood specialist, Eleanor protested that she wanted "nothing to do with doctors or tests!" Finally, to pacify him, she had the tests done and then flew to Poland. Results could wait until she returned home.

The tests revealed that Mrs. Roosevelt was seriously ill. Despite her protests, Gurewitsch insisted on a radical reduction of her travels.

In a conversation with the Rev. William Turner Levy, a priest and confidante, Eleanor disclosed her diagnosis, aplastic anemia (deficient bone marrow production of red blood cells).

"Dr. Gurewitsch has told me that I have two years to live." She held up a small bottle, "This is the medicine that I will be taking. It will work beautifully—but only for two years." Sensing Levy's discomfort,

Eleanor added, "Well, that's more than many people can count on. The important thing is that I use the time well. Less important things must go by the board." Because she treasured spending time with the brilliant Episcopal priest and English teacher, Eleanor insisted they open their schedule books to block out times to spend together.

MRS. ROOSEVELT AS A PATIENT

Blood transfusions, periodically necessary, triggered allergic reactions that sent her temperature as high as 105 degrees. By April 1962, the anemia was compounded by low white blood cells. Doctors prescribed prednisone, a corticosteroid, to stimulate bone marrow and increase the production of red blood cells. That treatment fueled controversy after her death, because steroids suppress immune function.

Although she had an unshakable cough for several weeks early in the summer of 1962, Eleanor insisted on having her annual picnic for the boys from Wiltwyck School on July 6. She could not disappoint them! After the boys left Val-Kill with two bags of candy each and her promise to come to the school to read stories and bring ice cream and cake, she pronounced the day a success. That evening she consulted with thirty Democratic leaders; Dr. Gurewitsch ordered another transfusion.

On July 10, Mrs. Roosevelt informed Gurewitsch that she had had the transfusion—"2 bags full, so I should need nothing more for a long time."

Eleanor did not want a prolonged dying. On the other hand, she feared "being buried alive" and asked both Gurewitsch and Franklin Jr. to be "absolutely certain of her death before her burial took place." Eleanor stipulated to her executors, "I want Dr. David Gurewitsch or any doctor in charge [at the time of my death] to open veins to be sure I am dead, then I want the funeral as soon as possible with no embalming" and a closed casket.

She wanted to be buried *before* the press was notified. Her secretary Maureen Corr teased that honoring that request might prove awkward if she died during a grave diggers' strike, given that so many cemetery workers in New York belonged to a union. Since Eleanor, a union member herself, had rarely crossed a picket line, surely she could not cross one dead. Amused, Eleanor replied, "We must hope to avoid that calamity!"

During the summer of 1962, she campaigned in New York City

for the Committee for Democratic Voters, a reform group. Eleanor insisted it was imperative for the party's future to run "young people who will make good Congressmen," more specifically, "young people who can think for themselves" (MD, August 29, 1962).

On August 3, 1962, after a transfusion triggered a 105-degree fever, her physician hospitalized her. Any form of the word *hospital* was anathema to Eleanor, who was always focused on her schedule and deadlines—and overcommitted. Moreover, Eleanor was impatient to finish writing her book *Tomorrow Is Now*. The doctor had overruled her, insisting that Eleanor had to go "that very hour to the hospital" (MD, August 13, 1962).

A TRIP TO CAMPOBELLO

Ignoring the advice of physicians, she traveled to Campobello to attend the dedication of the Franklin D. Roosevelt Memorial Bridge spanning the Lubec Narrows in the Bay of Fundy and linking the US mainland and Canada. Too sick to attend the ceremony, she rested in the cottage she had once loved. At close examination, what she wrote from Campobello in her column for August 15 was a disingenuous attempt to reassure readers alarmed about her health: "I am getting excellent rest and relaxation in the marvelous air up here after my bout with summer virus. . . . It is delightful to be here" (MD, August 15, 1962).

Eleanor knew her illness was more than a "summer virus." By this time, doctors were suspecting tuberculosis. Although exhausted by the trip, upon returning to Val-Kill Eleanor threw herself into finishing her book; she told herself that she must not inconvenience Elinore Denniston, who was assisting with the manuscript. Eleanor summarized the trip to Campobello in a letter to Anna, "Everything went smoothly [hardly!] and while I am feeling stronger all the time I imagine it will be quite a while before I feel entirely normal." Allida Black dismisses the notion of "feeling stronger all the time." No, Eleanor knew she was dying. "Yet she so wanted to complete [the book] that she endured dangerously high fevers, tremors and persistent fatigue, a raw throat, and bleeding gums to dictate the first draft. . . . ER kept working on *Tomorrow Is Now*—even when she grew too weak to hold a teacup and her voice dropped to a whisper."

Why was Eleanor so determined to complete this book? She told

Denniston, "I have something that I want terribly to say." Black added that Eleanor fought her condition "long enough to summon the strength to issue a final call to action."

ANOTHER HOSPITALIZATION

Although her appearance shocked some visitors to Hyde Park, she camouflaged her condition. When her labor friend Walter Reuther and his wife visited, they talked about their hopes for the Kennedy administration on labor issues. Mrs. Roosevelt admitted that she would not be able to address the International Union of Electrical Workers' national convention. Despite fever and aches, on the Sunday morning of their visit Eleanor, despite her high fever, "insisted that Reuther take her" to a service at St. James'.

On September 16, 1962, Mrs. Roosevelt was rehospitalized with a persistent fever and blood in her stools. This hospitalization attracted media interest and elevated the hospital's concern for managing her care, ensuring her privacy, responding to requests for medical updates, and limiting intrusions. After eleven days, doctors ordered X-rays for miliary tuberculosis, which spreads through the body via the bloodstream. Because lab results would not be back for four to six weeks, physicians prescribed isoniazid and streptomycin, the only miracle drugs of that era; Eleanor's body proved resistant to both drugs.

Eleanor wrote to Elliott, "I am trying to live up to my regimen but last Saturday I had a set back and the old bug reappeared in my lungs and I am back on antibiotics and as shaky as shaky can be." She reassured him, "But I am sure, I'll get over this quickly." Mrs. Roosevelt was at that time chairing President Kennedy's groundbreaking Commission on the Status of Women. After President and Mrs. Kennedy sent flowers, she drafted a disingenuous thank-you note: "The cause of my fever has been discovered and I should shortly be back on my regular schedule."

On September 27, Mrs. Roosevelt, chair of a fund-raising drive for the Wiltwyck School for Boys, got Kennedy to commit to serving as honorary chair of a new fund-raising campaign. She could not die until the cost of a new building had been underwritten.

Claire S. Kidd, the wife of the rector of St. James' Episcopal Church, Hyde Park, teasingly scolded her friend and St. James' famous parishioner: "Needless to say we are keeping tabs on your progress and know that you will soon be feeling much better—especially, if you are good and obey your doctor—Are you doing that? You must because we want you back in Hyde Park soon!"

A COMPLICATED PATIENT-PHYSICIAN RELATIONSHIP

Treatment was complicated, perhaps compromised, by Eleanor's relationship with David Gurewitsch, her primary physician. Their friendship was unorthodox; in medical historian Scott Webster's assessment, "beyond the usual bounds of doctor and patient." Eleanor, after leaving the White House in 1945, had asked him to be her personal physician. Initially, the arrangement pleased her family because Gurewitsch accompanied her on international travels, taking pictures and, at times, serving as her translator. Eleanor Seagraves, a niece, disclosed that her uncles—Eleanor's sons—had "hurt her, and I think that's why maybe she became very closely attached to people like David Gurewitsch" and writer Joseph Lash.

Insiders suspected that Eleanor had fallen in love with the handsome doctor despite the seventeen-year age difference. "ER's relationship with Gurewitsch fulfilled an emotional need for her," Webster explains. She "enjoyed the devotion of a younger man with whom she felt comfortable being herself" and was devastated when he fell in love with Edna Perkel. Webster comments, "ER's feelings of loneliness, combined with her fond regard for Gurewitsch, led her to despair when he and Perkel announced their marriage date."

On February 23, 1958, Gurewitsch and Perkel were married in Eleanor's apartment; Eleanor planned the ceremony and provided the reception! The newlyweds and Mrs. Roosevelt soon jointly purchased a property at 55 East 74th Street in New York City. Although living on separate floors, they often ate and socialized together. Mrs. Gurewitsch defended the relationship between her husband and Mrs. Roosevelt. "It is not unusual for a vigorous older woman to be attracted to a younger, handsome man. Their relationship made her feel alive, womanly. She could love this man because he could be trusted to keep within the bounds of an idealized love."

Dr. Gurewitsch's objectivity was influenced, if not impaired, by his idealization of and emotional devotion to his famous patient—and by their real estate investment. James Roosevelt in 1976 acknowledged that his mother stubbornly refused to see specialists recommended by

Dr. James Halstead, husband of Eleanor's daughter, Anna. Finally, after a consultation with Gurewitsch, Halstead—with Anna's full agreement—suggested that a "good internist" take over the case.

Outraged, Gurewitsch confronted Mrs. Roosevelt. "Jim and Anna don't think I can take care of you properly. They want me to turn you over to Dr. So-and-so." Eleanor was *not* amused. "Well, David, if you don't want to take care of me, I won't have *any doctor.*"

On the other hand, some might argue that Halstead, chief of medicine at the Metropolitan Hospital in Detroit, also complicated the family's objectivity. Gurewitsch discounted him as "perhaps a good administrator and researcher" but "ignorant of medical advances that were common knowledge in the medical profession." Gurewitsch was glad that Dr. Halstead lived in Michigan and could not daily second-guess or supervise his care.

Now, the Roosevelt children's resentment toward Gurewitsch that had been "constrained in the past could now be more openly expressed," Edna Gurewitsch reports. Yet at this stage of the crisis, the children "who had suffered him for so many years" now "could not dissociate him from their mother."

ELEANOR'S RIGHT TO DIE

Long before assisted living, hospice, and durable powers of attorney, the medical establishment interpreted a physician's role as Gurewitsch did: "A doctor's role is to preserve life and not to prolong dying." However, as Eleanor Roosevelt II concluded, it was not just Gurewitsch but the New York "medical establishment" who "could not allow a famous person to languish." Clearly, Eleanor's "wishes . . . continued to be ignored," her niece wrote. "Had she been stronger, she would no doubt have entered into one last battle: the right to die when you are very ill and ready to let go of life. She was not afraid of dying and certainly saw no sin in permitting a person who could no longer be useful to choose to let her body slip into death."

Edna Gurewitsch defended her husband: "With the diagnosis still not absolutely clear to him, he continued to pursue every avenue of inquiry." Despite differences in medical opinions, once tuberculosis was diagnosed Dr. Gurewitsch "became cautiously hopeful for the first time. He was determined to save her." Further, "knowing Mrs. Roosevelt as well as he did," he was "certain that if she knew she had a chance to live, she would grasp it." Excitedly, he spoke into her good ear, "We can cure you!" Eleanor cut him off, "David, I want to die."

In September 1962, in her hospital bed, Eleanor penned final letters to family members. Remarkably, she had kept close to most of her children's thirteen former spouses for the sake of her grandchildren. She wrote to Minnewa Roosevelt Bell—a previous Mrs. Elliott Roosevelt—"I am sorry to tell you that I had a setback of the bug I had all this summer and I am still struggling with complete weakness and I am not feeling very well much of the time." Eleanor closed the letter, "But some day it will pass like everything else."

At this point, James Roosevelt concluded his mother had lost her will to live:

> If she could no longer do the things she had been doing, she did not want to live. She told me over and over again whenever I saw her, "I do not want to be a burden to anyone." She hated it as she weakened and she could barely speak, much less write, lecture, travel, or host dinner parties, teas, and luncheons.

Hospitalization compromised Eleanor's privacy. The hospital, besieged by the media, struggled to release accurate medical updates. Aubrey Williams wrote to her about the media buzz: "Probably never in all history have so many people in all parts of the world watched to learn the latest report concerning the health of a private citizen as have watched [television] during these past few days."

Eleanor was hardly the model patient. The regimented hospital schedule, noise, and countless intrusions to check temperature and blood pressure irritated her. Having had staff her entire life, she was used to requesting, "I would like . . ." and hearing, "Yes, Mrs. Roosevelt." Eleanor refused medications, clenched her teeth to thwart nurses, spat out pills, stopped eating applesauce (once she discovered medications were in the applesauce), or secreted the medications "in the recesses of her mouth." Mrs. Roosevelt, long known to be gracious in any circumstance, now made no attempt to suppress her irritation with hospital routines. Thoroughly miserable, she told a nurse that she wanted to die. "The nurse responded that the Lord would take her in His own good time" and not until "she was finished with the work she was put on earth to do." Did she know to whom she was offering a spiritual cliché? Eleanor dismissed the admonition: "Utter nonsense."

Trude Lash, writing to their mutual friend, theologian Paul Tillich, captured Eleanor's distress: "There was only suffering for Mrs. Roosevelt from the first day in July when she was taken to the hospital for the first time. There was no moment of serenity. There was only anger, helpless anger at the doctors and nurses and the world who tried to keep her alive."

Anna, witnessing her mother's discomfort, confided in David Robinson, Eleanor's uncle, "There are so many indignities to being sick and helpless. . . . I find myself praying that whatever is the very best for her happens and happens quickly."

Long readily approachable, Eleanor now demanded absolute privacy. Clearly, she did not wish to be seen as a weak invalid.

John Roosevelt Boettiger, who had lived with his grandmother during graduate school, encountered a different Grandmere during the final weeks:

[I] found her really not wanting to receive me—certainly not angry at me nor dismissive but just not wanting me to hang around and be with her or see her in that kind of passive and helpless condition. . . . But I really had a clear sense that she wanted to make the visit brief and was finding it painful that she couldn't sustain the person that she had so long been for her grandchildren.

She explained her feelings in something of a good-bye letter to David Gurewitsch when he left for South America on a monthlong assignment on a hospital ship. "To me all goodbyes are more poignant now I like less and less to be long separated from those few whom I deeply love. Above all others you are the one to whom my heart is tied and I shall miss you every moment till we meet again."

She was not being dramatic. She had confessed to Trude Lash that there were "so few people that she really cared about." People, she had long believed, always "wanted something" from her. "But Mrs. Roosevelt," Maureen Corr had once challenged, "don't you think people love you for yourself?" Eleanor responded sharply, "No dear, I don't."

Eleanor's "No visitors!" decision angered friends who assumed that the Roosevelt children were acting as gatekeepers deciding who got in to see her. Eleanor Roosevelt could not have understood how her wish for privacy hurt friends who wanted an opportunity to say thank-you and good-bye.

HER FINAL DAYS

The elderly lady's pleas to go home were finally, reluctantly honored. Dr. Gurewitsch agreed to discharge her at night to avoid reporters. The patient grunted, "Now!" So, on October 18, 1962, the patient's stretcher was pushed through the corridors of New York's Presbyterian Hospital to a back entrance and a waiting ambulette (a small ambulance). The entourage breathed a sigh of relief for having evaded photographers and reporters camped out at the hospital's main entrance. Eleanor was driven for a last ride through Central Park on a beautiful afternoon. As the ambulance neared her residence, Gurewitsch groaned. Photographers, tipped off by a hospital employee, overran the sidewalk. The irate physician demanded privacy for his patient.

Daughter Anna intervened and allowed the photographers to get pictures. Joseph Lash captured the indignity: "she, who had had such dignity and pride of bearing was shown to the world stretcher-borne, her face puffy, her white hair straggly, her head sagging." Many newspapers, the following day, ran ghastly close-up photographs of the former First Lady. James Roosevelt labeled this incident his mother's "final embarrassment."

Being home boosted Eleanor's spirit. Realizing she had not thanked the stretcher-bearers, she instructed Maureen Corr, her secretary, "Please tell them that I think they did a magnificent job." Not merely a "good job," but a "magnificent" one!

Throughout 1962, Eleanor, "moved by a premonition that her time was ending," began sending checks "to fulfill promises and obligations far in advance of their due dates." Some covered godchildren's school tuition and others went to organizations whose fund drives she supported. Once home, Eleanor asked for one of her checkbooks and, with feeble hand, began writing checks; some checks she signed "ROSEVELT." She mailed Christmas gift checks early but ignored mounds of get-well letters, cards, and telegrams.

Eleanor had critics with long memories and a lack of social skills. One letter read aloud to family members provoked laughter:

Dear Mrs. Roosevelt—

My husband and I are conservative Republicans from Ohio. We have never really believed anything you have written or said. But I want you to know that I am praying for you. My husband is praying for you too, but he doesn't want anyone to know about it.

GATHERED TO HER PEOPLE

Eleanor's death could be described in words from the narrative of the patriarch Jacob: "And when Jacob had made an end of commanding his sons, he gathered up his feet into the bed, and yielded up the ghost, and was gathered unto his people" (Gen. 49:33).

Events unfolding in the political world that once would have galvanized Mrs. Roosevelt were ignored. In response to President Kennedy's naval blockade of Cuba, Nikita Khrushchev—whom Eleanor had vigorously debated, with Gurewitsch as her translator—"blinked" and withdrew Russian nuclear weapons from Cuba. The entire world, including individuals around Eleanor's deathbed, breathed a collective sigh of relief! When individuals tried reading newspaper headlines to her, Eleanor groaned, "Nobody makes sense." On November 4, with midterm elections two days away—the first election in five decades without her vigorous campaigning—Eleanor suffered a major stroke and lapsed into a coma.

On November 7, 1962, at 6:15 p.m., as dusk fell over the New York skyline and the smell of autumn scented the air, the heart of the Lioness of the Democratic Party stopped beating.

Eleanor Roosevelt Dies at 78

—Headline, *New York Times*

World Famous Ex-First Lady's Heart Gives Out

—Headline, *Indianapolis Star*

Thirty years to the day after FDR had been first elected president, Eleanor died at home, surrounded by her children Anna and John; John's wife, Anne; and two physicians. On the death certificate, Dr. George Hyman identified the cause of death as aplastic anemia, disseminated tuberculosis, and heart failure. Thirty days later, Dr. Gurewitsch would write to Joseph Lash, "It is really a miracle that she was able to carry on as actively as she did for as long as she did. . . . No medical knowledge is available which could have saved her."

Edna Gurewitsch described watching Mrs. Roosevelt leave the residence for the last time:

Around a quarter of nine, I saw from my bedroom window the simple casket leaving the house, it being placed into the hearse, and

Mrs. Roosevelt alone with David [being driven] away from 74th Street for the last time.

The hearse stopped at the corner for a red light. I was surprised that traffic lights were still working.

In "What Religion Means to Me," published thirty years before, Eleanor had penned words that would summarize her life's purpose:

> The fundamental, vital thing which must be alive in each human consciousness is the religious teaching that we cannot live for ourselves alone and that as long as we are here on this earth we are all of us brothers, regardless of race, creed, or color.

The author of the book of Hebrews wrote of our ancient ancestor Abel, "And by faith he still speaks, even though he is dead" (Heb. 11:4 NIV), a statement that can be said of Mrs. Roosevelt. Decades after her death, Anna Eleanor Roosevelt still speaks and prods and calls the nation to the full implementation of the Declaration of Independence. She still nudges timid individuals to believe that an individual can make a difference. Her life as a compassionate, remarkable child of God could be summarized in the words of the apostle Paul on the eve of his death, "I have fought a good fight, I have finished my course, I have kept the faith" (2 Tim. 4:7).

Conclusion

Eleanor's Legacy

In the death of Eleanor Roosevelt the world has suffered an irreparable loss. The entire world becomes one family orphaned by her passing.
— The Rev. Gordon Kidd, rector, St. James' Episcopal Church

No woman has ever so comforted the distressed, or so distressed the comfortable.

— Ambassador Clare Boothe Luce

United Nations Ambassador Adlai Stevenson, a gifted orator, faced a challenge as he approached the lectern in New York City's Cathedral Church of St. John the Divine. Eleanor Roosevelt's public memorial service had drawn ten thousand mourners and at least one cynic. William F. Buckley could not resist snarling, "Some came to pay their last respects. Others to make sure" that she was dead.

Stevenson began:

How much she had done — how much still unchronicled! We dare not try to tabulate the lives she salvaged, the battles, known and unrecorded—she fought, the afflicted she comforted, the hovels she brightened, the faces and places, near and far, that were given some new radiance, some sound of music, by her endeavors. What other single human being has touched and transformed the existence of so many others?

Eleanor had long pondered the prophet Micah's question: What does God require of humans? Attending religious services? Believing particular doctrines and dogmas? Being on the right side in denominational squabbles? No! Micah proclaimed: "to do justly, and to love mercy, and to walk humbly with thy God" (Mic. 6:8).

In an era when people sought to make their mark, make a name for themselves, or make lots of money, Eleanor spent her days *loving* mercy, *doing* justice, *walking* humbly, and encouraging others to embrace

Micah's credo. In innumerable encounters when she responded justly and kindly, only the recipient knew. Joseph Lash, her confidante and biographer, described her as "a woman of mercy right out of First Corinthians" (that is, chapter 13) and one "who achieved her greatest charge of happiness out of service to others."

SAINT ELEANOR OF HYDE PARK?

World religions recognize individuals who have demonstrated a high level of religious devotion and practice and have, to a notable degree, lived justly and kindly. Jews call such people *tzaddikim,* Buddhists call them *lamas,* Roman Catholics and the Greek Orthodox venerate them as *saints.* Protestants, however, are more cautious with the term *saint* because all believers are considered to be among the saints and, conversely, all fall far short of any saintly ideal.

After Eleanor's death, theologian Richard Niebuhr wrote to William Turner Levy, "She was a saint in both the classic and modern sense."

Calling Eleanor a *saint* will cause some readers to scowl: Saint Eleanor! *Really?* Or sputter, "But she was a Democrat" or "a liberal" or "a socialist"! Thomas Craughwell defines a saint as an individual "who tries to imitate Jesus Christ, who strives to practice the virtues to a heroic degree."

For two millennia, Christian believers have been inspired by individuals who, through God's mercy, love, and nudging, acted saintly in moments of testing, injustice, and deprivation. Medieval writers, according to Craughwell, would have scoffed at our naiveté for wanting flawless saints. Christian leaders were then "perfectly candid about saints whose early lives were far from saintly." Earlier generations of Christians could tolerate humanness mixed generously with devotion to God and humankind.

Eleanor demonstrated qualities Tessa Paul identifies as common in saints: piety, fortitude, humility, and courage. Eleanor's spirituality influenced her daily schedules, commitments, and checkbooks. Spirituality was the lens through which she saw the needs of the world and the needs of individuals. Paul suggests that "while all Christian saints are depicted in their devotion to God," each one had talent and personality, and, equally important, a personal "story of struggle."

Perhaps Anna Eleanor Roosevelt is a saint with a small *s,* although she would have vigorously dismissed such a label. Real saints, generally, respond, "Who, me?"

Reading about Eleanor's spirituality has, I hope, offered insight into how a justice-driven spirituality changes a life and the lives of those touched by that life. Hopefully, as a result of thinking about Eleanor's spirituality, readers will see that grace can work in and through *their* lives in the confluence of social, economic, religious, financial, or political opportunities often disguised as messes or catastrophes.

NO ORDINARY CELEBRITY

This post-Eleanor era is plagued by obsession with celebrities—some of the flash-in-the-pan variety, others famous for being infamous or outrageous. A rabid fascination with celebrities drives reality shows to create the celebrity du jour. Consequently, the world is parched by a critical shortage of real-to-the-bone saints, individuals who, in the words of Pope Francis on All Saints' Day 2013, "lived out their baptism" and remained "faithful to the Gospel and consistent with their identity as children of God . . . made courageous choices, at the cost of being derided, misunderstood, marginalized."

The world desperately needs Eleanors, saints whose words and lives become sticky notes on the walls of our souls, consciences, and imaginations. The world needs Eleanors to nudge us "to act justly and to love mercy" but to practice our spirituality humbly. Amid rampant injustice and economic inequality, God stirs the hearts of saints or saints-in-the-making to challenge bigotry, greed, foolishness, stupidity, and sin. Pope Francis, whom Eleanor would surely have admired, insists that we should express gratitude to God, "who has placed [such people] in our midst as contagious and living examples of a way of life and death which is faithful to the Lord Jesus and his Gospel."

Eleanor would have appreciated the writings of contemporary voices in spirituality like Joan Chittister, Brian McLaren, Joyce Rupp, Thomas Moore, Richard Rohr, Diana Butler Bass, and numerous others who are read by individuals searching for spiritual moorings in a time of social, political, and economic unsettledness.

You may have heard words attributed to Irenaeus, when bishop of what is now Lyon, France, exclaimed, "The glory of God is a human being fully alive." If anyone has been "fully alive," it was Eleanor. Cissy Patterson, publisher of the *Washington Times-Herald*, praised Eleanor: "Mrs. Roosevelt has solved the problem of living better than anyone I know."

In 1930, Eleanor was pondering writing a book about Uncle Theodore. In one draft words she used to describe him I think apply to her: "He was no amateur in life."

Given the long string of wounds Eleanor survived, her life could have turned out differently and the world would have been impoverished.

If Eleanor had died soon after Franklin or had slipped into quiet retirement like previous First Ladies, she would still have left a deep footprint from her White House years. Those seventeen years as a widow, outliving the average life expectancy of her era by five years, provided opportunities to leave a deeper, global footprint. Although she joked about her physical looks, "at present I look like Methuselah," she quickly added:

> I feel no older than my youngest friends and I am quite sure that I come through a busy day not much more exhausted than many of my friends who are half my age. There are always so many things to be done that you have not accomplished, that you are always looking forward instead of backwards and that is one of the secrets, I think, of having strength and energy. As you grow older too you find it easier to think about other people and forget about yourself and that gives you more interests and interest gives energy and the capacity to do whatever you really need to do.

As a girl memorizing New Testament verses in French, soul aching after the latest emotional wound, what did Eleanor hope for? As she sat by the hour in a cherry tree, what did Eleanor hope for? What thoughts about "someday" wandered the corridors of her imagination? What if someone had whispered, "*Someday, Eleanor, you* will be beloved by millions. *Someday*, you will make a difference in the world. *Someday*, your words and insights will be cherished. *Someday . . .*"

Eleanor's ideas still resonate. Eleanor's words will make sense to humans a century or two centuries from now.

Eleanor has no epitaph on the large, white, marble grave marker in the rose garden at Hyde Park. I would love to chisel into the marble, "Despite everything, she thrived!"

THE HUNGER TO BE REMEMBERED

Supposedly death and public speaking are the things most commonly feared. However, I believe the dominant, unspoken fear is being forgotten. With sufficient money one can, with a checkbook and a pen stroke, endow something or donate a sufficient amount to an institution to have one's name placed on a building, stadium, auditorium, scholarship, or professorship. Ultimately, few of us will be long remembered. Eventually, everyone who knew and loved us and those who hated us will die, too.

That is why I researched the lives of Eleanor's loudest critics, particularly the segregationist southern politicians who despised Eleanor because she challenged their plantation thinking. Eleanor angered the power brokers because she saw—and wanted them to see—individuals for their souls and minds rather than skin hues. Eleanor longed for them to courageously abandon soul-depleting prejudice and experience freedom from their indentured past. She wanted her critics to join her in working toward a new America that lived out the Declaration of Independence *and* the Beatitudes of Jesus.

Some pundits who bashed Eleanor obsessively had, for a time, large radio audiences, large readership for their newspaper columns, or political power. However, decades later, their names lie in the dustbins of American history. Psalm 9:6 leaped out at me after a long day of writing, and, quite frankly, questioning my ability to see this project into print: "Their memorial is perished with them."

No one today, in all likelihood, visits the graves of Theodore Bilbo, Charles Coughlin, Joseph McCarthy, Westbrook Pegler, or Alice Roosevelt Longworth. Their memorials perished with them.

Today in Hyde Park, however, regardless of the weather, individuals of all ages and backgrounds, some from nations that did not exist in Eleanor's lifetime, stand at her grave. A few have only a faint idea of who Eleanor was, informed by the string of facts in the National Park Service site brochure. Some have little inkling that the rights they take for granted were first ideas and abstractions that Eleanor championed and fought for as stated in the Universal Declaration of Human Rights.

Adlai Stevenson reminded his audience that Eleanor Roosevelt *chose* to "light candles" rather than curse the darkness. She understood that some of her dreams would be achieved only in some future day. She knew from reading the book of Hebrews that the greats in biblical narrative lived ahead of their times. Few lived to see the results of the investment of their lives.

What is said of our ancient ancestor Abel in the book of Hebrews is true of Eleanor: "By faith [she] still speaks, even though [she] is dead" (11:4 NIV). Eleanor's name remains the subject of repeated library queries and online searches. Her words, ideas, and hopes for humankind will find their way into research papers, reports, columns, sermons, blogs, books, and Web sites and will zing through cyberspace. Though dead, she *still* speaks!

All those mornings and nights when she picked up the gavel to call a UN committee session into order, few believed, fewer hoped, she could create in the diplomatic ideological chaos anything close to a universal declaration of human rights. Many nights she went back to her hotel disappointed by the session. But, after a night's sleep, she returned to that chair and gavel.

In 1933, in her first published book, *It's Up to the Women*, she wrote words that have stood the test of time. What she said of women applies to all:

> I think we shall have fulfilled our mission well if when our time comes to give up active work in the world we can say we never saw a wrong without trying to right it; we never intentionally left unhappiness where a little effort would have turned it into happiness, and we were more critical of ourselves than we were of others.

Without a doubt, Eleanor fulfilled her mission.

Notes

Front Matter

1   *In the mid-1930s* Daniel Patrick Moynihan, "Remarks," Session on the Centennial of Eleanor Roosevelt's Birth. 130th Congress. *Congressional Record*—Senate 13347 (October 5, 1984).

1   *Although it was early* This narrative is drawn from several sources, which report and emphasize different details of this gathering: Schiff, *Lighting the Way*, 209–17; Krueger, *And Promises to Keep*, 26–29; Reed, *Simple Decency & Common Sense*, 16–18; A. Black, *Casting Her Own Shadow*, 40–41, 213; Eleanor Roosevelt, *This I Remember*, 173–74; Cook, *Eleanor Roosevelt*, 2:564–65.

2   *The most important person* C. Black, *Franklin Delano Roosevelt*, 1122.

2   *If there hadn't been an Eleanor* Gottlieb, Gottlieb, Bowers, and Bowers, *1,000 Years, 1,000 People*, 43.

3   *"You must do"* Eleanor Roosevelt, *You Learn by Living*, 30.

5   *Eleanor believed lyrics* John Oxenham, "In Christ There Is No East or West," 1908; Eliza Hewitt (1851–1920), "My Faith Has Found a Resting Place"; Maltbie D. Babcock, "This Is My Father's World," 1901; Peter Scholtes, "They'll Know We Are Christians by Our Love," 1966.

6   *"Hate is strong"* Henry Wadsworth Longfellow, "I Heard the Bells on Christmas Day," 1863.

6   *"I don't want"* Oliver, "I Don't Want to Live a Small Life," 67.

Chapter 1: What Religion Meant to Her

7   *"I think anyone"* Lash, *Friend's Memoir*, 150.

7   *"Predominately a Protestant"* Eleanor Roosevelt Papers (hereafter cited as ER Papers), 1928 Campaign, File 3022, Franklin Delano Roosevelt Presidential Library (hereafter cited as FDRPL); see also Hamby, *Man of Destiny*, 383.

8   *"a woman of faith"* Elliott Roosevelt and James Brough, *Mother R.*, dedication page.

8   *"she was a woman"* Lash, *Eleanor and Franklin*, 391.

8   *"It's all very well"* Lash, *Friend's Memoir*, 245.

9   *"favorable word"* Ibid., 69.

9   *Eleanor always* Nina Roosevelt Gibson, July 8, 2015, interview.

10   *"In general, she"* Lash, *Friend's Memoir*, 243.

10   *"the greatest philosopher"* Berggren and Rae, "Jimmy Carter and George W. Bush, 615.

11   *"healthy" Christian spirituality* Benson and Eklin, *Effective Christian Education*, 10.

12   *"Many of us"* Eleanor Roosevelt, *India and the Awakening East*, 201.

12   *"Nobody can make you"* Albion, *Quotable Eleanor*, xi.

13   *Psychologists agree* Hart, Limke, and Budd, "Attachment and Faith Development," 122; Bowlby, *Secure Base;* L. Miller, *Spiritual Child*, 6.

13   *"Parenting choices"* L. Miller, *Spiritual Child*, 6.

13   *"For three years"* Eleanor Roosevelt, "Seven People."

13   *"I could not but sense"* W. T. Levy, *Extraordinary Mrs. R.*, 240.

13   *"A Christian and a Democrat"* A. Cohen, *Nothing to Fear*, 5.

14   *Years later, a grandchild* Nina Roosevelt Gibson, July 8, 2015, interview.

14   *65 percent* Orgill, *Dream Lucky*, 141.

14   *Biographer Joseph Lash* Lash, *Eleanor and Franklin;* Parks and Leighton, *Family in Turmoil.*

15   *"forbid us to be"* Lash, *Friend's Memoir*, 29; John Roosevelt Boettiger, interview by Harold Ivan Smith, July 23, 2014.

16   *"Show us a vision"* Elliott Roosevelt and James Brough, *Mother R.*, 152.

17   *"a sense of obligation"* Eleanor Roosevelt, "The Church and Youth." Lecture at Foundry Methodist Church, Washington, DC, May 24, 1942. ER Papers, Articles and Speeches (hereafter cited as A&S), 1942; see also Cahill, *Wise Woman*, 172.

17   *"paying witness"* Orgill, *Dream Lucky*, 140.

17   *"why the solution"* A. Black, *Casting Her Own Shadow*, 41.

18   *"felt a responsibility"* Lash, *Friend's Memoir*, 149.

18   *"in every situation"* Lash, *Eleanor and Franklin*, 392.

18   *One recipient of such help* *Time*, "Must This Man Go?"

18   *"great religious revivals"* Eleanor Roosevelt, *This Troubled World*, 45.

19   *"follow the life"* Eleanor Roosevelt, "Place of Spiritual Forces."

19   "When religion becomes" Eleanor Roosevelt, "What Religion Means," 324.

Chapter 2: Childhood from Hell

21   *"Mine was a very miserable"* Carl T. Rowan, draft of article, "Mrs. F.D.R. Knew Tragedy of Alcohol in Those Close to Her" (September, 1957). [Anna Halstead Papers, 1957, Box 60, folder 12, FDRPL.]

21 *"I do not feel"* Ward, *Before the Trumpet*, 282.

21 *"such a funny child"* Eleanor Roosevelt, *This Is My Story*, 17–18.

21 *"a very miserable"* Lash, *Friend's Memoir*, 108.

21 *"realize how ghastly"* Cited in Ward, *Before the Trumpet*, 260.

21 *"It is useless to resent"* Wigal, *Wisdom of Eleanor Roosevelt*, 45, citing Eleanor Roosevelt, *This I Remember*.

23 *drop her* Cook, *Eleanor Roosevelt*, 1:48.

23 *"traumatized little girl"* Ward, *Before the Trumpet*, 269.

23 *"Without the immediate"* Cook, *Eleanor Roosevelt*, 1:48–49.

23 *"Very well, but remember"* Eleanor Roosevelt, *This Is My Story*, 10.

24 *"Her father made her"* S. Williams, "Eleanor Roosevelt," transcript; see also Eleanor Roosevelt, *This Is My Story*, 10.

24 *"who looked upon"* Eleanor Roosevelt, "Seven People," 54.

24 *"acting as a gondolier"* Eleanor Roosevelt, *This Is My Story*, 8.

24 *"You're not afraid"* ER Papers, 1939, Box 3036, FDRPL.

24 *"How could a child of mine"* Lash, *Friend's Memoir*, 129.

24 *"It seemed never"* Cook, *Eleanor Roosevelt*, 1:58.

24 *"the coveront experience"* Eleanor Roosevelt, *This Is My Story*, 11–12.

25 *"You have no looks"* Cook, *Eleanor Roosevelt*, 1:62.

25 *"an impossible person"* Caroli, *Roosevelt Women*, 241.

25 *"have no right"* Ibid.

26 *"Elliott Roosevelt Insane"* Ward, *Before the Trumpet*, 276.

26 *"flagrant man-swine"* Ibid., 275, 276; see Mann, *Wars of the Roosevelts*.

26 *"Elliott Roosevelt demented"* S. Williams, "Eleanor Roosevelt," transcript

26 *"The Bible illustrated"* Eleanor Roosevelt, *This Is My Story*, 2.

26 *"abandoned the severe"* Glendon, "God and Mrs. Roosevelt," 23.

27 *Years later, Eleanor* Eleanor Roosevelt, "What Religion Means," 323.

27 *"It was something"* Elliott Roosevelt and James Brough, *Mother R.*, 96.

27 *"a day set apart"* Eleanor Roosevelt, "What Religion Means," 323.

27 *Eleanor's childhood curiosity* Eleanor Roosevelt, *You Learn by Living*, 28.

28 *"No matter what"* Cook, *Eleanor Roosevelt*, 1:70.

28 *"I slept in my mother's"* Eleanor Roosevelt, *This Is My Story*, 13.

28 *"hours on end"* S. Williams, "Eleanor Roosevelt," transcript.

28 *"My mother was"* Eleanor Roosevelt, *This Is My Story*, 1; Teague, *Mrs. L*, 151.

28 *"I fell short"* ER Papers, 1951–52, A&S, Box x, FDRPL.

28 *"feared to think"* Cook, *Eleanor Roosevelt*, 1:72.

28   *"put sugar on"*   Ibid.

29   *Anna repeatedly*   Eleanor Roosevelt, *This Is My Story*, 18.

29   *"I felt a curious barrier"*   Ibid., 17.

29   *Over time, the family*   D. Roosevelt, *Grandmere*, 61.

29   *"By nature I was"*   ER Papers, 1939, Box 3036, FDRPL.

29   *"I suppose it is"*   ER Papers, 1951–52, A&S, Box x, FDRPL.

29   *"Please Mother dearest"*   Elliott Roosevelt to Mrs. V. G. Hall, May 19, 1892, 1 Early Family Papers, ER Box 1, FDRPL.

30   *"There seems also"*   Elliott Roosevelt to Mrs. Lloyd, March 4, 1893, ER Papers, FDRPL.

30   *Elliott vowed*   Ibid.

30   *"Perhaps, in rejecting"*   Goodwin, *No Ordinary Time*, 93.

30   *"Bi-Chloride of Gold"*   Cordery, "Roosevelt, Elliott," 448.

30   *"My darling little"*   Elliott Roosevelt to Eleanor Roosevelt, October 9, 1892, ER Papers, FDRPL.

31   *He apologized for*   Ibid.

31   *Mrs. Hall groused*   Caroli, *Roosevelt Women*, 242.

31   *Grandmother Hall did not*   Papers of Anna Hall Roosevelt, 1875–1993, Box 6, FDRPL.

31   *Eleanor never forgot*   Eleanor Roosevelt, *This Is My Story*, 19.

31   *Theodore promised*   Lash, *Eleanor and Franklin*, 51.

31   *During one visit*   Ward, *Before the Trumpet*, 283.

32   *when her brothers*   Eleanor Roosevelt, *This Is My Story*, 32.

32   *Elliott tried*   D. Roosevelt, *Grandmere*, 59.

32   *After that episode*   Dalton, *Theodore Roosevelt*, 141.

32   *"hints of abuse worse"*   Ibid, 140.

32   *"I live in constant"*   Cook, *Eleanor Roosevelt*, 1:92.

33   *On August 13*   Caroli, *Roosevelt Women*, 243.

33   *"One has to pause"*   Cook, lecture, October 22, 2012; see also Graham, "Paradox of Eleanor Roosevelt," 3–5.

33   *in essence, a suicide*   Brinkley, *Rightful Heritage*, 43.

33   *"for the rest of her"*   W. T. Levy, *Extraordinary Mrs. R.*, 140.

33   *"selective forgetting"*   Worden, *Grief Counseling*.

33   *"I have a curious feeling"*   Eleanor Roosevelt, *This Is My Story*, 363.

33   *"Elliott Roosevelt Dies"*   "The Obituary Record." *New York Times*, August 16, 1894, 4.

33   *"I did want to see"*   Dalton, *Theodore Roosevelt*, 141.

33 *"simply refused to believe"* Eleanor Roosevelt, *This Is My Story*, 34.

34 *"I had no tangible thing"* Ibid.

34 *"There was no closure"* D. Roosevelt, *Grandmere*, 60.

34 *"reappeared briefly"* S. Williams, "Eleanor Roosevelt," transcript.

34 *assumptive "world"* Janoff-Bultman, "Aftermath of Victimization."

34 *As I argue* H. I. Smith, *GriefKeeping*, 164.

35 *"Perhaps she feared"* Eleanor Roosevelt, *This Is My Story*, 35.

35 *Mrs. Hall disapproved* Cook, *Eleanor Roosevelt*, 1:92.

35 *Mrs. Hall, obsessed* Cook, lecture.

35 *Her uncles* Ward, *Before the Trumpet*, 303.

35 *She emerged only* Cook, *Eleanor Roosevelt*, 1:93–94.

35 *"the grimmest childhood"* Cited in Toor, *Eleanor Roosevelt*, 26.

36 *A young girl* Eleanor Roosevelt, *This Is My Story*, 43.

36 *"When I was a child"* Draft for "Books I Read as a Child," *Parents-Children Magazine*, December 1928, ER Papers, Box 3022, FDRPL.

36 *"As you know I never"* Cook, *Eleanor Roosevelt*, 1:92.

36 *"If anything"* Ward, *Before the Trumpet*, 282.

36 *for some reason, rationalized* Eleanor Roosevelt, *This Is My Story*, 35.

36 *"a comfortable perch"* Cook, *Eleanor Roosevelt*, 1:99.

37 *three locks* Dalton, *Theodore Roosevelt*, 141; Brands, *Traitor to His Class*, 37; Peyser and Dwyer, *Hissing Cousins*, 25.

37 *"To keep my uncles"* Ward, *Before the Trumpet*, 304, 365; Cook, *Eleanor Roosevelt*, 1:517.

37 *"Whether or not"* Cook, *Eleanor Roosevelt*, 1:517–18.

37 *"I thought this"* Eleanor Roosevelt, *This Is My Story*, 29.

37 *"stern, unsmiling"* Cook, *Eleanor Roosevelt*, 1:70.

37 *"I was not supposed"* Eleanor Roosevelt, *This Is My Story*, 45–46.

38 *"Many a tear"* Ibid., 45.

38 *If Eleanor was* Ibid.

38 *"desperately afraid"* Ibid; see also Ward, *Before the Trumpet*, 291.

38 *"If she remembered"* Ward, *Before the Trumpet*, 291.

38 *adverse childhood experiences* Dong, Anda, et al., "Interrelatedness of Multiple Forms," 780.

38 *"little reason" to assume* Jung, *Sexual Trauma*, 68, 71.

39 *"any single category"* Anda, "Health and Social Impact," 14.

39 *"between sobs"* Eleanor Roosevelt, *Autobiography*, 7.

40 *"Public figures"* Chafe, *Bill and Hillary*, 3–4.

40 *"It is the way"* Eleanor Roosevelt, "What Religion Means," 324.

40 *"In a world"* Lash, *Friend's Memoir*, 81.

41 *"My aunt's feet"* Eleanor Roosevelt II, *With Love, Aunt Eleanor*, 78.

Chapter 3: Nourishing a Parched Soul

43 *"It was the first time"* Freedman, "Souvestre," 488; Eleanor Roosevelt, *This Is My Story*, 65.

44 *"better than any home"* Youngs, *Personal and Public Life*, 100.

44 *"lived in many places"* James Roosevelt and Bill Libby, *My Parents*, 13.

44 *"first time in all my life"* Eleanor Roosevelt, *This Is My Story*, 65.

44 *"I felt that I"* Toor, *Eleanor Roosevelt*, 28.

44 *Five years had passed* Ward, *Before the Trumpet*, 365.

44 *Mrs. Hall received* Cook, *Eleanor Roosevelt*, 1:82.

45 *"made to walk"* Ibid., 1:94.

45 *"she felt socially awkward"* D. Roosevelt, *Grandmere*, 62.

45 *"discovery of a new room"* Moore, "Spiritual Situation."

45 *"supreme favorite"* Cook, *Eleanor Roosevelt*, 1:114, 116.

45 *"under the loving care"* D. Roosevelt, *Grandmere*, 64.

46 *"truly unique liberal"* Ibid.

46 *To encourage thinking* "'First Lady of the World' Who Went to School Near Wimbleton Park, *Heritage* (October 12, 2012). Wimbledon Society. http://www.wimbledonguardian.co.uk/heritage/news/9979990.The_first _lady_of_the_world_who_went_to_school_near_Wimbledon_Park/.

46 *"lesbian proclivities"* Steel, "Souvestre," 727; Freedman, "Souvestre," 489.

47 *"the underdog"* Eleanor Roosevelt, A&S, 1951–1952, FDRPL.

47 *"with considerable"* Cook, *Eleanor Roosevelt*, 1:116.

47 *"to be looked down upon"* Eleanor Roosevelt, "What Religion Means," 323.

47 *"I was too young"* Ibid.

48 *"still live in"* Cook, *Eleanor Roosevelt*, 1:26.

48 *"My grandmother was"* S. Williams, "Eleanor Roosevelt," transcript.

49 *"the only way to know"* Eleanor Roosevelt, *Autobiography*, 31.

49 "We simply fell" Eleanor Roosevelt, *This Is My Story*, 83.

50 *"one talent she had"* ER Papers, Box 3058, A&S, 1957–62, FDRPL; Eleanor Roosevelt, *Autobiography*.

50   *As Eleanor and her aunt*   "Mrs. Roosevelt Talks about the Hall Family," A&S, 1962, FDRPL.

50   *"a liberal education"*   Eleanor Roosevelt, *This Is My Story*, 88.

51   *At some point*   Ibid., 89.

51   *Over that summer*   Cook, *Eleanor Roosevelt*, 1:115–16.

51   *"had her hands full"*   Eleanor Roosevelt, *Autobiography*, 33.

51   *weather made for*   Ibid., 34.

52   *"even when success"*   Marie Souvestre to Eleanor Roosevelt, July 7, 1902, ER Papers, Box 3: Family and Personal Correspondence, FDRPL.

52   *For long intervals*   Youngs, *Personal and Public Life*, 115.

52   *"I was the first girl"*   Eleanor Roosevelt, *Autobiography*, 37.

53   *"a great sorrow"*   Cook, *Eleanor Roosevelt*, 1:173.

53   *"trip brought home"*   Eleanor Roosevelt, *This Is My Story*, 132.

53   *"had its seeds"*   Toor, *Eleanor Roosevelt*, 29.

53   *"counted for much"*   Steel, "Souvestre," 727.

53   *"never turned away"*   Cook, *Eleanor Roosevelt*, 1:124.

53   *"always taken the public"*   Youngs, *Personal and Public Life*, 104.

54   *"As I grew older"*   Eleanor Roosevelt Correspondence, Moo-Mort Box 3334, FDRPL.

54   *"discouraged me"*   Ibid.

55   *"Each one of us"*   J. Morgan, "Violence Is the Dark Side," 131.

55   *"second period"*   D. Roosevelt, *Grandmere*, citing Collier and Horowitz, *American Saga*, 121.

55   *"Never again"*   Cook, *Eleanor Roosevelt*, 1:115.

Chapter 4: A Woman of Faith

57   "What did she believe"   A. Black, September 16, 2015, interview.

58   *"What you were taught"*   J. Roosevelt and Shalett, *Affectionately, FDR*, 106–7.

62   *"Dear Lord, Lest I"*   A. Black, September 16, 2015, interview.

63   *"a prayer was not"*   Lash, *Friend's Memoir*, 80.

63   *After reading*   Ibid., 80, 197.

Chapter 5: Challenged and Betrayed

65   *"very high standards"*   Eleanor Roosevelt, *This Is My Story*, 111.

65   *Alice Roosevelt, a bridesmaid*   Persico, *Franklin and Lucy*, 64.

65   *"traitors to their class"*   Brands, *Traitor to His Class*, 275–76.

66   *No one would have predicted*   Goodwin, "Most Influential First Lady," 123.

66   *Eleanor was hardly*   Curtis Roosevelt, interview by Mimi Geerges; see also J. Pottker, *Sara and Eleanor*, 101–2.

66   *"when the right time"*   Ward and Burns, *Roosevelts*, 115.

66   *"You were never quite sure"*   Lash, *Eleanor and Franklin*, 294, 162.

67   *"You may choose"*   Eleanor Roosevelt II, *With Love*, 6.

67   *before an argument erupted*   Eleanor Roosevelt, "On My Own," 69.

67   *Little wonder*   It should be noted that contrary to biographers' accounts, Roosevelt children and grandchildren agree they did not view Sara as "the heavy" in their family dynamic. Nina Roosevelt Gibson, July 8, 2015, interview; Curtis Roosevelt, lecture.

67   *"either getting over"*   D. Roosevelt, *Grandmere*, 97.

67   *"biggest and the most beautiful"*   Eleanor Roosevelt, *This Is My Story*, 164.

67   *"Poor Eleanor's mother's heart"*   Ward and Burns, *Roosevelts*, 143.

67   *"might have lived"*   Eleanor Roosevelt, *This Is My Story*, 168; W. T. Levy, *Extraordinary Mrs. R.*, 187.

67   *"devotion to the memory"*   W. T. Levy, *Extraordinary Mrs. R.*, 145.

67   *"To this day"*   Eleanor Roosevelt, *This Is My Story*, 165.

67   *"Sometimes I think"*   Cook, *Eleanor Roosevelt*, 1:525.

68   *"I was young"*   Eleanor Roosevelt, *This Is My Story*, 165.

68   *"The deep sorrow"*   D. Roosevelt, *Grandmere*, 97.

68   *Eleanor sat for hours*   Hamby, *Man of Destiny*, 46–47.

69   *Secretary Daniels*   Ward and Burns, *Roosevelts*, 202.

70   *"She never forgot"*   Ibid., 204.

70   *experience demonstrated*   Cook, *Eleanor Roosevelt*, 1:206–7. Brochure, Sara Delano Roosevelt Memorial House, New York City, May 22, 2012.

70   *Soon after the Roosevelts*   Willis, *FDR and Lucy*, 18, 19.

71   *When Eleanor was*   Elliott Roosevelt and James Brough, *Mother R.*, 29.

71   *"Franklin deserved"*   Persico, *Franklin and Lucy*, 107.

71   *As the epidemic*   R. G. Grant, *Smithsonian World War I*, 332; G. J. Meyer, *World Undone*, 705.

71   *Worldwide morbidity*   Brahms, *Notable Last Facts*, 171.

71   *"the only thing"*   Peyser and Dwyer, *Hissing Cousins*, 153.

71   *"way that my Aunt"*   S. Williams, "Eleanor Roosevelt," transcript.

72   *"The greatest hurt"*   Ibid.

72   *"I shall never be able"*   Persico, *Franklin and Lucy*, 60.

72   *"The bottom dropped out"* Lash, *Love, Eleanor*, 66.

72   *Elliott says* Elliott Roosevelt and James Brough, *Mother R.*, 29.

73   *"since discovering"* Persico, *Franklin and Lucy*, 176; D. Roosevelt, *Grandmere*, 197.

73   *"Franklin must have"* de Kay, *Roosevelt's Navy*, 239.

73   *"It became almost"* Ward and Burns, *Roosevelts*, 214.

73   *"No longer would she"* Goodwin, "Most Influential First Lady," 123.

74   *"Her life was a sad one"* Eleanor Roosevelt, *This Is My Story*, 300.

74   *"If you've never"* Curtis Roosevelt, interview by Mimi Geerges.

74   *"political partnerships"* Collier and Horowitz, *American Saga*, 292; Ward and Burns, *Roosevelts*, 214.

74   *"Mrs. Paul Johnson"* Ward and Burns, *Roosevelts*, 384.

75   *visited and laughed* Willis, *FDR and Lucy*, 12.

75   *"I doubt father"* M. Walker, "Rutherfurd," 472.

75   *under "great pressure"* Curtis Roosevelt, *WGBH Forum* interview.

75   *"Eleanor was able"* Hay, *All the Presidents' Ladies*, 116; Goodwin, "Sublime Confidence," 42.

75   *"an armed truce"* James Roosevelt and Bill Libby, *My Parents*, 101. Eleanor Roosevelt II admits that while Eleanor "remained Uncle Franklin's loyal partner," "I sensed. . . a brief sadness in my aunt for never having forgiven Uncle Franklin." *With Love, Aunt Eleanor*, 60.

75   *Eleanor declined* Elliott Roosevelt and James Brough, *Mother R.*; Eleanor Roosevelt to Harry S Truman, March 26, 1955, cited in Neal, *Eleanor and Harry*, 236; see Brinkley, *Rightful Heritage*, 595.

76   *"a return to normalcy"* Kane and Podell, *Facts about the Presidents*, 343.

76   *"He was in agony"* Ward and Burns, *Roosevelts*, 236.

76   *Eleanor carefully* Persico, *Franklin and Lucy*, 149; see also Carlson, "FDR's Loyal Mistress," 46.

76   *"You must do"* Eleanor Roosevelt, *You Learn by Living*, 30.

77   *"emerged from this"* Carlson, "FDR's Loyal Mistress," 46.

77   *some thread of deception* In 1985, Hugh Gregory Gallagher chronicled the efforts in *FDR's Splendid Deception: The Moving Story of Roosevelt's Massive Disability and the Intense Efforts to Conceal It from the Public*.

77   *Few photos of FDR* Rothstein, "Roosevelt's Legacy, Burning Brightly," C27.

77   *"Large numbers"* Binning, Esterly, and Sracic, *Encyclopedia of American Parties*, 364.

77   *"Franklin was going"* Eleanor Roosevelt, *This Is My Story*, 335.

78 *"somewhat acrimonious"* Ibid., 336.

78 *"over Franklin's soul"* Weatherford, *American Women's History*, 295.

78 *slept or stayed* Hamby, *Man of Destiny*, 101; See also K. Smith, *Gatekeeper*, 56–63.

79 *"Missy did all"* Goodwin, *No Ordinary Time*, 21.

79 *Eleanor "accommodated"* Hamby, *Man of Destiny*, 101.

79 *"We didn't like her one bit"* Hervieux, *Forgotten*, 118.

79 *over Eleanor and Sara's* Rowley, *Franklin and Eleanor*, 137.

80 *"Have something you want"* Eleanor Roosevelt, *This Is My Story*, 352.

80 *that "dirty little man"* David McCullough quoted in transcript of "FDR," *American Experience*, 1996, http://www.pbs.org/wgbh/americanexperience /features/transcript/fdr-transcript/; see also, T. Morgan, *FDR*, 135.

81 *"Remember the ladies!"* Hogan and Taylor, *My Dearest Friend*, 110.

81 *"excruciating charade"* Persico, *Franklin and Lucy*, 162; M. Leff, "Franklin D. Roosevelt," 370.

82 *no longer expected* G. Collins, *America's Women*, 357.

82 *Had Eleanor remained* A. Black in Louis Gould, *American First Ladies*, 429, 430.

82 *won the governorship* T. Morgan, *FDR*, 295; John Braeman, "Roosevelt," 3:1319.

83 *Reporters seeking comment* Lash, *Eleanor and Franklin*, 320.

83 *"better than anything"* Cook, *Eleanor Roosevelt*, 1:399.

84 *"I cannot say"* Eleanor Roosevelt, *This I Remember*, 74–75.

85 *"I knew he was"* Ibid., 76.

85 *"I'll just have to"* A. Black, *Casting Her Own Shadow*, 21.

85 *compared to Edith* See Gould, *Edith Kermit Roosevelt*.

86 *"I did not want"* Eleanor Roosevelt, *This I Remember*, 74.

86 *"ER prepared"* Cook, *Eleanor Roosevelt*, 1:498.

87 *"In the old days"* Hickok, *Reluctant First Lady*, 92.

Chapter 6: Helping the Little People

89 *"Dear God"* Goodwin, *No Ordinary Time*, 629; Gould and Hickok, *Walter Reuther*, 345.

89 *"It has been said"* S. Williams, "Eleanor Roosevelt," transcript.

89 *Out of the bags* C. Fleming, *Our Eleanor*, 98; Cook, *Eleanor Roosevelt*, 2:329–30.

90 *"My dear, you will never"* "Best Advice," draft for *Reader's Digest*, June 1957. ER Papers, A&S, 1957–62, Undated Box 1422, FDRPL.

90 *"I would be lost"* C. Smith, *Presidents*, 88, 89.

91 *"I'm afraid that you won't"* Hickok, *Reluctant First Lady*, 44.

91 *"transform the role"* Goodwin, *"No Ordinary Time."*

91 *Harry Hopkins had worked* Lowitt, "Hopkins," 246–47.

91 *"dingy, almost seedy"* West, *Upstairs at the White House*, 27.

92 *"plain foods"* Goodwin, *No Ordinary Time*, 198–99.

92 *"Mrs. Roosevelt and I"* Nesbitt, *White House Diary*, 41.

92 *"Mrs. Roosevelt didn't"* Shapiro, "First Kitchen"; West, *Upstairs at the White House*, 27.

92 *Ernest Hemingway* Vaill, *Hotel Florida*, 215.

93 *accommodate the First* West, *Upstairs at the White House,* 30.

93 *"knew the taste"* Shapiro, "First Kitchen."

93 *$2,000 a month* Nesbitt, *White House Diary*, 79.

93 *filled with houseguests* Ibid., 142, 143.

94 *When Eleanor realized* Lash, *Eleanor and Franklin*, 506.

94 *"In this motion I see"* FDR "The Great Communicator," Master Speech Files, 1898, 1910–45, File 1030:1937 January 20, Inaugural Address. FDRPL, 8–9.

95 *Lady Bird Johnson* Gillette, *Lady Bird Johnson*, 109.

95 *"to assess conditions"* Knepper, *Dear Mrs. Roosevelt*, 4.

96 *"a wonderful woman"* Lyons, "Kennedy Says Democracy All Done."

96 *Later that reporter* Salsini, "No Little People."

97 *"the rabbit story"* Eleanor Roosevelt, *Autobiography*, 178.

97 *"But you must help me"* A. Black, *What I Hope to Leave Behind*, 13–15.

98 *"required all citizens"* Ibid., 416.

98 *three hundred thousand pieces* Blair, "Write Me," 415.

99 *"Sometimes I say things"* Lash, *Eleanor and Franklin*, 363.

99 *Neither woman could* Pratte, "My Day," 355.

100 *Given the volume* Beasley and Belgrade, "First Lady," 42.

100 *Eleanor's earnings* Flynn, *Country Squire*, 118.

100 *Westbrook Pegler* Pegler, "Fair Enough."

100 *"do-gooder"* Brandon, "Enfant-Terrible"; Peyser and Dwyer, *Hissing Cousins*, 51.

100 *critics charged* Flynn, *Country Squire*, 118.

101 *yearly income* Petro, "Spare a Dime?," 1.

101 *"It was a wonder"* Nesbitt, *White House Diary*, 190.

101 *In 1939, some 4,729* Eleanor Roosevelt, *Autobiography*, 170.

101 *"She and other women"* Belgrade, "Radio Broadcasts," 426.

101 *her predecessor Lou Hoover* H. Pryor, *Lou Henry Hoover*, 130, 146

101 *"even after marriage"* Ibid., 144.

102 *That statement was* Moe, *Roosevelt's Second Act.*

102 *Actually, Eleanor knitted* Swan, "Eleanor Roosevelt and Her No-Nonsense Knitting."

102 *Eleanor's travel* Powers, "Travels," 518.

102 *"Mrs. Roosevelt Spends"* Goodwin, *No Ordinary Time*, 29.

102 *Of course, Eleanor* Tobin, *Man He Became*, 305–6.

102 *One irate White House* Eleanor Roosevelt, *This I Remember*, 92.

103 *"to do good"* E. Thomas, *War Lovers*, 23.

104 *"Every man ought"* *Book of Common Prayer* (1945), 611.

104 *"Almighty God"* Ibid., 599.

104 *Eleanor assumed* Folsom and Folsom, *FDR Goes to War*; Lash, *Love Eleanor*, 279.

104 *FDR informed* T. Fleming, *New Dealers' War*, 68.

104 *Franklin began* Ibid., 72.

105 *"We don't want"* Wright, *Campaigning for President*, 183.

105 *Roosevelt was reelected* Kane and Podell, *Facts about the Presidents*, 381.

105 *Sara Roosevelt, eighty-six* Elliott Roosevelt, *Eleanor Roosevelt, with Love*, 54.

105 *"It is dreadful"* Lash, *Love, Eleanor*, 356.

105 *Daisy Suckley* Ward and Burns, *Roosevelts*, 389.

106 *"From the time"* Eleanor Roosevelt, *This Is My Story*, 187.

106 *"My idea of hell"* Ward and Burns, *Roosevelts*, 390.

106 *"She went to father"* James Roosevelt and Bill Libby, *My Parents*, 113; see also Davis, *War President*, 283.

106 *"I just can't"* Asbell, *Mother and Daughter*, 137.

107 *"Hyde Park is now"* Goodwin, *No Ordinary Time*, 276.

107 *"I can't help but"* Asbell, *Mother and Daughter*, 141.

107 *"Yesterday, December 7"* Ward and Burns, *Roosevelts*, 394.

107 *"Whatever is asked"* Ibid., 392.

109 *"In support of her belief"* Goodwin, *No Ordinary Time*, 204.

Chapter 7: Refugees and Regrets

111 *"I should have done more"* Gruber, *Inside of Time*, 351.

112 *"impersonal and casual"* Cook, *Eleanor Roosevelt*, 1:390.

112 *"parochial narrowness"* Collier and Horowitz, *American Saga*, 191.

112 *"I'd rather be hung"* Ward, *Before the Trumpet*, 252; Cook, *Eleanor Roosevelt*, 1:390.

112 *"an interesting little man"* Lash, *Eleanor and Franklin*, 214.

112 *"Certain Jews were"* Persico, *Franklin and Lucy*, 240.

112 *"Mr. Baruch has given"* Cook, *Eleanor Roosevelt*, 2:141.

113 *"to blend into"* Mart, "Eleanor Roosevelt, Liberalism, and Israel," 62.

113 *German economy had* vanden Heuvel, "America and the Holocaust," 2.

114 *Many American Jews* Sarna, *American Judaism*, 258.

114 *"Having the fullest confidence"* Cook, *Eleanor Roosevelt*, 2:304.

114 *"no comparably curt"* Ibid., 305.

114 *"Franklin, I think"* Barker-Benfield and Clinton, *Portraits of American Women*, 471.

115 *"enormous German and Catholic vote"* Cook, *Eleanor Roosevelt*, 2:305.

115 *United States had its own* Elson, "Did F. D. R. Do Enough?"

115 *"full and immediate knowledge"* Cook, *Eleanor Roosevelt*, 2:304.

115 *"From Geneva comes"* S. Smith, *First Lady of Radio*, 57.

115 *In late January* Issacson, *Einstein*, 431.

115 *"It is critical"* vanden Heuvel, "America and the Holocaust."

116 *"Jewish-sponsored"* Cook, *Eleanor Roosevelt*, 2:559.

116 *twelve hundred editorial columns* L. Leff, *Buried by the Times*, 255.

116 *"cease and scrap"* Pressman, *50 Children*, 79.

117 *"that would refer to Jews"* Feingold, *Bearing Witness*, 102; Sarna, *American Judaism*, 260; Diner, "Interview: Ford's Anti-Semitism."

117 *Would Americans* Nasaw, *Patriarch*, 431, 498, 509; Maier, *When Lions Roar*.

118 *"We do not hate"* Eleanor Roosevelt to Carola von Schaffer-Bernstein, September 6, 1939, 100. Personal Letters, 1939, Bem-Bi, ER Papers, FDRPL.

118 *"You who believe in God"* Grunwald and Adler, *Women's Letters*, 543.

118 *"Once we hold the power"* Heiden, *History of National Socialism*, 100; Riebling, *Church of Spies*, 61–62; Pietrusza, *Rise of Hitler*, 77; Ludecke, *I Knew Hitler*, 374.

119 *"I have regarded myself"* Brands, *Traitor to His Class*, 515; *New York Times*, "Hitler Escapes Bomb Explosion."

119 *"No man can count"* S. Smith, *First Lady of Radio*, 178.

119 *In a speech in April* Langer, *Mind of Hitler*, 39; Hitler, speech delivered April 12, 1922, in *Speeches of Adolf Hitler*; Pietrusza, *Rise of Hitler*, 77, citing Ludecke, *I Knew Hitler*, 374; A. Black, *Eleanor Roosevelt Papers*, 2:225.

119 *"In standing guard"* M. Gilbert, *Holocaust*, 28; Eleanor Roosevelt, *Moral Basis of Democracy*, 77.

120 *"great majority of people"* Eleanor Roosevelt, *Moral Basis of Democracy*, 76–77.

120 *"A country always loses"* Wortman, *Fighting the Shadow War*, 83.

120 *A Fortune poll* *Fortune*, April 1939, 102.

120 *Kristallnacht* M. Gilbert, *Holocaust*, 69–70.

121 *Cuban president* Thomas and Witts, *Voyage of the Damned*, 78.

121 *the number of passengers* Ibid., 295, 303.

122 *"Can't something be done?"* Goodwin, *No Ordinary Time*, 175–76.

122 *Breckenridge Long* Cook, *Eleanor Roosevelt*, 2:559.

122 *"Franklin, you* know" Goodwin, *No Ordinary Time*, 175–76.

122 *"Saving Jewish lives"* Pressman, *50 Children*, 74.

122 *Given nine million* Mills, *Prices in a War Economy*, 4; Unemployment Statistics during the Great Depression. http://www.u-s-history.com/pages/h1528.html.

122 *"File No Action FDR"* Wyman, *Paper Walls*, 97.

122 *"You always stand for the right"* Albert Einstein to Eleanor Roosevelt, July 26, 1941, FDRPL, FDR Digital Collections.

123 *SS* Quanza Berenbaum, "Holocaust," 239.

123 *"helped to fuel"* Glendon, "God and Mrs. Roosevelt," 23.

123 *"Get two people"* Pressman, *50 Children*, 71.

123 *"I should prefer"* Breitman and Lichtman, *FDR and the Jews*, 150.

123 *Laura Delano Houghteling* Cited in Pressman, *50 Children*, 73.

123 *Agnes Waters* Ibid., 72.

124 *"directed to the children"* "Dorothy Thompson Pleads for Child Exiles," *Washington Post*, April 23, 1939, 1; Scharf, "Roosevelt," 491.

124 *Helen Hayes, a prominent* Pressman, *50 Children*, 72.

124 *drum major for the "nos"* Ibid., 73.

125 *"How utterly without mercy"* S. Smith, *First Lady of Radio*, 178.

125 *more than a million Jews* Winik, *Year That Changed History*, 301.

125 *"I cannot take any more!"* Beschloss, *Conquerors*, 43.

125 *eyewitness reports* H. Levy, *Henry Morgenthau, Jr.*, 347.

126 *Fourteen months* Gallup, *Gallup Poll*, 351, 357.

126 *"I realize quite well"* Grunwald and Adler, *Women's Letters*, 342.

128 *"Open our eyes"* Lash, *Friend's Memoir*, 291.

128 *Fritz Kuhn* Pressman, *50 Children*, 69–70.

129 *Cousin Alice outraged* Ward, *Roosevelts*, 375.

129 *Although he probably* Rozett and Spector, *Encyclopedia of the Holocaust*, 392–93.

129 *Winik blasts* Winik, *Year That Changed History,* 470–72, 535.

130 *sheer numbers of the dead* Kolatch, *Inside Judaism*, 251–52.

130 *Black charges that FDR* C. Black, *Franklin Delano Roosevelt*, 495.

130 *"And whoever saved a life"* Mishnah Sanhedrin 4:9; Jerusalem Talmud, Tractate Sanhedrin 37a.

130 *survivors found themselves* Dinnerstein, *Survivors of the Holocaust*, 16–17; see also Stargardt, *German War*, 548–51; Radosh and Radosh, *Safe Haven*, 210.

130 Manchester Guardian Gilbert, *Holocaust*, 817.

130 *thirty Jews were murdered* Von Tempo, "Refugees."

131 *another 1.5 million* Gruber, *Haven*, 262.

132 *What other American* A. Black, *Eleanor Roosevelt Papers*, 1:140.

133 *"Though every face"* Eleanor Roosevelt, *On My Own*, 55.

133 *Then the boy sang* Ibid., 56.

133 *"As I looked"* Ibid.

135 *That diplomats repeatedly* Radosh and Radosh, *Safe Haven*, 252–53; A. Black, *Eleanor Roosevelt Papers*, 2:323; Wyman, *Abandonment of the Jews*, 157.

135 *Ernest Bevin* Acheson, *Present at the Creation*, 173.

135 *Fort Ontario* Gruber, *Haven*, 15, 211.

136 *Eleven refugees boarded* Baron, "Haven from the Holocaust," 23–24.

137 *President Harry Truman* Gruber, *Inside of Time*, 184–87; Gruber, *Haven*, 292–93; Baron, "Haven from the Holocaust," 32–33.

137 *In that post* Keyles, *Naked to the Bone*, 185–86.

Chapter 8: Children of God

139 *"Whether in praise"* Carl T. Rowan, *Boston Globe*, October 14, 1962, quoted in Persico, *Franklin and Lucy*, 362.

139 *One warm March day* Holway, *Red Tails, Black Wings*, 44; Moye, *Freedom Flyers*, 51.

140 *"General [Hap] Arnold"* Moye, *Freedom Flyers*, 53.

140 *Eleanor, as a trustee* Ibid.; Williams, *Eleanor Roosevelt's Niggers.*

141 *"Desegregation is against the Bible"* William Carter quoted in "Fighting Back (1957–1962)," from *Eyes on the Prize: America's Civil Rights Movement 1954–1985,* PBS, transcript, http://www.pbs.org/wgbh/amex/eyesontheprize/about/pt_102.html.

142 *"I'd sure like to help"* Hitchens, *God Is Not Great*, 179.

142 *"The Southern institution"* Eastland, "Segregation and the South."

142 *"High places"* Hervieux, *Forgotten*, 164.

143 *"I do not see how"* Eleanor Roosevelt, "Race, Religion and Prejudice," 630.

143 *Martha Bulloch Roosevelt* Robinson, *My Brother Theodore Roosevelt.*

144 *Segregation in Warm Springs* Moye, *Freedom Flyers*, 51; J. Smith, *FDR*, 264.

144 *"no victim"* Oshinsky, *Polio*, 65, 66.

144 *Because of what she had seen* Powers, "Travels," 518.

145 *Eleanor immediately terminated* Parks and Leighton, *Family in Turmoil*, 46; H. Nesbitt, *White House Diary, 78;* Haygood, *Butler.*

145 *"The Roosevelt White House"* Parks and Leighton, *Family in Turmoil*, 46; Haygood, *Butler*

145 *"Did you persuade Eleanor"* "Best Advice," draft for *Reader's Digest*, June 1957. ER Papers, A&S, 1957–62, Undated Box 1422, FDRPL.

146 *her eyebrow-raising article* Eleanor Roosevelt, "Some of My Best Friends Are Negro."

146 *Many southern blacks* Bell-Scott, *Firebrand and First Lady, 70.*

147 *The only ongoing direct interaction* Hanson, *Mary Bethune*, 30; Boehm and Reed, "Bethune," 18–19; Kirby, *Black Americans in Roosevelt's Era*, 25.

147 *Murray, who drafted* Letter of Transmittal, President's Commission on Status of Women, Washington, DC: U.S. Government Printing Office, p. i.

147 *"I've got to get legislation"* W. White, *Man Called White*, 169–70.

147 *More than forty-seven hundred Americans* Teel, "Anti-Lynching Movement," 29–30.

147 *In 1933, twenty-four* Bess, *Choices under Fire*, 28.

148 *plans for a lynching* Anderson, "We Fight! Red Tails."

148 *"Somebody's been priming"* W. White, *Man Called White*, 169

148 *Claude Neal* Anderson, "Spectacle Lynching of Claude Neal."

149 *according to J. Edgar Hoover* Ibid.

149 *"I feel like a skunk"* Rowley, *Franklin and Eleanor*, 222.

149 *eleven assassination attempts* A. Black, "Outspoken Women."

150   *"Raping, mobbing, lynching"*   75 *Congressional Record*, Session 3, 893, 873 (1938); *Washington Afro-American*, "Bilboisms," 3.

150   *"no better friend"*   76 *Congressional Record*, Session 1, 4652, 4671 (1939).

150   *"I might entertain"*   78 *Congressional Record*, Session 1, 6253 (1943).

150   *One popular ditty*   Buckley, *American Patriots*, 232.

151   *Rumors metamorphosed*   A. Black, *Casting Her Own Shadow*, 87.

151   *"As far as I know"*   Eleanor Roosevelt, *It Seems to Me*, 186.

151   *Stunned by the negative*   Collins, *America's Women*, 107.

151   *"I feel obliged"*   Eleanor Roosevelt to Mrs. Henry Roberts, February 25, 1939. National Archives and Records Administration, "American Originals," http://www.archives.gov/exhibits/american_originals/eleanor.html.

152   *"I don't care if she sings"*   Collins, *America's Women*, 107.

152   *Anderson "had gone from"*   Ibid.

153   *Paradoxically, black men*   Anderson, "We Fight! Red Tails."

153   *"A Jim Crow army"*   Ward and Burns, *War*, 111.

153   *"desire of Headquarters"*   D. Miller, *Master of the Air*, 230.

153   *"We have never been willing"*   Eleanor Roosevelt, *Moral Basis of Democracy*, 43, 48.

153   *Eleanor barraged*   Goodwin, *No Ordinary Time*, 423; Hervieux, *Forgotten*, 120.

154   *Stimson publicly stated*   Office of Air Force History, *Blacks in the Armed Forces*, 13

154   *Stimson blatantly failed*   Goodwin, *No Ordinary Time*, 172; Hervieux, *Forgotten*, 119.

154   *"These colored boys"*   McGuire, *Jim Crow Army*, 129.

154   *By 1945, some 1.2 million"*   Kennedy, *American People in World War*, 344.

154   *an African-American woman*   Bess, *Choices under Fire*, 37.

154   *"I'd rather see Hitler win"*   Hervieux, *Forgotten*, 113.

155   *"sanded away stereotypes"*   Kennedy, *American People in World War*, 344.

155   *Sojourner Truth Housing Project*   Knepper, *Dear Mrs. Roosevelt*, 324.

155   *"It is blood on your hands"*   Ibid., 325–26.

155   *"Negro situation was too hot"*   A. Black, *Casting Her Own Shadow*, 92.

156   *One particularly hot day*   Salsini, "No Little People"; Hershan, *Woman of Quality*, 164.

156   *"For the first time"*   Lash, *World of Love*, 209.

157   *Southerners wanted to*   Fleegler, "Theodore G. Bilbo," 27; Atkins, "Bilbo," 50.

157   *"I spent four years"*   Patterson, *Great Expectations*, 23.

158 *Thurgood Marshall* Van West, "Columbia Race Riot, 1946"; J. Williams, *Thurgood Marshall*, 121

158 *"Give 'em hell, Harry!"* P. White, *Whistle Stop*, 224.

159 *"I think what most of us"* Eleanor Roosevelt, *Tomorrow Is Now*, 51.

160 *"In seeking a strong civil rights plank"* Martin Luther King Jr., "Testimony to the Committee on Platform and Resolutions."

160 *Critics had long assailed* "Eleanor Roosevelt," Primary Resources: FBI Files," *American Experience*, PBS, http://www.pbs.org/wgbh /americanexperience/features/primary-resources/eleanor-fbi/2/.

161 *"more savage, systematic, and unrelenting"* Lash, *Eleanor and Franklin*, 672.

161 *"primary test of prophesy"* Quoted in Cone, *Cross and Lynching Tree*, 61.

161 *"I have learned"* Eleanor Roosevelt, *Tomorrow Is Now*, 52.

161 *"You must remember"* Quoted in A. Black, *Eleanor Roosevelt Papers*, 2:376.

162 *"We have to make sure"* Ibid., 2:360.

162 *When Eleanor tired* Ibid., 1:889.

162 *"Never has a tinier minority"* Olson, *Freedom's Daughters*, 194.

163 *"so incensed by the violence"* A. Black, "Civil Rights," 95; A. Black, *Casting Her Own Shadow*, 127–28.

163 *"one of the most difficult"* A. Black, *Casting Her Own Shadow*, 128–29; Eleanor Roosevelt, *Tomorrow Is Now*, 52.

164 *"He was [not] worth a damn"* Ball, *Defiant Life*, 86.

Chapter 9: One Nation under God

165 *Though the term is common* Zubovich, "Short Career of Judeo-Christianity."

168 *"differences in religious belief"* Eleanor Roosevelt, *Moral Basis of Democracy*, 12, 42.

168 *Alfred Smith* Slayton, *Empire Statesman*, 479, 310–15.

170 *"I think I believe"* Glendon, "God and Mrs. Roosevelt," 24.

171 *moment of silent* A. Black, interview with author, September 16, 2015.

171 *"took a lot of heat"* Ibid.

172 *"principal American Catholic"* Fogarty, "Spellman," 499.

172 *"the American Pope"* Cooney, *American Pope.*

172 *"his politicking, close ties"* Ibid., 179, 205.

172 *The Catholic Church* Gannon, *Cardinal Spellman Story*, 211.

173 *Spellman built or remodeled* Tiffany, "Spellman," 412.

173 *"flaccid liberal"* Cooney, *American Pope*, 176.

174 *Protestants voiced outrage* A. Black, *Eleanor Roosevelt Papers*, 2:176–83.

176 *"most religiously diverse"* Eck, *New Religious America*, 338.

176 *"Almost any other religion"* Eleanor Roosevelt, *If You Ask Me*, 122–23.

177 *"The new spirituality is"* Moore, "Spiritual Situation."

178 *"The United States is"* Eleanor Roosevelt, *Tomorrow Is Now*, 51.

178 *"if everybody"* Eleanor Roosevelt, *It's Up to the Women*, 188.

Chapter 10: Her Final Years

179 *"I don't want"* Oliver, "When Death Comes," 11.

179 *"greatest convention speech"* Henry, *Eleanor Roosevelt and Adlai Stevenson*, 120.

179 *Arriving in Los Angeles* Ibid., 174.

180 *Anna Rosenberg* Ibid., 175.

180 *"People loved her"* Lash, *World of Love*, 523.

180 *"angry and disheartened"* Henry, *Eleanor Roosevelt and Adlai Stevenson*, 176; Elliott Roosevelt and James Brough, *Mother R.*, 259.

180 *"Don't you know"* Lash, *Years Alone*, 302.

181 *"In the seven years"* Time, "Eleanor Roosevelt."

181 *In old age Ludlow* Eleanor Roosevelt, *This Is My Story*, 26.

181 *overscheduled April day* Lash, *World of Love*, 515.

182 *"I got home from Boston"* Ibid., 531.

183 *"You see, I had to come"* William Ryan, "Remarks in the House," 15–20. Note: Remarks made on March 18, 1963; not published until 1966.

183 *"who learns to pray"* Chittister, *Breath of the Soul*, 114.

183 *"My interest or sympathy"* Lash, *Friend's Memoir*, 291.

183 *"into the dark corners"* Gallagher, "Remarks in the House," 61; Eleanor Roosevelt, *Autobiography*, 413.

184 *As she kept watch* Belafonte and Shnayerson, *My Song*, 254–59.

184 *"I know I should slow down"* Toor, *Eleanor Roosevelt*, 102.

184 *"Restrict your activities"* Elliott Roosevelt to Eleanor Roosevelt, September 12, 1962, ER Papers, 1957–62, Box 3624, FDRPL.

184 *"I have tried . . . not to worry"* Lash, *Years Alone*, 332.

186 *"Make us ever mindful"* Evening Prayer, *Book of Common Prayer* (1892), 327.

186 *"GOD . . . make us"* *Book of Common Prayer* (1928), 489.

186 *"So live, that when"* Bryant, "Thanatopsis," 781.

187 *"when one passes"* Eleanor Roosevelt, interview by Edward R. Murrow, *This I Believe*, CBS Radio Network, January 22, 1954.

187 *"In a recent radio broadcast"* Harry S Truman Official Papers, Box 911, Harry S Truman Presidential Library.

188 *"I'm really too busy"* Interview with Eleanor Wotkyns by Emily Williams, June 12, 1978, 58–59, Eleanor Roosevelt Oral Histories, Box 5, FDRPL.

188 *"Christ's teaching"* Gordon Kidd, Box 4841, Eleanor's Death, FDRPL.

188 *"if you pay much attention"* Lash, *Centenary Portrait*, 184.

188 *"nothing to do with"* Anna R. Halstead Papers, Box 61, FDRPL.

188 *"Dr. Gurewitsch has told"* W. T. Levy, *Extraordinary Mrs. R.*, 244.

189 *"2 bags full"* Lash, *World of Love*, 550.

189 *"being buried alive"* Gurewitsch, *Kindred Souls*, 290.

189 *"I want Dr. David Gurewitsch"* ER—Burial Instructions 1955, in John A. Roosevelt Papers, Box 4, FDRPL.

189 *"We must hope"* Gurewitsch, *Kindred Souls*, 263.

190 *"Everything went smoothly"* Asbell, *Mother and Daughter*, 352.

190 *"Yet she so wanted"* A. Black, introduction to *Tomorrow Is Now*, xiii.

191 *"I have something that"* Ibid.

191 *"insisted that Reuther"* O'Farrell, *She Was One of Us*, 203.

191 *"I am trying to live up"* Eleanor Roosevelt, 1957–62, Box 3624, FDRPL.

191 *"cause of my fever"* Eleanor Roosevelt to John F. Kennedy, October 2, 1962, Small Collections JFK, Kennedy Presidential Library; see also Box 32, President's Office Files.

191 *chair of a fund-raising* Eleanor Roosevelt to John F. Kennedy, September 27, 1962, Small Collection, FDRPL.

191 *"Needless to say"* Claire S. Kidd, Undated 1962 Correspondence, Box 1832, 1957–62, FDRPL.

192 *"beyond the usual bounds"* Webster, "Gurewitsch," 219; see also Lerner, "Final Diagnosis," 13–16.

192 *"hurt her, and I think"* Eleanor Seagraves, Box 5, p. 48, FDRPL.

192 *"ER's relationship with Gurewitsch"* Webster, "Gurewitsch," 221.

192 *"enjoyed the devotion"* Ibid., 220.

192 *"It is not unusual"* Gurewitsch, "Remembering Mrs. Roosevelt."

193 *"Jim and Anna don't think"* Asbell, *Mother and Daughter*, 344.

193 *"perhaps a good"* Lash, *World of Love*, 557.

193 *"constrained in the past"* Gurewitsch, *Kindred Souls*, 282.

193 *"A doctor's role"* Ibid.

193   *"could not allow a famous person"* Eleanor Roosevelt II, *With Love, Aunt Eleanor*, 198.

193   *"With the diagnosis"* Gurewitsch, *Kindred Souls*, 282–85.

194   *"I am sorry to tell you"* Eleanor Roosevelt Correspondence, 1959–62, Box 3625, FDRPL.

194   *"If she could no longer"* James Roosevelt and Bill Libby, *My Parents*, 297.

194   *"Probably never in all history"* Aubrey Williams to Eleanor Roosevelt, October 12, 1962, Aubrey Williams Files, Box 60, FDRPL.

194   *Eleanor refused medications* Asbell, *Mother and Daughter*, 354.

195   *"There was only suffering"* Lash, *Years Alone*, 329.

195   *"so many indignities"* Ibid., 331.

195   *"[I] found her really not"* John Roosevelt Boettiger, Oral History, August 1, 1979, p. 56, FDRPL.

195   *"To me all goodbyes"* Gurewitsch, *Kindred Souls*, 259.

195   *"so few people"* Lash, *Years Alone*, 329.

195   *"don't you think people"* Persico, *Franklin and Lucy*, 363.

196   *"she, who had had"* Lash, *Years Alone*, 330.

196   *"final embarrassment"* James Roosevelt and Bill Libby, *My Parents*, 298.

196   *"Please tell them"* Lash, *Years Alone*, 330.

196   *"moved by a premonition"* Asbell, *Mother and Daughter*, 354.

196   *"My husband and I"* Gurewitsch, *Kindred Souls*, 281.

197   *"Nobody makes sense"* Lash, *Years Alone*, 330.

197   *"It is really a miracle"* Gurewitsch, *Kindred Souls*, 286.

197   *"Around a quarter of nine"* Ibid., 285–86.

198   *"The fundamental, vital"* Eleanor Roosevelt, "What Religion Means to Me," 324.

Conclusion

199   *"In the death of Eleanor Roosevelt"* *New York Daily News*, "Services for Mrs. Roosevelt."

199   *"No woman has ever"* Morris, *Price of Fame*, 654.

199   *"Some came to pay"* W. T. Levy, *Extraordinary Mrs. R.*, 248; Ponte, "William F. Buckley."

199   *"How much she had done"* W. T. Levy, *Extraordinary Mrs. R.*, 248–49.

200   *"a woman of mercy"* Lash, *Love, Eleanor*, x.

200   *"She was a saint"* Levy, *Extraordinary Mrs. R.,* 154.

200   *"who tries"* Craughwell, *Saints Behaving Badly*, xii.

200 *"perfectly candid about saints"* Ibid.

200 *"while all Christian saints"* Paul, *Encyclopedia of Saints*, 6.

201 *"lived out their baptism"* Pope Francis, "Saints Lived Out Their Baptismal Seal."

201 *"who has placed"* Ibid.

201 *"The glory of God"* Irenaeus, *Against Heresies* 4.20.

201 "Mrs. Roosevelt has solved" Persico, *Franklin and Lucy*, 363.

202 "no amateur in life" Eleanor Roosevelt, 1930 draft, "Precis of a Book," ER Papers, Box 3022, FDRPL.

202 *"At present I look like"* Eleanor Roosevelt, undated draft, "Strength and Energy of Eleanor Roosevelt," A&S, FDRPL.

204 *"I think we shall have fulfilled"* Eleanor Roosevelt, *It's Up to the Women*, 262.

Bibliography

Acheson, Dean. *Present at the Creation: My Years in the State Department.* New York: W. W. Norton, 1969.

Albion, Michele Wehrwein, ed. *The Quotable Eleanor Roosevelt.* Gainesville, FL: University Press of Florida, 2013.

Anda, Robert. "The Health and Social Impact of Growing Up with Alcoholic Abuse and Related Adverse Childhood Experiences: The Human and Economic Costs of the Status Quo." Conference in Anacortes, WA, June 2007.

Anderson, Carol. "Spectacle Lynching of Claude Neale." Emory University, February 13, 2013.

———. "We Fight! Red Tails, Black Soldiers, and the Civil Rights Movement." Lecture at the Truman Forum, Kansas City, MO, September 24, 2014.

Asbell, Bernard, ed. *Mother and Daughter: The Letters of Eleanor and Anna Roosevelt.* New York: Coward, McCann & Geoghegan, 1982.

Atkins, Stephen. "Bilbo." In *Encyclopedia of Right-Wing Extremism in Modern American History,* 48–51. New York: ABC-CLIO, 2011.

Ball, Howard A. *A Defiant Life: Thurgood Marshall and the Persistence of Racism in America.* New York: Crown Publishers, 1998.

Barker-Benfield, G. J., and Catherine Clinton. *Portraits of American Women: From Settlement to the Present.* New York: Oxford University Press, 1998.

Baron, Lawrence. "Haven from the Holocaust. Oswego, New York: 1944–1946." *New York History* 640 (January 1983): 5–34.

Beasley, Maurine, and Paul Belgrade. "Eleanor Roosevelt: First Lady as Radical Pioneer." *Journalism History* 11 (Autumn–Winter 1984): 42–45.

Belafonte, Harry, and Michael Shnayerson. *My Song: A Memoir.* New York: Knopf, 2011.

Belgrade, Paul S. "Radio Broadcasts." In *The Eleanor Roosevelt Encyclopedia,* ed. Maurine H. Beasley, Holly C. Shulman, and Henry R. Beasley, 425–29. Westport, CT: Greenwood, 2001.

Bell-Scott, Patricia. *The Firebrand and the First Lady: Portrait of a Friendship; Pauli Murray, Eleanor Roosevelt, and the Struggle for Social Justice.* New York: Knopf, 2016.

Benson, Peter L., and Carolyn H. Eklin. *Effective Christian Education: A National Study of Protestant Congregations; A Summary Report on Faith, Loyalty and Congregational Life.* Minneapolis: Search Institute, 1990.

Berenbaum, Michael. "Holocaust." In *The Eleanor Roosevelt Encyclopedia,* ed.

Maurine H. Beasley, Holly C. Shulman, and Henry R. Beasley, 239–41. Westport, CT: Greenwood, 2001.

Berggren, D. Jason, and Nicol C. Rae. "Jimmy Carter and George W. Bush: Faith Foreign Policy and an Evangelical President Style." *Presidential Studies Quarterly* 36, no. 4 (2006): 606–32.

Beschloss, Michael R. *The Conquerors: Roosevelt, Truman and the Destruction of Hitler's Germany, 1941–1945*. New York: Simon & Schuster, 2002.

Bess, Michael. *Choices under Fire: Moral Dimensions of World War II*. New York: Random House, 2008.

Binning, William C., Larry E. Esterly, and Paul Sracic. *Encyclopedia of American Parties, Campaigns, and Elections*. Westport, CT: Greenwood, 1999.

Black, Allida M. *Casting Her Own Shadow: Eleanor Roosevelt and the Shaping of Postwar Liberalism*. New York: Columbia University Press, 1996.

———. "Civil Rights." In *The Eleanor Roosevelt Encyclopedia*, ed. Maurine H. Beasley, Holly C. Shulman, and Henry R. Beasley, 89–96. Westport, CT: Greenwood, 2001.

———, ed. *The Eleanor Roosevelt Papers*. Vol. 1, *The Human Rights Years, 1945–1948*. Detroit: Thomson Gale, 2007.

———, ed. *The Eleanor Roosevelt Papers*. Vol. 2, *1949–1952*. Richmond: University of Virginia Press, 2012.

———. Introduction to *Tomorrow Is Now*, by Eleanor Roosevelt, xviii–xliv New York: Penguin Books, 2012.

———. "Outspoken Women: What Eleanor Roosevelt and Betty Ford Taught about Leadership." Lecture presented at Ford Presidential Museum, Grand Rapids, MI, April 24, 2014.

———, ed. *What I Hope to Leave Behind: The Essential Essays of Eleanor Roosevelt*. New York: Carlson, 1995.

Black, Conrad. *Franklin Delano Roosevelt: Champion of Freedom*. New York: Public Affairs Press, 2003.

Blair, Diane Marie. "'I Want You to Write Me': Eleanor Roosevelt's Use of Personal Letters as a Rhetorical Resource." *Western Journal of Communication* 72, no. 4 (2008): 415–33.

Boehm, Randolph, and Linda Reed. "Bethune, Mary McLeod." In *The Eleanor Roosevelt Encyclopedia*, ed. Maurine H. Beasley, Holly C. Shulman, and Henry R. Beasley, 47–52. Westport, CT: Greenwood, 2001.

Boettiger, John Roosevelt. Interview by Harold Ivan Smith, July 23, 2014.

Bowlby, John. *A Secure Base: Clinical Applications of Attachment Theory*. New York: Routledge, 2006.

Braeman, John. "Roosevelt, Franklin." In *Encyclopedia of the American Presidency*, ed. Leonard W. Leavy and Louis Fisher, 3:1318–28. New York: Simon & Schuster, 1994.

Brahms, William B., ed. *Notable Last Facts: A Compendium of Endings,*

Conclusions, Terminations and Final Events throughout History. Haddonfield, NJ: Reference Desk Press, 2005.

Brandon, Henry. "A Talk with an 83-Year-Old Enfant-Terrible." *New York Times Magazine,* August 6, 1967.

Brands, H. W. *Traitor to His Class: The Privileged Life and Radical Presidency of Franklin D. Roosevelt.* New York: Doubleday, 2008.

Breitman, Richard, and Allan J. Lichtman. *FDR and the Jews.* Cambridge, MA: Belknap Press of Harvard University Press, 2013.

Brinkley, Douglas. *Rightful Heritage: Franklin D. Roosevelt and the Land of America.* New York: Harper, 2016.

Bryant, William Cullen. "Thanatoposis." In *A Treasury of Great Poems,* ed. Louis Untermeyer, 779–81. New York: Galahad Books, 1955.

Buckley, Gail. *American Patriots: The Story of Blacks in the Military from the Revolution to Desert Storm.* New York: Random House, 2001.

Bureau of the Census. *Statistical Abstract of the United States: 1989.* Washington, DC: U.S. Printing Office, 1989.

Cahill, Susan, ed. *Wise Woman: Over Two Thousand Years of Spiritual Writing by Women.* New York: Norton, 1997.

Carlson, Peter. "FDR's Loyal Mistress." *American History* 45, no. 4 (December 2010): 45–47.

Caroli, Betty Boyd. *The Roosevelt Women: A Portrait in Five Generations.* New York: Basic Books, 1998.

Chafe, William H. *Bill and Hillary: The Politics of the Personal.* New York: Farrar, Straus & Giroux, 2012.

Chittister, Joan. *The Breath of the Soul: Reflections on Prayer.* Mystic, CT: Twenty-Third Publications, 2011.

Cohen, Adam. *Nothing to Fear: FDR's Inner Circle and the Hundred Days That Created Modern America.* New York: Penguin, 2009.

Collier, Peter, and David Horowitz. *The Roosevelts: An American Saga.* New York: Simon & Schuster, 1994.

Collins, Gail. *America's Women: 400 Years of Dolls, Drudges, Helpmates, and Heroines.* New York: William Morrow, 2003.

Cone, James H. *The Cross and the Lynching Tree.* Maryknoll, NY: Orbis Books, 2011.

Cook, Blanche Wiesen. *Eleanor Roosevelt.* Vol. 1, *1884–1933.* New York: Viking, 1992.

———. *Eleanor Roosevelt.* Vol. 2, *The Defining Years, 1933–1938.* New York: Viking, 1999.

———. Lecture at the New York Historical Society, October 22, 2012.

Cooney, John. *The American Pope: The Life and Times of Francis Cardinal Spellman.* New York: Times Books, 1984.

Cordery, Stacey A. "Roosevelt, Elliott." In *The Eleanor Roosevelt Encyclopedia,* ed. Maurine H. Beasley, Holly C. Shulman, and Henry R. Beasley, 446–48. Westport, CT: Greenwood, 2011.

Craughwell, Thomas J. *Saints Behaving Badly: The Cutthroats, Crooks, Trollops, Con Men and Devil-Worshippers Who Became Saints.* New York: Image/Random House, 2006.

Dalton, Kathleen. *Theodore Roosevelt: A Strenuous Life.* New York: Alfred A. Knopf, 2004.

Davis, Kenneth S. *FDR, the War President, 1940–1943: A History.* New York: Random House, 2000.

de Kay, James Tertius. *Roosevelt's Navy: The Education of a Warrior President, 1882–1920.* New York: Pegasus Books, 2012.

Diner, Hasia. "Interview: Ford's Anti-Semitism." PBS, *American Experience,* http://www.pbs.org/wgbh/americanexperience/features/interview/henryford-antisemitism/.

Dinnerstein, Leonard. *America and the Survivors of the Holocaust: The Evolution of a United States Displaced Persons Policy, 1945–1950.* New York: Columbia University Press, 1982.

Dong, Maxia, Robert F. Anda, Vincent J. Felitti, Shanta R. Dube, David F. Williamson, Theodore J. Thompson, Clifton M. Loo, and Wayne H. Giles. "The Interrelatedness of Multiple Forms of Childhood Abuse, Neglect, and Household Dysfunction." *Child Abuse & Neglect* 28 (2004): 771–84

Eastland, James O. "The Supreme Court, Segregation and the South." Speech in the United States Senate, May 27, 1954.

Eck, Diana L. *A New Religious America: How a "Christian Country" Has Now Become the World's Most Religious Nation.* San Francisco: HarperSan Francisco, 2001.

Elson, John. "History: Did F. D. R. Do Enough?" *Time,* April 18, 1994, 83.

Feingold, Henry. *Bearing Witness: How America and Its Jews Responded to the Holocaust.* Syracuse, NY: Syracuse University Press, 1995.

Fleegler, Robert L. "Theodore G. Bilbo and the Decline of Public Racism, 1931–1947." *Journal of Mississippi History,* Spring 2006, 1–27.

Fleming, Candace. *Our Eleanor: A Scrapbook Look at Eleanor Roosevelt's Remarkable Life.* New York: Atheneum Books for Young Readers, 2005.

Fleming, Thomas. *The New Dealers' War: FDR and the War within World War II.* New York: Basic Books, 2001.

Flynn, John T. *Country Squire in the White House.* New York: Doubleday, Doran & Company, 1940.

Fogarty, Gerald P. "Spellman, Joseph Francis." In *The Eleanor Roosevelt Encyclopedia,* ed. Maurine H. Beasley, Holly C. Shulman, and Henry R. Beasley, 498–502. Westport, CT: Greenwood, 2011.

Folsom, Burton, Jr., and Anita Folsom. *FDR Goes to War: How Expanded Executive Power, Spiraling National Debt, and Restricted Civil Liberties Shaped Wartime America.* New York: Threshold, 2011.

Francis, Pope. "Saints Lived Out Their Baptismal Seal." Vatican Press Service, Vatican City, November 1, 2013.

Freedman, Russell. "Souvestre, Marie." In *The Eleanor Roosevelt Encyclopedia*, ed. Maurine H. Beasley, Holly C. Shulman, and Henry R. Beasley, 488–90. Westport, CT: Greenwood, 2001.

Gallagher, Cornelius E. "Remarks in the House." In *Anna Eleanor Roosevelt, 1884–1962: Memorial Addresses of the House of Representatives*. 88 *Congressional Record,* 1st session, 61. Washington DC: U.S. Government Printing Office, 1966.

Gallagher, Hugh Gregory. *FDR's Splendid Deception: The Moving Story of Roosevelt's Massive Disability and the Intense Efforts to Conceal It from the Public.* New York: Dodd, Mead, 1985.

Gallup, George. *The Gallup Poll: Public Opinion, 1935–1971.* New York: Random House, 1972.

Gannon, Robert I. *The Cardinal Spellman Story.* New York: Doubleday, 1962.

Gilbert, Daniel. *Stumbling on Happiness.* New York: Scribner, 2006.

Gilbert, Martin. *The Holocaust: A History of the Jews of Europe during the Second World War.* New York: Holt, Rinehart & Winston, 1985.

Gillette, Michael L. *Lady Bird Johnson: An Oral History.* New York: Oxford University Press, 2012.

Glendon, Mary Ann. "God and Mrs. Roosevelt." *First Things,* May 2010, 21–24.

Goodwin, Doris Kearns. "Eleanor Roosevelt: America's Most Influential First Lady Blazed Path for Women and Battled for Social Justice Everywhere." *Time,* April 13, 1998, 121–24.

———. "Franklin D. Roosevelt: 'Sublime Confidence.'" In *Power and the Presidency,* ed. Robert A. Wilson, 19–43. New York: PublicAffairs, 1999.

———. "No Ordinary Time." Interview by Brian Lamb. *Booknotes.* C-SPAN, January 1, 1995.

———. *No Ordinary Time: Franklin and Eleanor Roosevelt and the Home Front in World War Two.* New York: Simon & Schuster, 1994.

Gottlieb, Agnes Hooper, Henry Gottlieb, Barbara Bowers, and Brent Bowers. *1,000 Years, 1,000 People: Ranking the Men and Women Who Shaped the Millennium.* New York: Barnes & Noble, 2006.

Gould, Jean, and Lenora Hickok. *Walter Reuther: Labor's Rugged Individualist.* New York: Dodd, Mead, 1972.

Gould, Lewis L. *Edith Kermit Roosevelt: Creating the Modern First Lady.* Lawrence: University of Kansas Press, 2013.

Gould, Louis L., ed. *American First Ladies: Their Lives and Their Legacy.* New York: Garland, 1996.

Graham, H. Davis. "The Paradox of Eleanor Roosevelt: Alcoholism's Child." *Virginia Quarterly Review* 63 (1987): 3–26.

Grant, R. G. *World War I: The Definitive Visual History.* New York: Dorling Kindersley, 2014

Gruber, Ruth. *Haven: The Unknown Story of 1,000 World War II Refugees.* New York: Coward-McCann, 2000.

———. *Inside of Time: My Journey from Alaska to Israel.* New York: Coward-McCann, 2003.

Grunwald, Lisa, and Stephen J. Adler. *Women's Letters: America from the Revolutionary War to the Present.* New York: Random House, 2005.

Gurewitsch, Edna P. *Kindred Souls: The Friendship of Eleanor Roosevelt and David Gurewitsch.* New York: St. Martin's Press, 2002.

———. "Remembering Mrs. Roosevelt." *American Heritage* 33, no. 1 (December 1981): 10–19. http://www.americanheritage.com/print/54223?page -show200,000.

Hamby, Alonzo. *Man of Destiny: FDR and the Making of the American Century.* New York: Basic Books, 2015.

Hanson, Joyce A. *Mary Bethune and Black Women's Political Activism.* Columbia: University of Missouri Press, 2003.

Hart, Jonathan, Alicia Limke, and Phillip R. Budd. "Attachment and Faith Development." *Journal of Psychology and Theology* 38, no. 2 (2010): 122–28.

Hay, Peter. *All the Presidents' Ladies: Anecdotes of the Women behind the Men in the White House.* New York: Viking, 1988.

Haygood, Wil. *The Butler: A Witness to History.* New York: Atria, 2013.

Heiden, Konrad. *A History of National Socialism.* London: Routledge, 2013

Henry, Richard. *Eleanor Roosevelt and Adlai Stevenson.* New York: Palgrave/Macmillan, 2010.

Hershan, Stella K. *A Woman of Quality: Eleanor Roosevelt.* New York: Crown, 1970.

Hervieux, Linda. *Forgotten: The Untold Story of D-Day's Black Heroes, at Home and at War.* New York: Harper, 2015.

Hickok, Lenora A. *Eleanor Roosevelt: Reluctant First Lady.* New York: Dodd, Mead, 1962.

Hitchens, Christopher. *God Is Not Great: How Religion Poisons Everything.* New York: Twelve, 2007.

Hitler, Adolf. Speech delivered April 12, 1922. In *The Speeches of Adolf Hitler, April 1922–August 1939,* ed. Norman H. Baynes, 1:19–20. New York: Oxford University Press, 1942.

Hogan, Margaret A., and C. James Taylor, eds. *My Dearest Friend: Letters of Abigail and John Adams.* Cambridge, MA: Belknap Press of Harvard University Press, 2007.

Holway, John B. *Red Tails, Black Wings: The Men of America's Black Air Force.* Las Cruces, NM: Yucca Tree Press, 1997.

Isaacson, Walter. *Einstein: His Life and Universe.* New York: Simon and Schuster, 2007.

Janoff-Bulman, Ronnie. "The Aftermath of Victimization: Rebuilding Shattered Assumptions." In *Trauma and Its Wake,* ed. C. R. Figley, 15–35. New York: Brunner/Mazel, 1985.

Jung, K. Elan. *Sexual Trauma: A Challenge Not Insanity; Sexual Trauma, Its Victims and How They Have Shaped Our World.* Queensbury, NY: Hudson Press, 2010.

Kane, Joseph Nathan, and Janet Podell. *Facts about the Presidents: A Compilation of Biographical and Historical Information.* 8th ed. New York: H. W. Wilson, 2009.

Kennedy, David. *The American People in World War II.* New York: Oxford University Press, 1999.

Keyles, Bettyann Holtzmann. *Naked to the Bone: Medical Imaging in the Twentieth Century.* New Brunswick, NJ: Rutgers University Press, 1997.

King, Martin Luther, Jr. "Testimony to the Committee on Platform and Resolutions, Democratic National Committee, August 11, 1956." In *The Papers of Martin Luther King, Jr.* Vol. 3, *Birth of a New Age, December 1955–December, 1956,* ed. Clayborne Carson, 335–37. Berkeley: University of California Press, 1997.

Kirby, J. B. *Black Americans in the Roosevelt Era: Liberalism and Race.* Knoxville: University of Tennessee Press, 1980.

Knepper, Cathy D., ed. *Dear Mrs. Roosevelt: Letters to Eleanor Roosevelt through Depression and War.* New York: Carroll & Graf, 2004.

Kolatch, Alfred J. *Inside Judaism: The Concept, Customs, and Celebrations of the Jewish People.* Middle Village, NY: Jonathan David Publishers, 2006.

Krueger, Thomas A. *And Promises to Keep: The Southern Christian Conference for Human Welfare, 1938–1948.* Nashville: Vanderbilt University Press, 1968.

Langer, Walter C. *The Mind of Hitler: The Secret Wartime Report.* New York: Basic Books, 1972.

Lash, Joseph P. *Eleanor and Franklin: The Story of Their Relationship Based on Eleanor Roosevelt's Private Papers.* New York: Norton, 1971.

———. *Eleanor Roosevelt: A Friend's Memoir.* Garden City, NY: Doubleday, 1964.

———. *Eleanor: The Years Alone.* New York: W. W. Norton, 1972.

———. *Life Was Meant to Be Lived: A Centenary Portrait of Eleanor Roosevelt.* New York: W. W. Norton, 1984.

———. *Love, Eleanor: Eleanor Roosevelt and Her Friends.* Garden City, NY: Doubleday, 1982.

———. *A World of Love: Eleanor Roosevelt and Her Friends, 1932–1962.* Garden City, NY: Doubleday, 1984.

Leff, Laurel. *Buried by the Times: The Holocaust and America's Most Important Newspaper.* Cambridge: Cambridge University Press, 2005.

Leff, Mark H. "Franklin D. Roosevelt." In *The Reader's Companion to the American Presidency,* ed. Alan Brinkley and Davis Dyer, 366–85. New York: Houghton-Mifflin, 2000.

Lerner, Barron H. "Final Diagnosis." *Washington Post,* February 8, 2000, Health 13–16.

Levy, Herbert. *Henry Morgenthau, Jr.: The Remarkable Life of FDR's Secretary of the Treasury.* New York: Skyhorse Publishing, 2010.

Levy, William Turner, with C. E. Russell. *The Extraordinary Mrs. R.: A Friend Remembers Eleanor Roosevelt.* New York: John Wiley & Sons, 1999.

Lowitt, Richard. "Hopkins, Harry Lloyd." In *The Eleanor Roosevelt Encyclopedia,* ed. Maurine H. Beasley, Holly C. Shulman, and Henry R. Beasley, 246–49. Westport, CT: Greenwood, 2001.

Ludecke, Kurt. *I Knew Hitler: The Story of a Nationalist Socialist Who Escaped the Bloody Purge.* New York: Scribner's, 1937.

Lyons, L. "Kennedy Says Democracy All Done." *Daily Boston Globe,* November 10, 1940, C1, C2.

Maier, Thomas. *When Lions Roar: The Churchills and the Kennedys.* New York: Crown Books, 2014.

Mann, William J. *The Wars of the Roosevelts: The Ruthless Rise of America's Greatest Political Family.* New York: HarperCollins, 2016.

Mart, Michelle. "Eleanor Roosevelt, Liberalism, and Israel." *Shofar: An Interdisciplinary Journal of Jewish Studies* 24, no. 3 (2006): 58–89.

McGuire, Philip, ed. *Taps for a Jim Crow Army: Letters from Black Soldiers in World War II.* Lexington: University of Kentucky Press, 1993.

Meyer, G. J. *A World Undone: The Story of the Great War, 1914–1918.* New York: Delta, 2006.

Miller, Donald L. *Master of the Air: America's Bomber Boys Who Fought against Nazi Germany.* New York: Simon & Schuster, 2006.

Miller, Lisa. *The Spiritual Child: The New Science of Parenting for Health and Lifelong Thriving.* New York: St. Martin's, 2015.

Mills, Frederick C. *Prices in a War Economy: Some Aspects of the Present Price Structure in the United States.* Washington, DC: National Bureau of Economic Research, 1943.

Moe, Richard. *Roosevelt's Second Act: The Election of 1940 and the Politics of War.* New York: Oxford University Press, 2013.

Moore, Thomas. "The Spiritual Situation." *Spirituality & Health,* July–August 2010, 12.

Morgan, John D. "Violence Is the Dark Side of Spirituality." In *Making Sense of Death: Spiritual, Pastoral, and Personal Aspects of Death, Dying, and Bereavement,* ed. Gerry R. Cox, Robert A. Bendiksen, and Robert G. Stevenson, 127–36. Amityville, NY: Baywood, 2003.

Morgan, Ted. *FDR: A Biography.* New York: Simon & Schuster, 1986.

Morris, Sylvia Jukes. *Price of Fame: The Honorable Clare Boothe Luce.* New York: Random House, 2014.

Moye, J. Todd. *Freedom Flyers: The Tuskegee Airmen of World War II.* New York: Oxford University Press, 2012.

Nasaw, David. *The Patriarch: The Remarkable Life and Turbulent Times of Joseph P. Kennedy.* New York: Penguin, 2012.

Neal, Steve, ed. *Eleanor and Harry: The Correspondence of Eleanor Roosevelt and Harry Truman*. New York: Lisa Drew, 2002.

Nesbitt, Henrietta. *White House Diary*. Garden City, NY: Doubleday, 1948.

New York Daily News. "Services for Mrs. Roosevelt." November 11, 1962, 3G.

New York Times. "Hitler Escapes Bomb Explosion by 15 Minutes." November 9, 1939, A1.

O'Farrell, Brigid. *She Was One of Us: Eleanor Roosevelt and the American Worker*. Ithaca, NY: Cornell University Press, 2010.

Office of Air Force History. *Blacks in the Armed Forces during World War II: The Problem of Race Relations*. Washington, DC: Office of Air Force History, 1980.

Oliver, Mary. "When Death Comes." In *New and Selected Poems*, 10–11. Boston: Beacon Press, 1992.

———. "I Don't Want to Live a Small Life." In *Red Bird Poems*, 67. Boston, MA: Beacon Press, 2009.

Olson, Lynne. *Freedom's Daughters: The Unsung Heroines of the Civil Rights Movement from 1830 to 1970*. New York: Scribner's, 2001.

Orgill, Roxane. *Dream Lucky: When FDR Was in the White House, Count Basie Was on the Radio, and Everyone Wore a Hat*. Washington, DC: Smithsonian Books, 2008.

Oshinsky, David M. *Polio: An American Story*. New York: Oxford University Press, 2005.

Parks, Lillian Rogers, and Frances Spatz Leighton. *The Roosevelts: A Family in Turmoil*. Englewood Cliffs, NJ: Prentice-Hall, 1981.

Patterson, James. *Great Expectations*. New York: Oxford University Press, 1996.

Paul, Tessa. *The Complete Illustrated Encyclopedia of Saints*. New York: Anness Publishing/Hermes House, 2009.

Pegler, Westbrook. "Fair Enough: Mrs. Roosevelt's Public Life." *Washington Post*, February 12, 1942.

Persico, Joseph E. *Franklin and Lucy: Mrs. Rutherfurd and the Other Remarkable Women in FDR's Life*. New York: Random House, 2008.

Petro, Diane. "Brother Can You Spare a Dime? The 1940 Census." *Prologue* 44, no. 1 (Spring 2012): 1–5.

Peyser, Marc, and Timothy Dwyer. *Hissing Cousins: The Untold Story of Eleanor Roosevelt and Alice Roosevelt Longworth*. New York: Nan Talese/Doubleday, 2015.

Pietrusza, David. *1932: The Rise of Hitler and FDR; Two Tales of Politics, Betrayal, and Unlikely Destiny*. New York: Lyons, 2015.

Ponte, Lowell. "Memories of William F. Buckley." *Newsmax*, February 28, 2008.

Pottker, Jan. *Sara and Eleanor: The Story of Sara Delano Roosevelt and Her Daughter-in-Law, Eleanor Roosevelt*. New York: St. Martin's Press, 2004.

Powers, Kelly A. J. "Travels." In *The Eleanor Roosevelt Encyclopedia*, ed. Maurine H. Beasley, Holly C. Shulman, and Henry R. Beasley, 518–25. Westport, CT: Greenwood, 2001.

Pratte, Alf. "My Day." In *The Eleanor Roosevelt Encyclopedia,* ed. Maurine H. Beasley, Holly C. Shulman, and Henry R. Beasley, 354–58. Westport, CT: Greenwood, 2001.

Pressman, Stephen. *50 Children: One Ordinary American Couple's Extraordinary Rescue Mission into the Heart of Nazi Germany.* New York: HarperTorch, 2014.

Pryor, Helen B. *Lou Henry Hoover: Gallant First Lady.* New York: Dodd, Mead, 1969.

Radosh, Allis, and Robert Radosh. *A Safe Haven: Harry S Truman and the Founding of Israel.* New York: Harper Perennial, 2010.

Reed, Linda. *Simple Decency & Common Sense: The Southern Conference Movement, 1938–1963.* Bloomington: Indiana University Press, 1991.

Riebling, Mark. *Church of Spies: The Pope's Secret War against Hitler.* New York: Basic Books, 2015.

Robinson, Corinne. *My Brother Theodore Roosevelt.* New York: Charles Scribner's, 1921.

Roosevelt, Curtis. Interview by Mimi Geerges. *Mimi Geerges Show.* XM Satellite Radio, June 15, 2015.

———. Interview. *WGBH Forum.* WGBH Public Radio, Boston, April 25, 2014.

———. Lecture at Harvard, February 27, 2010.

Roosevelt, David. *Grandmère: A Personal History of Eleanor Roosevelt.* New York: Warner Books, 2002.

Roosevelt, Eleanor. *An Autobiography of Eleanor Roosevelt.* New York: Da Capo Press, 1993.

———. *If You Ask Me.* New York: D. Appleton-Century, 1946.

———. *India and the Awakening East.* New York: Harper, 1953.

———. *It Seems to Me: Selected Letters of Eleanor Roosevelt.* Edited by Leonard C. Schlup and Donald W. Whisenhunt. Lexington: University of Kentucky Press, 2001.

———. *It's Up to the Women.* New York: Frederick A. Stokes, 1933.

———. *The Moral Basis of Democracy.* New York: Howell, Soskin, 1940.

———. *On My Own.* New York: Harper and Brothers, 1958.

———. "The Place of Spiritual Forces in the Life of the Nation." *Journal of the Department of History (The Presbyterian Historical Society) of the Presbyterian Church in the U.S.A.* 15, no. 7/8 (September-December, 1933): 392–95.

———. "Race, Religion and Prejudice." *New Republic,* May 1942.

———. "The Seven People Who Shaped My Life." *Look,* June 19, 1951, 54–56, 58.

———. "Some of My Best Friends Are Negro." *Ebony,* February 1953, 16–26.

———. *This I Remember.* New York: Harper & Brothers, 1949.

———. *This Is My Story.* New York: Harper & Brothers, 1937.

———. *This Troubled World.* New York: L. C. Kinsey, 1938.

———. *Tomorrow Is Now.* New York: Penguin Books, 2012.

———. "What Religion Means to Me." *Forum* 88 (December 1932): 322–24.

———. *You Learn by Living*. Philadelphia: Westminster Press, 1960.

Roosevelt, Eleanor, II. [Eleanor Wotkyns]. *With Love, Aunt Eleanor: Stories from My Life with the First Lady of the World*. Petaluma, CA: Scrapbook Press, 2004.

Roosevelt, Elliott. *Eleanor Roosevelt, with Love: A Centenary Remembrance*. New York: Dutton, 1984.

Roosevelt, Elliott, and James Brough. *Mother R.: Eleanor Roosevelt's Untold Story*. New York: G. P. Putnam, 1977.

Roosevelt, James, and Bill Libby. *My Parents: A Differing View*. Chicago: Playboy Press, 1976.

Roosevelt, James, and Sidney Shalett. *Affectionately, FDR: A Son's Story of a Courageous Man*. New York: Harcourt & Brace, 1959.

Rothstein, Edward. "Roosevelt's Legacy, Burning Brightly." *New York Times*, June 28, 2013, C25.

Rowley, Hazel. *Franklin and Eleanor: An Extraordinary Marriage*. New York: Farrar, Straus & Giroux, 2010.

Rozett, Robert, and Samuel Spector. *Encyclopedia of the Holocaust*. New York: Facts on File, 2000.

Ryan, William. "Remarks in the House." In *Anna Eleanor Roosevelt, 1884–1962: Memorial Addresses of the House of Representatives*. 88 *Congressional Record*, 1st session, 15–20. Washington DC: U.S. Government Printing Office, 1966.

Salsini, Barbara. "There Were No Little People in Her World." *Milwaukee Journal*, November 2, 1970.

Sarna, Jonathan D. *American Judaism: A History*. New Haven, CT: Yale University Press, 2004.

Scharf, Lois. "Roosevelt, Eleanor." In *Historical Dictionary of the New Deal: From Inauguration to Preparation for War*, ed. James S. Olson, 427–30. Westport, CT: Greenwood, 1985.

Schiff, Karenna Gore. *Lightening the Way: Nine Women Who Changed Modern America*. New York: Miramax, 2005.

Shapiro, Laura. "Washington Chronicles: The First Kitchen." *New Yorker*, November 22, 2012, 74.

Slayton, Robert A. *Empire Statesman: The Rise and Redemption of Al Smith*. New York: Free Press, 2001.

Smith, Carter. *Presidents: Every Question Answered; Everything You Could Possibly Want to Know about the Nation's Chief Executives*. San Diego, CA: Thunder Bay Press, 2014.

Smith, Harold Ivan. *GriefKeeping: Learning How Long Grief Lasts*. New York: Crossroad, 2004.

Smith, Jean Edward. *FDR*. New York: Random House, 2007.

Smith, Kathyrn. *The Gatekeeper: Missy LeHand, FDR, and the Untold Story of the Partnership That Defined a Presidency*. New York: Touchstone, 2016.

Smith, Stephen Drury. *The First Lady of Radio: Eleanor Roosevelt's Historic Broadcasts*. New York: New Press, 2014.

Stargardt, Nicholas. *The German War: A Nation under Arms, 1939–1945*. New York: Basic Books, 2015.

Steel, D. A. "Souvestre, Marie Claire." In *Oxford Dictionary of National Biography*, ed. H. C. G. Matthew and Brian Harrison, 51:726–27. New York: Oxford University Press, 2004.

Swan, Orange, "Eleanor Roosevelt and Her No-Nonsense Knitting. The Knitting Needle and the Damage Done (blog). February 13, 2013. http://theknittingneedleandthedamagedone.blogspot.com/2013/02/eleanor-roosevelt-and-her-no-nonsense.html.

Teague, Michael. *Mrs. L: Conversations with Alice Roosevelt Longworth*. London: Gerald Duckworth, 1981.

Teel, Leonard Ray. "Anti-Lynching Movement." In *The Eleanor Roosevelt Encyclopedia*, ed. Maurine H. Beasley, Holly C. Shulman, and Henry R. Beasley, 28–30. Westport, CT: Greenwood, 2001.

Thomas, Evan. *The War Lovers: Roosevelt, Lodge, Hearst, and the Rush to Empire, 1898*. New York: Little, Brown, 2010.

Thomas, Gordon, and Max Morgan Witts. *Voyage of the Damned*. New York: Stein & Day, 1974.

Tiffany, G. E. "Spellman, Francis." In *The New Catholic Encyclopedia*, 13:411–12. Detroit: Gale, 2013.

Time. "Eleanor Roosevelt." February 22, 2002. content.time.com/time/magazine/article/0,9171,212515,00.html.

———. "Must This Man Go?" January 29, 1934.

Tobin, James. *The Man He Became: How FDR Defied Polio to Win the Presidency*. New York: Simon & Schuster, 2013.

Toor, Rachel. *Eleanor Roosevelt*. New York: Chelsea House, 1989.

Vaill, Amanda. *Hotel Florida: Truth, Love, and Death in the Spanish Civil War*. New York: Farrar, Strauss & Giroux, 2014.

Van West, Carroll. "The Columbia Race Riot, 1946." In *The Tennessee Encyclopedia of History and Culture*, ed. Carroll Van West, 191–92. Nashville, TN: Rutledge Hill Press, 2003.

vanden Heuvel, William J. "America and the Holocaust." *American Heritage*, July–August 1999.

Von Tempo, Carl Joseph. "Refugees." In *The Eleanor Roosevelt Encyclopedia*, ed. Maurine H. Beasley, Holly C. Shulman, and Henry R. Beasley, 431–35. Westport, CT: Greenwood, 1997.

Walker, Melissa. "Rutherfurd, Lucy Mercer." In *The Eleanor Roosevelt Encyclopedia*, ed. M. H. Beasley, H. C. Shulman, and H. R. Beasley, 470–73. Westport, CT: Greenwood, 1997.

Ward, Geoffrey C. *Before the Trumpet: Young Franklin Roosevelt, 1882–1905*. New York: Konecky and Konecky, 1985.

Ward, Geoffrey C., and Ken Burns. *War: An Intimate History, 1941–1945*. New York: Knopf, 2007.

———. *The Roosevelts: An Intimate History*. New York: Knopf, 2014.

Washington Afro-American. "Bilboisms." April 29, 1939.

Washington Post. "Dorothy Thompson Pleads for Child Exiles," April 23, 1939, 1.

Weatherford, Doris. *American Women's History*. New York: Macmillan General Reference, 1994.

Webster, Scott W. "Gurewitsch, Arno David." In *The Eleanor Roosevelt Encyclopedia*, ed. Maurine H. Beasley, Holly C. Shulman, and Henry R. Beasley, 219–21. Westport, CT: Greenwood, 2001.

West, J. B., and Mary Lynn Kotz. *Upstairs at the White House: My Life with the First Ladies*. New York: Coward, McCann & Geoghegan, 2014.

White, Philip. *Whistle Stop: How 31,000 Miles of Train Travel, 352 Speeches, and a Little Midwest Gumption Saved the Presidency of Harry Truman*. Lebanon, NH: ForeEdge/ University Press of New England, 2014.

White, Walter. *A Man Called White: The Autobiography of Walter White*. Athens: University of Georgia Press, 1995.

Wigal, Donald, ed. *The Wisdom of Eleanor Roosevelt*. New York: Citadel Press, 2003.

Williams, David J. *Eleanor Roosevelt's Niggers*. Winter Haven, FL: Neptune Press, 1976.

Williams, Juan. *Thurgood Marshall: American Revolutionary*. New York: Broadway Books, 2000.

Williams, Sue, writer and director. "Eleanor Roosevelt." *American Experience*. Aired January 10, 2000. Transcript, http://www.pbs.org/wgbh /americanexperience/features/transcript/eleanor-transcript/.

Willis, Resa. *FDR and Lucy: Lovers and Friends*. New York: Routledge, 2004.

Winik, Jay. *1944: FDR and the Year That Changed History*. New York: Simon & Schuster, 2015.

Worden, J. William. *Grief Counseling and Grief Therapy: A Handbook for the Mental Health Practitioner*. 4th ed. New York: Springer, 2009.

Wortman, Marc. *1941: Fighting the Shadow War; A Divided America in a World at War*. New York: Atlantic Monthly Press, 2016.

Wright, Jordan M. *Campaigning for President*. Washington, DC: Smithsonian, 2007.

Wyman, David S. *Abandonment of the Jews: America and the Holocaust, 1941–1945*. New York: Pantheon, 1984.

———. *Paper Walls: America and the Refugee Crisis, 1938–1941*. New York: Pantheon, 1968.

Youngs, J. William. *Eleanor Roosevelt: A Personal and Public Life*. 2nd ed. New York: Pearson, 2006.

Zubovich, Gene. "The Strange, Short Career of Judeo-Christianity." *Aeon*, March 22, 2016. https://aeon.co/ideas/the-strange-short-career-of-judeo -christianity.

CPSIA information can be obtained
at www.ICGtesting.com
Printed in the USA
LVHW032300211218
601414LV00001B/11/P

9 780664 261641